Extending the Supply Chain

Extending the Supply Chain

How Cutting-Edge Companies Bridge the Critical Last Mile into Customers' Homes

Kenneth Karel Boyer,
Markham T. Frohlich,
and G. Tomas M. Hult

AMACOM

American Management Association
New York • Atlanta • Brussels • Chicago • Mexico City • San Francisco
Shanghai • Tokyo • Toronto • Washington, D.C.

Special discounts on bulk quantities of AMACOM books are available to corporations, professional associations, and other organizations. For details, contact Special Sales Department, AMACOM, a division of American Management Association, 1601 Broadway, New York, NY 10019.
Tel.: 212-903-8316. Fax: 212-903-8083.
Web site: www.amacombooks.org

This publication is designed to provide accurate and authoritative information in regard to the subject matter covered. It is sold with the understanding that the publisher is not engaged in rendering legal, accounting, or other professional service. If legal advice or other expert assistance is required, the services of a competent professional person should be sought.

Library of Congress Cataloging-in-Publication Data

Boyer, Kenneth Karel
     Extending the supply chain : how cutting-edge companies bridge the critical last mile into customers' homes / Kenneth Karel Boyer, Markham T. Frohlich, and G. Tomas M. Hult. — 1st ed.
         p.   cm.
     Includes bibliographical references and index.
     ISBN 0-8144-0836-2
     1. Business logistics.   2. Grocery trade.   3. Retail trade.   I. Frohlich, Markham T.   II. Hult, G. Tomas M.   III. Title.

HD38.5.B698   2004
658.7'88—dc22

                                                                    2004000846

Printing Hole Number

10   9   8   7   6   5   4   3   2   1

CONTENTS

There are things that work and then there are things that work well. We watched in wonder and confusion from 1997 to 2000 as investors shoveled money at scores of start-up companies with grand but ill-thought-out plans to deliver everything from pet supplies to groceries to customer doorsteps. It was not that we thought this was a bad idea—on the contrary, we believe that there is a substantial, untapped market for consumer-direct products. Instead, we were amazed at the apparent lack of thought underlying the supply chains that were to deliver this smorgasbord of products. It seemed that people were so caught up in the idea of the Internet that they forgot that products could not be beamed through the wires, but still had to be physically delivered.

As we examined companies in our classes and research, we became convinced that there was a great deal of opportunity in the last-mile supply chain—if only companies would carefully sift through various decisions regarding supply chain, marketing, and information technology. First and foremost, we saw a need to tightly link marketing and supply chain decisions. Certainly these decisions ought to be linked in all organizations, but the desire to deliver directly to customers places extra pressure on the natural conflicts between marketing and supply chain. Second, we began to see that delivering to customers is a changing pool of quicksand—opportunities for improving and cutting the length of the supply chain abound, but so do obstacles, which can quickly pull a company down. Thus, there is a need for companies to examine their supply chain strategies to clearly determine what their goals are and how last-mile supply chains can benefit both companies and customers. Finally, the Internet is a phenomenal tool, but like any other tool, it can be misapplied. Many companies take orders over the Internet, but they are unable to streamline the order-taking or fulfillment process. We seek to understand how taking orders over the Internet (or some other automated system) can reduce labor, improve accuracy, and provide customers with greater convenience and more control over their purchases.

We are grateful to the many individuals and corporations that assisted us in our research over the last three years. Supply chain management is an applied field. We can observe and compare the experiences of a number of companies, but we need to have access to them. We have benefited from the open exchange of ideas with executives of numerous last-mile retailers and manufacturers. This book represents a compilation of insights gained from conversations, surveys, and interviews with scores of executives and customers.

In particular, we would like to thank the following individuals and companies for their generous participation—both in terms of time and access for interviews and data collection. Monica Luechtefeld and Kathleen Stockham of Office Depot; Roger Whiteside, Nigel Robertson, Robert Gorrie, Andy McWilliams, Anne Marie Foley, and Claire Harper of Ocado; Jason Ackerman, Daniel Radek, and Neal Bayless of FreshDirect; Ed Holmes and Julie Goggans of PublixDirect; Terry Moore and Lisa Selip of Lowes Foods; Mike Spindler, Karisa Greiner, and Cyndi Metallo of MyWebGrocer; Robin Lassiter, Christina Thanassoulis, and Dave Merefield of Sainsbury's; Jason Abbott, Amy Boyle, Bob Krajeski, Pam Powell, Dea Parker, and Sandy Shook of Albertson's; Claude Germain, John Mozas, Scott Robinson, and Stephen Tallevi of Grocery Gateway. All of these individuals and companies have been valuable in helping study their companies and customers, as well as providing a sounding board for our numerous ideas.

In addition, we would like to thank the following individuals who assisted in some manner with data collection, analysis, or presentation in our various studies. Leslie Zielke, University of Washington, Bothell; Krystle Canaii, University of Miami; Andrea McGee, Paul Myler, Kathy Mullins, Tiffany Norwood, Michael Reed, and Mary Upshur, Michigan State University. We also wish to thank the many individuals who have offered insights into last-mile supply chains in telephone or personal discussions, including David Porter, SmartBox Inc., Tom Coyne, Diamond Phoenix, Paul Demery, *Internet Retailer*, and Chris Manella, Ensenda, Inc. Financial support was provided for much of this research by the U.S. National Science Foundation (under the Information Technology Research Program), and administrative support was provided by the Marketing & Supply Chain Management Department and the Center for

International Business Education and Research at Michigan State University and the London Business School.

Finally, the people who listened to our ideas and tribulations during the writing and revision process also deserve a hearty acknowledgment. Christina McLaughlin at AMACOM guided us through the editorial process with numerous constructive suggestions and patience in pulling us through to a better book. Most important, we could not accomplish anything without the ever-present love and support of our families: Graham, Julia, and Mary Boyer; Laurie and Daniel Hult; Diane and Nicholas Frohlich—*thanks*!

Best regards from our doorsteps while awaiting a home delivery,

Kenneth Karel Boyer, Ph.D.
Michigan State University

Markham T. Frohlich, Ph.D.
Boston University

G. Tomas M. Hult, Ph.D.
Michigan State University

PREFACE

Groceries and the Last-Mile Supply Chain

This book began as a study on Internet ordering for home-delivered groceries, but as you will find in the pages that follow, it has evolved into much more than that. For a start, all three of its coauthors, being both academics today and managers in their former careers, were never entirely comfortable with the way that the whole dot-com saga of Internet home delivery seemed to have started with such promise in the 1990s, only to have imploded with so much scorn by 2001. Although companies such as Webvan (and many others around the globe) had tried to build a profitable business model out of Internet home delivery, no one had really answered the question about whether or not it could ever make money to our satisfaction. Moreover, if it could be profitable, then what was the best strategy to really maximize its potential?

Luckily, we were not alone in our curiosity about Internet-based home delivery—the U.S. government's National Science Foundation (NSF) was also interested. In 2002, the NSF awarded us a grant to investigate this intriguing new way of potentially doing business. In the ensuing two years leading up to this book, we studied Internet-based home delivery in numerous companies in the United States and Europe, interviewed dozens of managers, and surveyed well over 5,000 of their home-delivery customers. We also shadowed "personal shoppers" through grocery store aisles from Seattle to London, shivered through the frozen food sections of giant warehouses, and talked with anybody else involved in the home-delivery process, from the frontline van drivers to the back-office IT staff to the marketing professionals trying to stimulate demand. We've even tried many of these online services ourselves to see what it is really like to be a customer on the receiving end of these businesses.

Every good management study has a starting point (or focus) where initial lessons are learned, hypotheses are tested, and preliminary conclusions are drawn. This is called "controlling for industry," which simply means that by first analyzing a single sector you don't have to worry too much about potentially distorting factors that may arise, such as varying customers, government regulations, standards, or terminology. In other words, controlling for industry lets you compare "apples to apples" as you work your way through mounds of interview notes, personal observations, and raw data leading up to the first set of conclusions.

From their initially "tight" focus, the best such managerial studies then branch out and consider the entire range of business possibilities. That is exactly the plan that we followed in our own research and the analyses underlying this book. The starting point for our study was where many of the most spectacular dot-com failures occurred—in Internet groceries. Where there was smoke there must have been some fire, and the best place to begin such an ambitious study was in the very same industry where so many well-funded companies (such as Webvan) had spectacularly failed a few years ago. From that point, as you'll see in the chapters that follow, we broadened the study's scope to include all of the major possible types of Internet-based home-delivery strategies—*regardless of industry*. Indeed, if there is one thing we learned early in this study, it is that what seems to work in one type of retailing more often than not works with all other kinds of retailers.

First, let's take the case of groceries. Familiarity tends to make us take most things in life for granted, and grocery stores are no different. When you think of groceries, you probably think of parking lot mayhem, pushing a cart around with one wobbly wheel, forgetting to take a number at the deli (and missing your turn to someone who showed up later, but remembered to pull a ticket), steering the kids away from the cookies, candies, comic books, and toys, and, of course, when checking out, discovering only three of a dozen lines are open (and you get behind the person who is paying with an out-of-state check).

Yes, that is pretty much grocery shopping as we all "fondly" know it as consumers, but surprisingly enough, groceries are also a business that managers from *all* other industries can learn from. In fact, groceries have pioneered many business innovations and practices for well over a hundred years, ranging from brand management to bar codes to today's self-checkout. Nothing in our daily lives is more basic than eating, but the struggle behind the scenes to win us as customers has been anything but boring; in fact, it's been as intense as any battle in the history of modern business. New methods spell extra profit in the grocery business, which is why time and again leading managerial practice comes from this most basic of industries.

Arguing that groceries is a good starting point for understanding many forms of business, the Internet, and home delivery may, at first glance, seem a little strange. When you read the weekly magazines and daily newspapers it seems like almost everything wonderful in modern business practice comes from either the auto industry, hi-tech start-ups, aerospace and defense, or the omnipresent consultants, who seem to know everything. After all, we are talking about cans of soap, boxes of diapers, jugs of milk, and bags of onions. But what makes this sector so interesting to study and learn from is its degree of competition. It is competition like you would not believe. Competition that not only wants to steal your customers today, but that also wants to buy you up or put you out of business tomorrow. It is competition that is as much fueled by corporate offices pushing new practices downward as it is by hourly clerks in stores around the world coming up with great ideas that ricochet across the industry.

In particular, there are three reasons that make the grocery industry such a worthy one to closely watch for the next big managerial trends. The first is the "pace" of the industry, and its unmerciful rate of change. The second reason is that along with fierce competition come low margins, and the need to innovate to stay profitable. The final reason that groceries are such an interesting battleground to study first is the repetitive nature of the business and the sheer volumes involved—if it can work in that sector, then chances are that it will work anywhere else in retail.

The three coauthors of this book have more than fifty years of managerial and academic experience between us, and we have honestly never seen a more dynamic and interesting industry to study than groceries. Grocery shopping is a habit of a lifetime, a habit that is the same for billions of people around the world. Since most of our experience is confined to the United States and Europe, we will keep our comments to these two regions, but they could just as easily apply to comparisons between the United States and large parts of Asian/Pacific, South American, and some Mideast and African nations. In the United Kingdom and the rest of Europe, the average basket size still contains around sixty to ninety items, and whatever the currency, the average bill still works out to around $100.

This is good news, because it means that this book's lessons are not confined to the United States or a particular industry. Instead, our arguments and

findings apply to grocery stores around the world, and by extension, this book
is potentially just as relevant to all types of retailers around the globe as it is to
groceries. After all, how different are groceries from many other forms of retail?

The final point we would like to make concerns not the nature of the
battles that have dominated the grocery industry (and most other retail industries), but where they inevitably take place. If you think about it, some industrial battles literally take place in secret. They happen behind closed doors in
research centers, in engineering departments, in laboratories, and at universities.
They also often happen months or even years before the products (or services)
are ever offered to customers. Retailers should be so lucky. The battleground
for all retailers—including groceries—takes place right in front of customers.
As in professional sports, there are no secrets in retail. You figuratively set your
"play"—be it price, product, place, or promotion—and then you throw your
doors open to see what the customers think. If they like what you offer, you'll
soon enough know. If they don't, it may take a little longer to figure it out, but
soon enough, the mistakes become apparent.

In all forms of retail, you cannot somehow finesse your operations and
hope that they will work. You cannot haphazardly decide which SKUs to sell
in the extended supply versus those you should not. You also can't go cheap
on the information technology (IT), personnel, procedures, or policies that
back up the typical business. But most important, you cannot succeed by expecting that your customers will automatically change. If you are going to take
the good battle to your rivals using advanced supply chains, you are also going
to have to work closely with your customers to do it.

Don't worry—chances are that your business is ready for this leap forward.
Moreover, although your best customers probably already love your company,
a sizable percentage of them may hate shopping there. Change that around so
that your best customers love doing business with you via an extended supply
chain, and your company becomes almost unstoppable in its markets. Sadly,
botch the implementation, and chances are that you may lose a lot more than
you gain.

Doing nothing at all is probably most worrisome. Making no decision is,
in fact, making a decision. If you don't adopt an extended supply chain, one or
more of your competitors no doubt will (maybe they already have). If they beat
you to it, and get it right, then that is about the most miserable position you
can possibly be in as a manager. Suddenly, you find your company playing
catch-up, as the financial markets heckle you for reacting too slowly while your

competitor(s), having wooed the best customers (which often means the freest-spending and easiest to acquire), laugh at your efforts. The effect on your employees can be just about as devastating—they start to wonder what is going on with senior management. Questions and complaints begin to circulate around the break and lunchroom tables. Comments like these are heard: "Don't they know that some of our customers want a better way to shop?" "Why doesn't management offer home delivery to take a little of the pressure off the rest of operations?"

All this leads us up to the present day. The next major battle in all forms of retail (including groceries) is in the critical last-mile of the supply chain: from retailers to customers' homes. Yes, there will continue to be technological breakthroughs in traditional retail stores and upstream in the supply chain, but today the big action is at the other end—downstream at the consumer's doorstep. By some estimations, over the next decade anywhere from 2 percent to 10 percent of all shoppers will opt for home delivery service. This does not sound like much, until you remember how small the in-store margins often are, and how big the overall pies are when we talk about sectors like fashion, consumer electronics, and appliances, as well as groceries. Just 2 percent or 3 percent of the $450 billion–plus total grocery revenue per year would make your company about number nine or ten in terms of the twenty largest grocery stores. If you captured 10 percent of the customers who may eventually shop online—you'd be number one in the industry in the United States.

If your company doesn't implement the extended supply chain, but your competitors do, then the table is turned on you—usually for the worse. Your competitors grow in size at your expense, and over time, you will have the disheartening pleasure of watching many of your most profitable customers defect to these rivals, while the business press sings their praises for their vision, leadership, and skills. Read on—starting with the next series of chapters we will show you how it is done by companies that have already "gone to war" on their rivals—the companies that are already winning this most crucial of all contemporary retail battles . . . the home-delivery war.

Background on Grocery Home-Delivery Study

The research underpinning this book is based on a three-year U.S. National Science Foundation grant (Grant SES 0216839) awarded by the Information Technology Research and Decision Risk & Management Science Programs.

The title of the research project is "ITR: Internet Disintermediation of Food Delivery—Spanning the Last Mile," and the project is ongoing, running from August 1, 2002, until July 31, 2005. It investigates two main research questions:

1. Can the Internet as an interface for delivering groceries be a profitable business model?
2. What conditions, strategies, and investments best position companies to effectively capitalize on the Internet as a retail channel for groceries and foodstuffs?

The conceptual model for this study is summarized in Figure P-1. The important thing to note is that we investigated multiple aspects of Internet-based home delivery, including operations, marketing, performance, and the customer's experience.

Figure P-1. Conceptual model for grocery home-delivery study.

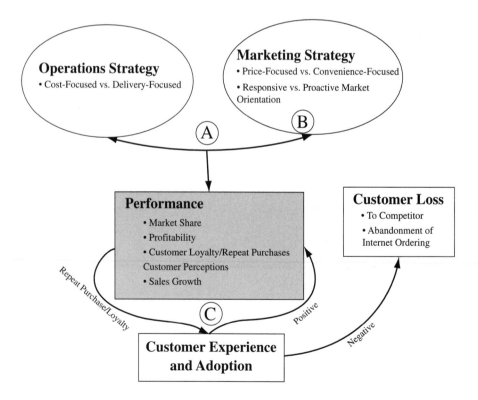

In terms of study methods, we conducted mini case studies and management interviews at seven leading grocery home-delivery companies, including Sainsbury's, Ocado, Grocery Gateway, Lowes Foods, PublixDirect, FreshDirect, and Albertson's. In addition to the grocery companies, we have also conducted studies with Office Depot and Federal Express. For the grocery study, we surveyed customers of all seven companies. In total, we collected over 2,900 surveys as shown in Figure P-2, which describes the major markets served by each grocer (for home delivery only), the methods used to collect the surveys, and the method the companies utilized to pick and deliver customer orders. We were able to include in the study all the major picking strategies found in home delivery, including the warehouse only model, in-store only strategy, and mixed warehouse plus in-store approach. To the best of our knowledge, we are the only team of researchers to have ever gained such unprecedented access to so many companies in order to do so. And, we think the results of this "holistic" study show up in this book. If it is being done somewhere out there in terms of Internet-based home delivery, we have probably seen and evaluated it.

It is also worth noting that throughout this study that the authors have taken a very hands-on approach to the entire process. We've done everything from actually picking orders to talking with CEOs in their boardrooms. We've stood in parking lots and looked at dented vans with anguished managers, and we've talked though the marketing strategies with marketers before their expensive advertisements hit the airwaves. Along the way, we have also studied countless company documents, spoken with staff and workers, met the engineers trying to make automated warehouses work, and even peeked around the corners at piles of returned items that no one really wanted us to see.

We will use results from our study to illustrate various principles throughout this book. Often, these results will be presented in an aggregated manner to disguise which company they come from—this is done to ameliorate the concerns all of these companies have regarding the sensitivity of their customer data and operating results in a very competitive and emerging business environment. We also make use of our personal experiences and examples gleaned from the popular press and our teaching experiences.

If you want more detailed information on our grocery study, such as copies of our academic research papers, please go to the following Web site: http://www.msugrocery.org/.

Figure P-2. Description of participating companies and data collection methods.

	Total	Lowes Foods	Albertson's	Grocery Gateway	Ocado	Sainsbury	PublixDirect	FreshDirect
Markets served by Home Delivery		North Carolina	Seattle, Portland, San Francisco, San Diego, Los Angeles, Las Vegas, Dallas	Toronto	London, UK	72% of UK	Miami	New York
Data Collection Methods								
Sample Selection		Stratified	Random	Stratified	Stratified	Stratified	Stratified	Stratified
Invitation to Customer		E-Mail	Opt-In at Checkout	E-Mail	Written letter	E-Mail	E-Mail	E-Mail
Incentive		Yes	No	Yes	Yes	Yes	Yes	Yes
Survey Method		Web Survey	Web Survey	Web Survey	Written Survey	Web Survey	Web Survey	Web Survey
Follow-Up Invitation		Yes	No	Yes	Yes	Yes	Yes	No
Customers Contacted	16,577	1,159	10,418	2,500	500	5,000	2,078	2,000
Responses	2,985	396	1,066	690	373	877	475	460
Response Rate	18.0%	34.2%	8.6%	27.6%	74.6%	17.5%	22.9%	23.0%
Order Pick Method		Store	Store	DC	DC	Store & DC	DC	DC
Order Delivery Method		Customer Pickup at Store	Home Delivery or Store Pickup	Home Delivery	Home Delivery—1 Hour Windows	Home Delivery—2 Hour Windows	Home Delivery	Home Delivery—Very Limited Evening Windows

Extending the Supply Chain

PART I

INTRODUCTION

CHAPTER 1

The Great Divide Between Customers and Retailers

Many people view the 1950s quite nostalgically as a time of happy families, increasing prosperity, and predictable world affairs. Much has changed since then. Back then, many people routinely got goods and services delivered to their homes. The milkman would drop off milk and other dairy products either once or twice per week. The dry cleaner often picked up dirty laundry, and returned the cleaned items. The Fuller Brush man sold a wide variety of brushes door-to-door. Diaper services that delivered freshly laundered cloth diapers and took away junior's odiferous old ones were plentiful. Some doctors even made house calls! As millions of people have noted, progress is not always forward.

Fast-forward more than fifty years, and much has changed. In general, most countries with developed economies have a substantially higher standard of living, and their citizens also are much busier in both their work and personal lives. Thus, in general, we have more money and less time, and yet home delivery of products virtually disappeared between 1950 and 1995. Shouldn't we have more ability to order products for home delivery, not less?

Given increased incomes, improved technology, and better management techniques, this book examines the resurgence of home delivery as a way to address the time pressures that weigh on the majority of consumers today. We argue that the combination of automated ordering systems (telephone, fax, and, most important, the Internet) and new supply chain management techniques allows companies to serve customers in new ways that add convenience, quality, customization, and enjoyable experiences to a business world that has increasingly been dominated by an emphasis on low price at the expense of service and any meaningful connection with customers.

New Strategies for New Times

The strategy that many companies are using to attack industry leaders in new ways involves extending the supply chain. Whereas Ford, McDonald's, and Wal-Mart all were (or are) masters at managing supply chains designed to minimize costs rather than create meaningful customer experiences, companies such as Dell, Amazon, and Office Depot are using the Internet not only to efficiently link with customers, but also to extend the supply chain the critical "last mile" into consumers' homes. The Dell model is widely known and examined for manufacturing firms, yet there have been few companies that have managed to successfully copy the entire system and apply it to nonmanufacturing environments. However, there is currently a wave of retailers that are refining this basic model and using it to extend the supply chain for a wide variety of products, including electronics, office supplies, and groceries.[1]

Fundamentally, there are two ways to compete in business: Offer low prices or differentiate your product or service in some manner such as improved quality, better service, more choices, etc. Offering low prices has a simple appeal to customers—we all would like to pay less. However, running a business to provide low costs that actually allow a profit is a bit more challenging. The elephant in any discussion of retailing in North America these days is Wal-Mart. While there are scores of factors underlying its success, the most fundamental one is that it has consistently worked to improve its supply chain with a relentless focus on squeezing out costs. Some of the supply chain techniques Wal-Mart has used to cut costs include vendor-managed inventory, real-time tracking of inventory and sales in individual stores, and cross-docking of fast-moving items in distribution centers. To compete with this, many companies are implementing everyday low prices; however, it is more of a challenge to back up this pricing with costs that allow organizations to remain profitable. Wal-Mart is very visible, hard to avoid, and must be watched carefully. Many retailers seem to be batting at this elephant with a flyswatter—inefficient supply chains that have substantially higher costs. This strategy is *not* going to remove the elephant.

Just ask any executive from Kmart, or the entire grocery industry. Consider a regional grocer such as Farmer Jack, which announced on June 12, 2003, that it was radically changing its pricing strategy to go to constant low prices, forsaking weekly specials. Yet they did not provide any operational details underlying this strategy, saying instead, "We have some great plans in the works."[2] The big grocers aren't much different. The stock values of America's top three grocery chains (Kroger, Albertson's, and Safeway) were, on average, 51 percent off their 2002 high of May 5, 2003.[3] Could this have anything to do with the fact that they are not actually lowering prices? A study by A.G. Edwards in a price survey of 215 items in January 2002 in the Dallas market found that prices at Kroger were on average 35.1 percent higher than competitors in the same region.[4] As the saying goes, you do the math.

Let's return to the alternative, the other fundamental business strategy: Differentiate your product. While we all want low prices, we are also generally willing to pay more for better quality, better service, more convenience, or a more customized product. Everyone has a pretty good idea of the things that differentiate a Rolex from a Swatch watch, a BMW from a Hyundai car, or even a room at an InterContinental Hotel from a room at a Holiday Inn. People tend to recognize a product or service that offers more: higher quality, more choice/customization, or faster service. The challenge is determining how much customers are willing to pay. Is a Rolex worth 50 percent more than a Swatch? One hundred percent more? Three times as much? Quantifying the monetary value of some differentiating feature of a product or a service is a fuzzy exercise. This can be either a benefit or a drawback: Companies that convince customers that their product is worth substantially more than a less differentiated product often earn much higher premiums. However, companies that are not as successful in convincing potential customers to pay a premium generally do poorly.

This problem is compounded in a retail environment, where selling commodity products does not offer much room for differentiation. The Crest toothpaste or Coca-Cola from Wal-Mart, Rite-Aid, or Kroger is exactly the same. This is why the majority of retailers pursue some type of low-price marketing strategy. In order to successfully differentiate themselves, retailers must offer services (not products) that appeal to consumers. In other words, they must have friendlier, faster, more convenient service, or have more selection. The challenge is getting customers to value this—and to pay for it. Let's try a mental comparison. If money were no object, where would you shop for clothes? Brooks Brothers? Neiman Marcus? Bergdorf Goodman? What differentiates these retailers from Wal-Mart, Target, and Sears? Are their clothes better? Probably, but probably not three, four, or five times better. So what does a "high-end" retailer do differently? They make the process of buying something more pleasant, less time-consuming (or, if you enjoy shopping, longer). They have less busy, nicer surroundings. In short, they make shopping a pleasant experience, rather than a trial to be endured. You can easily catalog your own experiences and, using this strict set, classify every shopping experience you've had recently as either price-oriented or experience-oriented.

In some ways, retailers that are either clearly price-oriented or experience-oriented have it easy—at least in the sense that they have a clear goal. It is when retailers are in between these extremes that defining their appeal to customers is difficult. Companies that lack the type of dominating, engineered for low-cost supply chain exemplified by Wal-Mart or the high-end, experience-oriented selling exemplified by Bergdorf Goodman must communicate to customers exactly where they stand, and how they are different. The past few decades have seen a huge increase in price-oriented retailers. According to a recent National Retail Federation study, 8 percent of retail sales were based on discount pricing in 1971 versus 78 percent in 2002. Yet, the pendulum is beginning to swing back toward service. According to consumer psychologist Lilliam Maresch, founder of Generation Insight (a market research firm), "People are yearning for that high touch after so many years of high tech. When you get consumers talking about service, they are very vocal and articulate."[5]

The quote above mentions high tech and high touch, which are the key elements of a fundamentally new way to bridge the two extremes of low cost versus high service. The last-mile supply chain delivers a product from the retailer (either from a manufacturing facility, a distribution center, or a store) directly to a customer. The delivery of a product serves to differentiate the experience, without causing the price to increase proportionately. In short, the last-mile supply chain offers a new approach to business that offers customers greater convenience at a price—a service that is appealing in an increasingly cash-rich, time-starved society.

The Dawning of Extended Supply Chains

Numerous authors have argued in the past five years that the era of mass production is giving way to an era where services and products are designed to create an experience that resonates with customers. Various terms have been introduced, such as mass customization, the experience economy, the support economy, or the loyalty effect.[6,7,8,9] Retailers and manufacturers such as Dell, Amazon, and Office Depot are effectively extending the supply chain directly to consumers' homes to provide the type of experience for which consumers will pay a premium. The extension of the supply chain allows companies to circumvent the relentless pressure to compete primarily on ever lower costs, as personified by the twentieth century giants Ford, McDonald's, and Wal-Mart. At the dawn of the twenty-first century, the Internet is a tool that allows customers unprecedented access to a vast variety of retailers, while logistics and production techniques have advanced to a point where goods can be delivered directly to customers with an enormous degree of quality, service, and customization.

The evolution of supply chain management essentially started with Ford's highly integrated River Rouge plant in the early twentieth century, in which raw materials would enter one side of the plant, and a finished Model T would exit the other end. Following World War II, Toyota redefined supply chain standards by strengthening its relationships with suppliers. The next evolutionary step was Wal-Mart's development of cross-docking and vendor-managed inventory to improve the supply chain linkages between manufacturers and retailers. Finally, Dell has been the exemplar of a manufacturer linking directly to consumers. Only in the last five years have retailers made substantial inroads, linking more directly with customers by covering the "last mile" into their homes. As shown in Figure 1-1, this extended supply chain represents a powerful opportunity to build stronger relationships with customers.

Our examination of the extended supply chain is based on insights from leading twenty-first-century companies and in-depth customer data from an emerging channel—consumer-direct groceries. This book presents a combined examination of the key components of last-mile supply chains, including marketing, supply chain fulfillment and delivery, and IT. The book combines insights and data from the authors' large-scale studies of multiple online grocers, Office Depot, and Federal Express, and from data gleaned from the popular press. The lessons and insights offered in this book apply to a broad range of retailers and manufacturing firms that are seeking to offer new services and differentiate their offerings from the predominant model, which emphasizes low prices. To introduce the power of extended or last-mile supply chains, we

Figure 1-1. The push for extended supply chains.

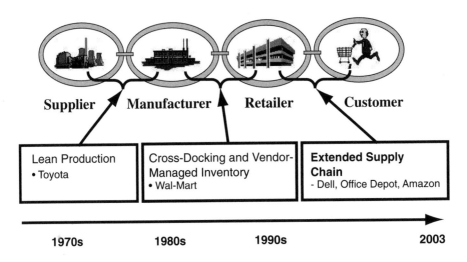

start off with a brief overview of the current state of the grocery industry, and the impact of extended supply chains.

The Grocery Industry

The grocery industry is an ideal example for examining extended supply chains that is at once universal—we all shop and eat—and also the most challenging supply chain environment. The grocery industry is characterized by hypercompetition with average profit margins of 1–2 percent of sales and highly perishable and fragile products with a low value-to-size ratio. Customers have widely varying tastes, and they tend to fixate on prices. For all these reasons, extending the supply chain for groceries (so that consumers have an experience that is more service-oriented) provides a unique opportunity for companies to differentiate themselves. For example, customers can place orders online from the comfort of their homes, and have their orders filled and delivered to their doorstep. There are substantial costs involved in extending the supply chain into consumer homes, which does not seem to fit with an extremely price-sensitive industry. And yet, it is precisely by turning this reasoning on its head that there is a quiet insurrection occurring. Extending the supply chain for groceries works, despite its challenges. It provides a means of enhancing the customer's experiences and breaking away from the crushing "price, price,

price" strategy exploited by leading retailers, such as Wal-Mart. It creates the type of customer experience that leads to greatly increased customer loyalty. The idea is to reforge links with customers that have been severed by decades of price promotions that have eroded customer loyalty to specific brands and to individual stores. If extending the supply chain can be used to create a loyalty effect in the ultrachallenging world of retail grocers, there are important lessons for a broader range of retailers and manufacturers.

As leading Internet retailers such as Amazon and Dell have shown, there is a market for products ordered online and delivered to customer homes. Yet, delivering products directly to customers is a challenging task—particularly with groceries. Perhaps the leading example of an Internet failure in this industry sector is Webvan, which burned through $700 million of investor capital in a little over a year in a highly visible effort to deliver groceries to customers' homes at prices competitive with traditional grocers. We argue that the spectacular failure of Webvan in 2001, and its contemporaries such as HomeGrocer and Streamline, was due primarily to two factors: (1) poor alignment between marketing and supply chain management, and (2) poor management of the supply chain. Fundamentally, Webvan was a symbol of putting the cart before the horse—the Internet can be an effective tool, but the real advantage is in extending the supply chain directly to consumers. The conventional wisdom has been that this last link will never be perfected, and over the period between 2002 and the end of 2003, several companies started or expanded their efforts to deliver groceries directly to customers. Just because earlier efforts weren't successful doesn't mean the war is over. In fact, major grocers including Albertson's, Tesco, Safeway, and Sainsbury's, and start-up companies such as Ocado and FreshDirect have seen sales of home-delivered groceries increase at rates above 50 percent per year over the last couple of years.

Book Layout

The extended supply chain creates opportunities to establish bonds with consumers where they live, but the opportunity comes with some unique challenges. The cost of delivering many small shipments to individual consumers (rather than large consolidated shipments to neighborhood stores) is substantially higher. Yet, companies such as Amazon, Lands' End, Office Depot, Grainger, etc. have already vaulted this barrier. We will devote the remainder of this chapter to two important topics. First, we profile the benefits of extended or last-mile supply chains for customers. Second, we introduce a frame-work of four strategies for extending supply chains into customer homes or places of business. This framework will be used as our central foundation to compare and contrast various retailers and manufacturers throughout the book. It also examines the grocery industry in particular to illustrate the framework. As is said about New York City, "If you can make it here, you can make it anywhere." The same saying can be applied to groceries—if supermarkets can use extended supply chains to break from the vicious cycle of lower and lower prices, then retailers and manufacturers in many other industries can too. The rest of the book is then laid out in two major sections:

- ◆ *Part 2, Strategies.* Chapters Two through Five examine each of the spe-cific strategies introduced later in this chapter in more detail. In each of these chapters, case studies of grocery firms and other retailer/manu-facturers are used to illustrate how these companies are bridging the last mile. Each of these chapters also examines the key advantages and challenges associated with that particular extended supply chain strategy.
- ◆ *Part 3, Transforming the Supply Chain.* Chapter Six starts this section off with an examination of how to mesh marketing and operational goals—something that all last-mile retailers realize is crucial, but few accomplish flawlessly. Chapters Seven through Nine then look sepa-rately at how marketing, supply chain design, and IT are being applied to change relationships with end customers.

Extended Supply Chains Attract Customers

We conclude this chapter with a brief discussion of the key advantages of ex-tended supply chains from a customer's perspective that will drive sales. While there are many challenges in bridging the last mile, it is these rewards that will unite companies and customers across the chasm between price-focused and service-focused retailing. We also introduce four strategies that retailers and manufacturers can utilize to extend their supply chains.

Convenience

Clearly, consumer-direct ordering (either over the Internet or by phone) is largely focused on customer convenience. People enjoy being able to order anytime and anywhere. While developed nations generally have scores of retail outlets within easy reach of most potential customers, shoppers get a certain enjoyment out of surfing the Web and placing orders for delivery. What businesses need to be careful about is how this transaction is conducted, how it is marketed to potential customers, and how it is executed.

Consider Amazon, which is widely regarded as one of the leaders of e-commerce. Is it more convenient to order a book online? Most people would answer yes without giving the question much thought. But the answer is really that *it depends*. On what? If I want something to read now or later today, then ordering from Amazon is less convenient since I can't get the book right away. In a few major cities, Barnes & Noble's online service, bn.com, will deliver that day. However, if I want a specific or obscure book title, going to the store is a wasted trip if it is not stocked by that store. Take for example a book that received an excellent review, but that is fairly low selling (say something like *The Natural History of the Oak Tree: An Intricate Visual Exploration of the Oak and Its Environment,* by Richard Lewington and David Streeter, DK Publishing, 1999). This book ranked as the 1,411,285th most popular book on Amazon (and, by the way, got a fantastic customer rating). This book is extremely unlikely to be in stock at almost any bookstore (the largest booksellers such as Barnes & Noble stock "only" 125,000 books in a superstore), thus online ordering offers a very convenient way to obtain it. Like Amazon, all last-mile supply chains must focus on providing increased convenience, but there also must be an understanding of the specific type of convenience (where direct to the consumer is more or less convenient).

Customization

Customization has been exploited by relatively few companies, yet it has the huge potential to offer products and services that consumers value and are willing to pay higher prices for. Dell Computer is the widely examined leader in customization. Starting from Michael Dell's dorm at the University of Texas, Dell has grown into the largest personal computer manufacturer in the world. Since its founding in 1984, the method of receiving orders has evolved from mail to telephone to online. The two fundamental advantages that Dell has exploited: first, cutting out the middleman and going direct to consumers to save costs; but more important, developing a supply chain that allows each consumer to order "her" personalized computer. Customers are allowed to choose the size of the hard drive, the speed of the processor, the type of input/output device (CD/DVD, zip disk, floppy disk), the type of monitor, and even the color of the computer. In a world where most products are commodities, offering customers *meaningful* customization is a huge advantage.

Why is the word *meaningful* emphasized? Because many companies offer customization that does not really offer great value to the customer, or that is so difficult to order that it loses appeal. Thus, we must contrast between *meaningful* and *minutia* in customization. Consider something like gift wrap or cards: Many retail Web sites offer the ability to have an item wrapped, or to enclose a card. This is customization, but it is mostly a qualifier—customers expect it, and they don't see it as a huge additional value. After all, there is nothing that special about wrapping a package before mailing it. This type of minutia customization is not only of slight value to customers, but it is also likely to confuse or trouble them by forcing them to make extra decisions. In contrast, consider Lands' End Custom: It allows customers to select one of nine colors, three rises, two back-pocket styles, two front-pocket styles, two leg styles, two fits (natural or relaxed) for a total of 432 possibilities *before* we even decide waist, hip, and inseam size, each of which can be selected in increments of a quarter inch. The end result provides well over 25,000 combinations of waist, hip, and inseam, which when multiplied by the 432 possibilities for color, rise, pockets, etc. comes to *over a million end possibilities*. This is *meaningful* customization, since each customer feels that he is getting his own customized pair of pants. Obviously, it would be impossible to stock all these combinations in a store or centralized distribution center. What have the results been for Land's End Custom? In the first year of operation, sales of custom chinos topped the company's initial goal of 10 percent of sales for the category. In addition, the company estimates that 25 percent of the buyers of custom pants and jeans are new to the company.[10]

A recent Harris Interactive poll found that less than half of Americans are content with buying clothing off the rack, and two-thirds have difficulty finding the right garments in the right size off the rack. Twenty percent say that finding clothing that fits is one of their greatest challenges.[11] Apparently, the entire apparel industry could benefit from more customization, yet this potential has been untapped. Take it from us (all three authors of this book are 6-foot, 3-inches, or taller), finding clothes that fit is not easy or convenient. We will see in Chapters Three and Nine how manufacturers can profitably use last-mile supply chains to offer customization directly to customers and help increase customer loyalty.

Quality

Quality is one of the most misused words in the business lexicon. Everyone wants quality. Everyone promises quality. After all, have you ever met a retailer who says, "What we sell is junk, but it is really cheap"? The point is that everyone says he has quality, but what is truly important is "relative quality." Most retailers promise quality products, but since they are selling commodity products, there is little incentive to actually improve quality. The Nikon digital camera bought at Best Buy is the same camera that can be bought at almost any other electronics outlet. So what does quality mean to a retailer? Mostly that the camera was not broken or dropped when in shipment or when being placed on the shelf. If there is a problem after purchase, then the retailer simply issues a credit, and returns the item to the manufacturer. Hence, quality here means little more than the product is what the manufacturer provided. It is the quality of service that offers retailers a chance to set themselves apart. Yet the recent trend has been for retailers such as Wal-Mart and Home Depot to greatly decrease the availability of service in favor of reducing prices.

In contrast, extended supply chains offer opportunities to provide service quality that is substantively better than normal supply chains. For the most part, the improved quality is offered by delivering orders directly from a manufacturer or distribution center, rather than from a store. The advantage here is that delivering from the manufacturer or distribution center cuts a link out of the supply chain. Most products sold in stores today are shipped according to the general flow shown in Figure 1-1. Suppliers ship parts and raw materials to a manufacturer that produces or assembles the end product, which is then shipped to a distribution center. The distribution center typically receives shipments from numerous manufacturers, breaks large truckload shipments up into smaller orders, and ships smaller trucks with numerous SKUs to individual stores. For example, Kraft produces Oreo cookies in its plant on the south side of Chicago, and then ships orders by the truckload to distribution centers. So a distribution center for Kroger might get an entire truckload of Oreos once a month. The distribution center stores the Oreos and ships smaller quantities to individual stores in combination with other items. So an individual Kroger store might get a shipment of a single case of Oreos once a week, but this shipment comes on the same truck with orders for cereal, cheese, disposable diapers, and hundreds of other products. Few customers of grocery stores, drugstores, etc., ever give much thought to how their products get to the store, yet this is precisely where an opportunity for improvement can be found.

By delivering straight to the consumer from the manufacturing facility or distribution center, the supply chain can be substantially shortened. A large part of the success of Dell is attributable to its shortening of the supply chain. By cutting out retailers, Dell has less inventory spread across the supply chain—hence, less potential for obsolete computers. Computers have a relatively short life span (often changing every two to three months in today's accelerated business climate), but this is nothing compared to any company offering perishable products for sale, such as food products. Here, shortening the supply chain can have a substantial impact on product quality/freshness. Consider Omaha Steaks, which has become a $300 million per year business by mailing premium steaks through the mail directly to customers. The increased costs of shipping to individual consumers are more than offset by the decrease in time to get the steak from processing to customers, and the accompanying improvement in product freshness. Online grocers such as FreshDirect (see Chapter Two) and Ocado (see Chapter Five) are capitalizing on this shortened supply chain to offer fresher, higher-quality products.

Experience

In many ways, this is the toughest advantage to capitalize on, but also one of the best opportunities for retailers. Most retailers have moved relentlessly toward the price-oriented, low-customer-contact, big-box experience over the past three decades. At best, the experience of shopping in a superstore is OK, but most of us prefer to get it done as quickly and painlessly as possible. Think of the greeters at many of the big-box retailers (Wal-Mart, Home Depot, Best Buy etc.)—do they do anything useful? Mostly they stand at the front of the store and say hello. So what! Didn't everyone in stores fifty years ago say hello and treat customers like they were valued? Seventy-five or a hundred years ago, your corner baker, grocer, hardware store owner, and druggist probably knew most of his customers by name. No more. Now, aside from the greeters, it is hard to find a human being to help in many of the big-box stores. How many times have you spent five to ten minutes wandering around these stores trying to get someone to answer a question, or to find a particular item? It almost seems like these retailers think they are doing you a favor by letting you shop in their stores, rather than the other way around.

So how do extended supply chains address the experience problem? They do this in one of two ways: by completely removing human interaction for routine purchases (let's face it, you get little "human" interaction when shopping in person at a big-box retailer), or by creating opportunities for *real* interaction. By far, the most common approach is the first—removing human interaction for routine purchases. When buying a commodity product like an airline ticket, a book, or a digital camera, many consumers can quickly find what they want and place an order with no human assistance. In fact, the Web site likely will provide more useful information than a person in a store ever could. For example, Amazon has capitalized on its ability to suggest other books/items that a customer may be interested in, based on previous purchases. In fact, one of the benefits of the low or no-contact experience is that customers can spend as little (or as much) time placing an order as they want. A specific book can be obtained on Amazon by a customer who has purchased previously in well under three minutes by using one-click ordering. On the other hand, many of Amazon's customers often spend an hour or more browsing through customer recommendations. Two things are important for the low/no-touch experience: The retailer must have a clear understanding of what/when this approach is attractive to customers, and he must offer reasonable alternatives to submit, process, or follow up on an order, since inevitably there will be exceptions and problems. In other words, call centers, e-mail correspondence, live chat, and a place to walk in and talk to a company representative will be used less often (as a lower proportion of total orders), but they will be used by many customers in situations where something abnormal happens in the transaction.

The second approach to handling customer experiences is to use extended supply chains to create *real* interaction. What does real interaction mean? At the point of direct customer contact, the moment of truth as it were, customers must feel like they are genuinely appreciated. This means that the delivery agent should be friendly, approachable, and, ideally, familiar to the customer. In other words, all the things that we don't typically receive in a big-box store. The advantage of extended supply chains is that delivery agents have an opportunity to create a real, meaningful customer experience at the customer's home or place of business, but that interaction can be managed and scheduled to occur in a brief amount of time (say, less than ten minutes). Thus, in a well-managed situation, customers can have a real, enjoyable experience, without the retailer having to sacrifice all efficiencies. As we will see in Chapters Six and Seven, companies that offer direct delivery have an opportunity to create stronger customer relationships through positive experiences. Interestingly, some companies that offer only indirect delivery can also capitalize on extended supply chains to improve customer experiences.

Strategies for Bridging the Last Mile

We propose four strategies for last-mile retailers to successfully deliver to customers' homes. However, we start with a brief examination of notorious failures in order to first show what does not work.

Past Failures

While retailers are effectively realizing that the Web provides opportunities for tapping new markets and adding sales growth not possible through traditional channels, there is also a growing awareness of the complex challenges that direct fulfillment entails. The first wave of last-mile retailers made bold promises during the Internet boom of 1998 to 2000, but mostly fell flat on their faces. The most prominent failures include Webvan, Pets.com, eToys.com, and Kozmo. In many ways, Webvan became the standard bearer for poor business planning by promising to provide groceries shipped directly to the customer's door in a prespecified, thirty-minute window at a price matching or beating that of existing grocers. Although this sounded excellent to customers, the operational challenge of fulfilling orders for low-margin, hard-to-handle groceries that required tight temperature controls left Webvan with a negative gross profit per delivery—before overhead costs of developing the Web site and brand were even incorporated. In short, Webvan went bankrupt—falling from a high market value of $7.9 billion to the $2.7 million that Louis Borders sold his 45 million shares for (at six cents per share) in July 2001, while burning through over $1 billion in start-up capital.[12] Another notorious flameout involved Pets .com, which spent $55.3 million in its first ten months of operations, mostly on high-profile television ads, including an infamous $2 million commercial during the 1999 Super Bowl. While this represented a tour de force in marketing brand development (the August 7, 2000, issue of *Advertising Age* called the Sock Puppet, the lovably loquacious icon of Pets.com, the "first bona fide advertising celebrity to be created in dot-com land"), it also represented a complete failure of fulfillment operations, given that it sold goods that cost $13.4 million for a price of $5.8 million.[13] Perhaps the Sock Puppet would have been more useful had it helped with deliveries rather than simply serving as a cute mouthpiece.

Two other notorious examples must be mentioned in any discussion of last-mile failures. During the Christmas of 1998, thousands of customers discovered that while Santa may be 100 percent reliable in delivering toys beneath the tree, retailers (including Toysrus.com, KBKids.com, and eToys.com) had substantial problems. Only 90 percent of over 1 million online orders were delivered on time by eToys.com—despite requiring purchasers to book orders by December 10 for delivery by December 24. Toysrus.com had similar problems. Thousands of customers were left hanging with unclear feedback regarding the status and whereabouts of their orders. The $100 rebate coupons offered to consumers to compensate them for their difficulties did little to combat the image of Toys 'R Us as Scrooge when children did not get coveted toys for Christmas.[14] Our final entrant in the hall of shame is Kozmo.com, which promised free delivery of almost anything from candy bars to CDs to videos in an hour, and managed to burn through $280 million in capital in its roughly year and a half existence from late 1999 to mid-2001. While this business model was described as dimwitted by many, and Kozmo never even got close to breaking even, many customers did love the service, as exemplified by Elizabeth Georges: ". . . I miss Kozmo—anyone who can bring me a dozen Krispy Kreme doughnuts and a DVD of *Gladiator* in under an hour with no delivery charge is my best friend."[15] As evidenced by this quote, there was a high degree of enthusiasm for Kozmo, but clearly some problems with its business model.

Despite the well-publicized disasters profiled above, there are now scores of companies that have employed more rational strategies for fulfilling orders received online for either customer pickup or home delivery. As discussed in Chapter One, this second wave of last-mile retailers shares two primary characteristics. First, their marketing focuses primarily on selling customers a value-added convenience, rather than a low-priced commodity. Gone is the idea that customers will flock to order online simply because it is the new cool thing; instead retailers must carefully target customers who want value-added convenience, and are willing to pay for it. Most of these retailers have implemented some type of delivery charge, and they have implemented constraints on when and where deliveries will be made. Essentially, retailers are now focusing on specific target markets, rather than trying to be all things to all people. The second characteristic that is shared in this second wave is a more rational, pragmatic approach to fulfilling orders. Much greater thought is being applied to supply chain decision making, and many lessons from the failed first wave of retailers are being incorporated into new supply chain designs.

Retail sales growth over the Web has consistently outpaced in-store sales over the past five years. While same-store sales have been largely stagnant, online sales continue to grow quickly, with $45.4 billion in 2002, $58.2 billion in 2003, and expected growth to $88 billion in 2005. Established retailers increasingly see online sales as a promising channel for growth. For example, Office Depot grew online sales by 23 percent in the first quarter of 2003, while total first quarter sales grew only by one percent, with same-store sales falling by 3 percent. With online purchases representing 19.3 percent of all sales, Office Depot clearly is only experiencing growth through its online channels. Similarly, outdoor gear retailer REI experienced a healthier overall 3.6 percent increase in sales at its sixty-five stores, yet its online sales grew by over 20 percent in the same period. Sears Canada Inc. experienced an online sales increase of 27 percent, from $94 million in 2001 to $120 million in 2002.[16] These retailers represent just a sampling of the hundreds that are finding that the online sales channel for home delivery or pickup offers opportunities for growth that simply do not exist with more traditional channels.

Successful Strategies

There are two key decisions associated with extending the supply chain. First, order fulfillment, or the picking of items for consumer orders, can be accomplished either in existing stores or in a centralized distribution center(s). Store-based order fulfillment generally involves a lower fixed capital investment, yet suffers from lower efficiency and more challenging inventory tracking than distribution centers. Second, delivery to the end consumer can be direct, as in delivery to the consumer's home, or indirect, wherein the consumer is required to pick up her order, or a third-party provider such as Federal Express or UPS provides the deliveries. Direct delivery is of greater value to the consumer, but also engenders increased delivery costs. Each of the four strategies shown in Figure 1-2 is a viable and attractive business model in the right circumstances.

The four strategies differ in terms of four critical factors: customer convenience, delivery cost, picking efficiency, and capital investment. Companies wishing to offer high levels of customer convenience deliver directly to consumers. For example, Office Depot delivered over $2 billion in office supplies

Figure 1-2. Strategies for extending the supply chain.

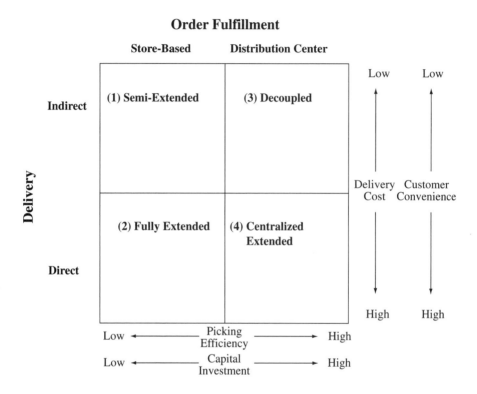

Order Fulfillment

directly to customer offices and homes in 2002. Office Depot employs a *central-ized extended* strategy because the large volume of consumer direct sales justifies a large capital investment in order to achieve picking efficiencies. In contrast, Tesco also delivers directly to customer homes (over $600 million of groceries and other household items in 2002), but it utilizes a *fully extended* strategy that involves picking orders from individual stores. This strategy allows Tesco to minimize capital investment for what is currently a niche market (about 1.5 percent of their total sales) and to make a profit on this business.

In contrast to Tesco and Office Depot, companies that want to minimize delivery costs either subcontract with third-party providers (such as UPS, Federal Express, or Airborne), or allow customers to pick up Internet orders at existing stores. Scores of companies follow a *decoupled* strategy to minimize delivery costs, while taking advantage of high picking efficiencies. Prominent examples of companies using this strategy include Dell, Amazon, NetFlix,

Caremark, and almost any catalog retailer such as Lands' End. Companies that choose to offer Internet ordering for pickup at a store do so to minimize capital investments and offer customers another channel. Companies such as REI, Best Buy, Rite Aid, and Lowes Foods To Go have used a *semi-extended* strategy to offer customers increased convenience at a low delivery cost and have forged stronger links with previously indifferent consumers.

Figure 1-3 provides an overview of the advantages and disadvantages of each of our four strategies, as well as examples of companies that are applying these strategies successfully. The figure provides a broad introduction to the extended supply chain strategies that will be examined throughout the remainder of this book. More detailed examinations of each of these strategies and case profiles of leading companies that utilize them are offered in Chapters Two through Five.

Action Steps

We have examined the potential benefits of last-mile supply chains and shown how they offer an opportunity to build stronger, more enduring, and profitable relationships with customers. We have also profiled four strategies for bridging the last mile. These strategies have numerous benefits as well as challenges; thus, we offer the following action steps as a starting point.

- ♦ Examine your company's supply chain and classify it as (1) predominantly price/cost-oriented, or (2) focused on differentiation. If it is price/cost-oriented, are you the leader in your business segment? If it is focused on differentiation, does cost ever lead you off track?

- ♦ Have you ever worried that Wal-Mart or some other price-oriented retailer/manufacturer will wipe your business out? If so, identify which of the potential benefits of last-mile supply chains your firm could most easily tap.

- ♦ Consider how last-mile supply chains may change your relationships with customers. How can you reap some benefits from this closer relationship?

- ♦ Choose one of the four strategies depicted in Figure 1-2 that best fits your goals for delivering directly to customers. You may want to consider things like total sales for your company, the value customers place

Figure 1-3. Overview of extended supply chain strategies.

	Advantages	Disadvantages	Examples
Semi-Extended	• Low, fixed investment cost • Increased foot traffic in stores and continued opportunities for impulse buys • Dual channel marketing • Low delivery cost	• High picking costs • Inventory tracking is difficult • High risk of stock-outs/substitutions • Low customer convenience	Best Buy Circuit City Lowes Foods REI Sears Canada Rite-Aid Walgreens
Fully Extended	• Low fixed investment cost • Halo effect • Dual channel marketing • High customer convenience	• High picking costs • Inventory tracking is difficult • High risk of stock-outs/substitutions • High delivery cost	Tesco Grainger Sainsbury Albertsons America Fresh
Decoupled	• Aggregated inventory • Low picking costs • Specialized and dedicated fulfillment • Fresher product & faster inventory turns • Ability to manufacture or assemble to order • Low risk of stock-outs/substitutions • Low delivery cost	• Low customer visibility • Low brand awareness • High fixed investment cost • Long lead time	Amazon Dell FreshDirect NetFlix Lands' End LL Bean Drugstore.com Caremark Omaha Steaks
Centralized Extended	• Aggregated Inventory • Low picking costs • Specialized and dedicated fulfillment • Fresher product & faster inventory turns • Ability to manufacture or assemble to order • Low risk of stock-outs/substitutions	• High delivery cost • Low customer visibility • Low brand awareness • High fixed investment cost • Long lead time	Office Depot Ocado Grocery Gateway Simon Delivers OfficeMax RoomstoGo Schwan's Dairy

on convenience for your products/services, your existing supply chain, etc. Follow this initial choice of strategies by a close reading of the chapter (Two through Five) on this strategy.

Notes

1. J. Swartz, "More Click on Item on Web, Pick it Up at Store," *USA Today* (December 5, 2002).

2. J. Dixon, "Farmer Jack Gambles on Big Change," *Detroit Free Press* (June 12, 2003), p. C-1.

3. R. Taylor, "Saving America's Grocers," *Brandweek* (May 5, 2003), p. 21.

4. Ibid.

5. John Reinan, "Retailers Boosting Emphasis on Service to Loyal Customers," *Minneapolis Star Tribune* (July 8, 2003), p. D-1.

6. James P. Womack, "Mass Customization: The New Frontier in Business Competition," *Sloan Management Review* (Cambridge: Spring 1993), Vol. 34, Issue 3, pp. 121–122.

7. B. Joseph Pine II and James H. Gilmore, "Welcome to the Experience Economy," *Harvard Business Review* (July/August 1998).

8. Shoshanna Zuboff and James Maxmin, *The Support Economy: Why Corporations Are Failing Individuals and The Next Episode of Capitalism* (Viking Press, 2002).

9. Frederick F. Reichheld, "Lead for Loyalty," *Harvard Business Review* (July/August 2001), Vol. 79, Issue 7, p. 76.

10. "More Lands' End Customers Ditching Standard Sizes in Favor of 'Size You,'" *Internet Retailer* (September 4, 2002), see www.internetretailer.com.

11. Ibid.

12. T. Rizzo, "The Death of Webvan," *Internet World* (August 1, 2001), pp. 4–5.

13. Data drawn from J. Weil, "Going Concerns—Did Accountants Fail to Flag Problems at Dot-Com Casualties?," *The Wall Street Journal* (February 9, 2001), p. C.1, and H. F. Schultz and D. E. Schultz, "Why the Sock Puppet Got Sacked," *Marketing Management* (July/August 2001), Vol. 10, No. 2, pp. 34–39.

14. D.G. Stankevich, "Was the Grinch Really Online?" *Discount Merchandiser* (March 2000), Vol. 40, No. 3, pp. 40–42.

15. Quote from M. Totty, "Listen Up, Retailers: These Five Consumers All Like Some Aspect of Shopping Online: So Why Don't They Do More of It?" *The Wall Street Journal* (September 24, 2001), p. R.9; financing information taken from J. Angwin, "Web Delivery Firm Kozmo Shuts Down," *The Wall Street Journal* (April 12, 2001), p. B.10.

16. Sales data for retailers taken from articles posted at www.internetretailer.com: "Online Retail Sales Will Nearly Double by End of 2005, eMarketer Projects"

(April 23, 2003); "Office Depot's Web Sales Grow 23% in Q1 While Total Sales Remain Flat" (April 17, 2003); "Sales Up More Than 20% at Outdoor Gear Retailers Altrec.com and REI.com" (April 22, 2003); "How Sears Canada's Fulfillment Network Supports Rising Web Sales" (April 17, 2003).

PART II

STRATEGIES

CHAPTER 2

Decoupled Extended Supply Chains

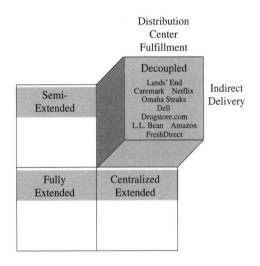

Distribution
Center
Fulfillment

Decoupled

Lands' End
Caremark   Netflix
Omaha Steaks
Dell
Drugstore.com
L.L. Bean   Amazon
FreshDirect

Indirect
Delivery

Semi-
Extended

Fully
Extended

Centralized
Extended

Over the past decade, the use of outsourcing and the Internet have proven to be two of the most dominant forces in modern management. It was inevitable that sooner (rather than later) these two trends would converge and intertwine into an even more powerful strategy. This is precisely what happened in the mid-1990s, and the outcome was the decoupled extended supply chain—arguably the most famous supply chain strategy of all time next to Toyota's celebrated just-in-time system. Mention the very phrase "dot-com," and you can't help but think of pioneering online retailers like Amazon and Dell. And it was with decoupled extended supply chains that these early e-businesses competed. They still do today, and it is no surprise that companies following this strategy are winning a lot of market share in a host of different retailing businesses. Without a doubt, the decoupled extended supply chain is a formidable strategy. So much so that many rivals (using other supply chain strategies) have still not figured out how to successfully counter it. Perhaps they never will.

The growing conventional wisdom in the 1990s was that outsourcing all noncritical processes was often the most effective way to compete in many businesses. We all know the mantra of outsourcing well—specialize in what you do best, and let your partners excel at what they can do even better. Outsourcing a few processes was good, and outsourcing everything not a core competence was usually even better. At the same time that companies voluntarily turned over their nonessential processes to others, they also needed to create even closer links with their upstream and downstream strategic partners and customers in the supply chain to coordinate information flows and products. This is where the Internet comes in. The Web allowed instantaneous sharing of information up and down the supply chain along with extremely precise tracking of all related activities and inventories. In good times, partners shared demand and forecast information to optimize their operations and maximize profits. In bad times, they used the instantaneously available information to buffer their operations from the mistakes of others somewhere else in the supply chain.

This is the strategy that companies like Amazon and Dell followed, and the hallmark of a decoupled extended supply chains remains delivery of products by specialized, third-party logistics partners. Amazon organizes the upstream supply chain and concentrates on its large warehouses strategically spotted around the world.[1] Delivery experts such as Federal Express, United Parcel Service (UPS), and Airborne handle the downstream distribution. Together, Amazon and its strategic delivery partners took on the giants of traditional retailing, and as we all know, they more than got Wal-Mart's and Barnes & Noble's attention. In fact, some would even argue that Amazon won at least the first few rounds of this battle, even though Walmart.com and bn.com have bravely battled back with their own decoupled extended supply chain strategies.

Dell's well-told story is nearly the same, except that it, of course, focused on assembly of desktop PCs, laptops, and servers.[2] In addition, another distinguishing feature of this supply chain strategy is the option to offer highly customized products. And what an unwelcome surprise Dell's decoupled extended supply chain strategy was to the reigning incumbents of the PC business in the

1990s, including Compaq, IBM, and Hewlett-Packard. Dell.com is famous for its PCs that are delivered direct to customers' businesses and homes, instead of through traditional retail channels. Moreover, virtually all of Dell's major products can be ordered in either standard form or heavily customized. Not surprisingly, when given a choice, some customers opt to customize their new computers. And it doesn't really need to be said (but we'll say it anyway) that more customized products not only mean happier customers, but also higher margins and greater insight into where consumers' tastes and preferences are headed next. When it comes time to deliver these computers, however, Dell turns it over to a select group of logistics companies (just like Amazon) whose own particular core competencies are in home deliveries and the related logistic processes involving returns.

The Basic Decoupled Extended Supply Chain Model

Although the economics of this model may, at first glance, seem relatively simple, it is actually quite difficult to orchestrate in practice, as summarized in Figure 2-1. There are six basic information flows that must *all* be carefully designed and managed in order for the overall decoupled extended supply chain to succeed. Four of these information flows are visible to end consumers, while two invisibly (at least to end customers) link the retailing and distributing partners in the business-to-business portion of the supply chain for outgoing deliveries and incoming returns.

The first (and arguably the most important) information flow is the ordering and payment system. While this is largely true for all extended supply chain strategies, it is absolutely critical for the decoupled extended supply chain. Think about it—by following this strategy, a company is *willingly* giving up any chance of ever having a firsthand or "direct" personal relationship with its customers at the moment that their goods are actually bought and delivered. Since these businesses will never have any direct personal interaction with end customers, it follows that the look and feel of their online stores must be superlative. This is where customers' positive (or negative) impressions of an online retailer are first formed, and as described in greater detail in Chapter Seven's discussion around marketing, online customers rarely give you more than one chance to get it right. Because it is their lifeline to customers, this information flow *is therefore always the primary responsibility of the retailer.* Indeed, both Amazon

Figure 2-1. Information flows of decoupled extended supply chains.

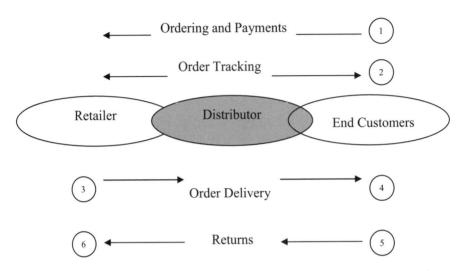

and Dell are widely recognized as having among the best online stores. Their Web sites offer fast loading, swift navigating, and easy purchasing. Behind the scene, each customer's data is carefully collected and analyzed to provide even better service the next time that he returns to shop. The IT underlying these systems is also as reliable as it can be. If you are a $40 billion, 24/7, online retailer such as Dell, then just fifteen minutes of unexpected downtime can easily cost you over $1 million in lost revenue.

The second vital information flow is for order tracking. Although not as critical in the overall strategy as the ordering and payment system, it is nevertheless an important feature. In general, the main responsibility for this resides more with the distributor, since the online retailer has outsourced delivery to it. Most major delivery companies have all the IT necessary to track parcels and packages across their distribution networks. Moreover, the best can feed this data to end consumers using tracking numbers, or back to retailers that want to show it via their Web site. Interested customers can then go online and track down their orders wherever they are in the transit pipeline. Retailers can likewise monitor the progress of their shipments anywhere around the world.

The third information flow—from retailer to distributor—is invisible to end consumers and a pure business-to-business transaction. These are commonly done via the Internet or EDI and, in the best of cases, involve bar codes and automated billing and payment systems. After all, there is no reason to pay for unnecessary shipping and accounting labor when automation can reduce costs at this step to virtually nothing.

The related fourth information flow is visible to customers, and at times, may be dependent upon their direct participation. This is especially true of high-value or bulky items that cannot be safely left on the front steps, or by the garage. In such instances, customers must be directly involved in the process to schedule deliveries when they are home.

The final two information flows are for returns. Not a pleasant thing to discuss, but these have historically proven to be the Achilles' heel of the decoupled extended supply chains. Everything is great up until the end customer decides that she doesn't want the product. At that point, transferring returning goods from customers to distributors to retailers frequently becomes a challenge—especially if time lapses, the product was damaged in transit, or the original packaging accidentally discarded. The information flow from customers to distributors for returns (number five in Figure 2-1) is, therefore, commonly one of the most problematic in the entire decoupled extended supply chain.

This is especially true if the customer cannot simply put the return item(s) in the regular mail, or is unwilling to incur the extra effort and/or expense of shipping it back via a common carrier. In such cases, the return pickup must be coordinated between the end customer and the original delivery company, along with the agreed form of counterpayment (refund, credit, return authorization number, etc.) and related paperwork. The final information flow—from the delivery company to retailer—is usually more routine than getting the return process started with customers, but unless carefully managed, it potentially carries a high per-transaction cost due to the less-than-truckload volumes commonly involved and restocking necessary upon its return to the shipping dock.

Notice throughout the above discussion the prominent role of third-party delivery partners in the downstream side of the typical decoupled extended supply chain. This suggests a contingent model for when this strategy is most favorably deployed. Ideally, the items being delivered are physically small, and the order volume is relatively low. As shown in Figure 2-2, items that companies like Amazon and Dell routinely sell are ideally suited to this supply chain strategy. They are relatively modest in size, and the order quantities are more often than not small. Since end customers typically pay for delivery in decoupled supply chains, it is important that they can readily afford the shipping charges with these items.

Figure 2-2. Trade-offs in decoupled extended supply chains.

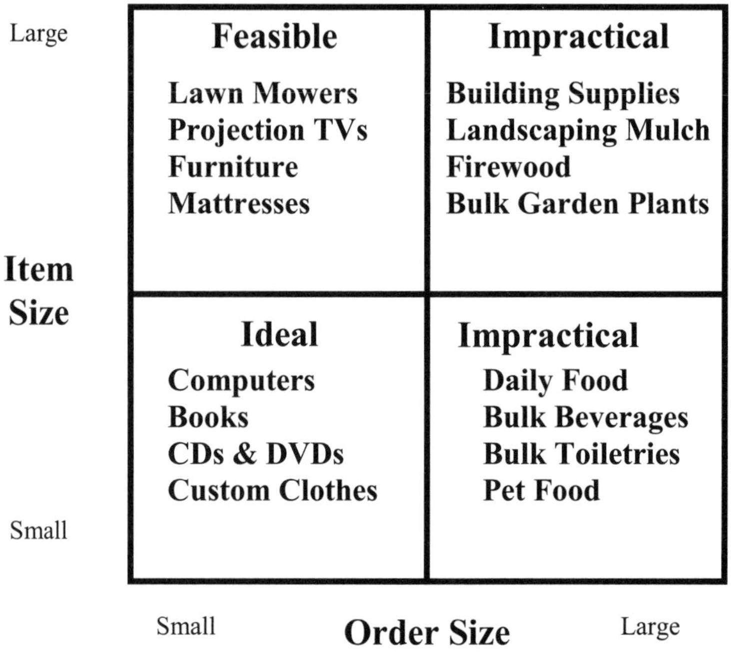

Large	**Feasible**	**Impractical**
	Lawn Mowers Projection TVs Furniture Mattresses	Building Supplies Landscaping Mulch Firewood Bulk Garden Plants
Item Size	**Ideal**	**Impractical**
	Computers Books CDs & DVDs Custom Clothes	Daily Food Bulk Beverages Bulk Toiletries Pet Food
Small		

Small · **Order Size** · Large

Decoupled extended supply chains can also deal with physically large products that are commonly ordered *in small volumes*. Although not as straightforward as the case is with smaller items, large products can often be accommodated by online retailers at the cost of bigger warehouses to store such bulky inventory. Similarly, customers must value the overall deal that they are getting on these products to help justify the extra shipping and handling charges. At the other extremes—small and large items *at high volumes*—these are almost always impractical for this supply chain strategy. Few people would ever be willing to pay the weekly delivery charges by UPS for household groceries, much less buy a load of firewood if it was going to be delivered overnight by Federal Express.

The Ability to Offer Customized Products

It seems like we have been hearing about the dawn of a new business strategy called "mass customization" for over a decade. Namely, this strategy involves products that are closely tailored to customers' individual preferences at near market-rate prices. This has been viewed as the Holy Grail of management—each customer is uniquely served, and yet the company does not go bankrupt in the process of delighting its clients. But in order to offer customers a customized product, you first need three basic elements. On the front end of the system you must have very fast incoming order processing. In the middle of the system, you need operations that are flexible enough to assemble individual orders (versus larger standardized batches) at a competitive price with relatively short lead times. Finally, on the back end, you have to put into place a rapid outgoing delivery system to get products back to the customer as quickly as possible. Bring these three elements together, and retailing magic happens. Customers place orders for products tailored to their tastes, operations economically and reliably fulfills them, and delivery partners swiftly put the item(s) back into the hands of the waiting shoppers.

As pioneering companies such as Dell demonstrate, the long wait for true mass customization is finally over. In fact, of the four supply chain strategies discussed in this book, only the decoupled extended strategy can handle mass customization. If you reflect on it, to mass-customize you need that critical lapse in time between when a customer places her order and when she expects to receive her product. That relatively brief interval is when your flexible operations comes into play to make what the customer wants. If you are shipping made-to-stock products out of a warehouse (or a store) using either a semi-extended (Chapter Three), fully extended (Chapter Four), or centralized extended (Chapter Five) supply chain, there is no buffered time in which to customize each customer's order. In other words, if you are seriously thinking of offering customized products to your customers, then you also need to begin carefully evolving your existing operations into a decoupled extended supply chain.

The Internet is, of course, the answer to the first part of a mass customization system. The Web lets customers mix and match options, and then electronically submit their final orders when they are ready. Equally important, the Web store and supporting configuration software can prevent customers from selecting combinations of options that are infeasible to make. Once the order is digitized, it stays that way throughout the production process. Information Technology schedules the customer's unique order, and humans with some supporting automation typically assemble-to-order the product. And from there, it functions like any other decoupled extended supply chain in that a third-party logistics provider usually takes over and delivers the products to end customers.

The Decoupled Extended Supply Chain in Groceries

As suggested by Figure 2-2, there is no pure example of this strategy in groceries due to the weekly nature and typical volume of purchases (sixty to one hundred items). There are, however, strong echoes of the strategy in an online grocer named FreshDirect. FreshDirect specializes in high-quality food preparation and delivery in New York City (mainly Manhattan). FreshDirect's strength is in its impeccably prepared, perishable foods, including fish, sausages, roasts, and baked items—in other words, "mass-customized groceries." It has built what one of its cofounders—Joe Fedele—proudly describes as "the most automated plant in food processing."[3] In fact, FreshDirect's operations blur the traditionally distinct line between kitchen/factory and warehouse by storing fresh "raw materials" like carcasses of beef, bakery items, and vegetables, and then cooking customer orders to preference. In terms of volume, FreshDirect can handle up to 16,000 orders per day.[4] The entire operation can best be described as a giant kitchen in an even bigger refrigerator. Throughout the entire production, packing, and shipping process, food is kept at (or below) 36 degrees Fahrenheit. FreshDirect also stocks a limited range of dry goods and nonperishables, but these are mainly of the convenience variety to complement the meals that are prepared and sold.

FreshDirect differs in practice from companies like Dell only in the way it delivers its products. Specifically, it operates its own fleet of delivery vans instead of subcontracting out to a third-party service. Of course, the key reason for this is that FreshDirect's products are perishable, which makes swift and reliable delivery absolutely imperative. In other words, delivery is a core competence that companies such as FreshDirect cannot afford to outsource to others. Coupled with this strategy is limiting the delivery area to a handful of Zip code areas in the Big Apple and initially night-only delivery.[5] Given the tough daytime traffic in Manhattan, it makes sense to deliver later in the day when the roads are less crowded, people are more likely to be home, and the mass-customized groceries can be delivered as fresh as possible.

Figure 2-3 shows the average response to a survey of 450 FreshDirect customers. As we would expect, the customers think that the service saves them

Figure 2-3. The average response to a survey of 450 FreshDirect customers.

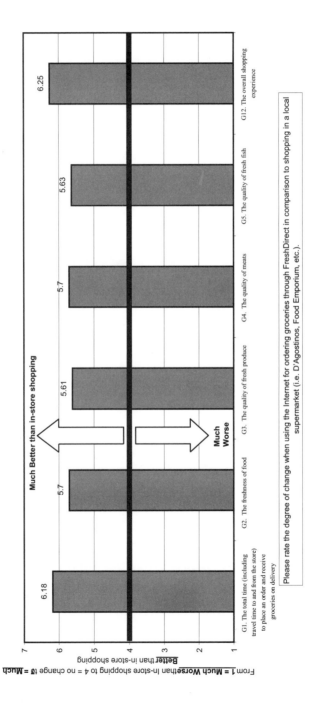

Please rate the degree of change when using the Internet for ordering groceries through FreshDirect in comparison to shopping in a local supermarket (i.e. D'Agostinos, Food Emporium, etc.).

From 1 = **Much Worse** than in-store shopping to 4 = no change to 7 = **Much Better** than in-store shopping

G1. The total time (including travel time to and from the store) to place an order and receive groceries on delivery

G2. The freshness of food

G3. The quality of fresh produce

G4. The quality of meats

G5. The quality of fresh fish

G12. The overall shopping experience

time (with an average rating of 6.18, where 4 means the time is about the same as a traditional supermarket and 7 is much better). What is more intriguing is the very high ratings for product freshness. Customers rate the freshness and quality of produce, meats, and fish as substantially better than what they can get in their local supermarket. This illustrates the capabilities of FreshDirect in particular and the decoupled extended supply chain in general to deliver fresh, customized products. The final question in Figure 2-3—regarding the overall shopping experience—has a mean response of 6.25, indicating that customers truly love this new method of shopping for groceries.

Perhaps one of the most interesting aspects of FreshDirect's business model (for the insight it gives into changing consumer habits) is that its ideal customer orders once a week from it, but also shops once per month at a bulk retailer, such as Costco or Sam's Club.[6] This goes right back to Figure 2-2—the strong point of such retailers is large-volume, bulky items (shown in the lower right-hand quadrant of the diagram) that are uneconomical to ship. You know—stuff like thirty-six packs of toilet paper, five-pound jars of peanut butter, and ten-gallon jugs of bleach. In other words, for certain industries, the overall market may end up splitting its total customer base between low-volume customized retailers and high-volume bulk specialists.

For about the same overall annual expense as shopping weekly at a traditional grocery store for everything, a shrewd customer splitting his business eats better during the week thanks to FreshDirect *and* only has to trundle off to the store once a month for bulky items. Don't forget that the customers we are largely talking about are busy career moms. By following such a plan, they are annually spared around forty extra shopping trips (three to four shops per month multiplied by twelve months), which easily adds up to over sixty prime-time hours. We are starting to see this in certain instances in the high-end grocery business in dense urban areas, and this trend is also occurring in clothes and fashion—the subject of the next section.

The Decoupled Extended Supply Chain in Fashion and Apparel

Most likely picking up on what Dell did to revolutionize the PC business, the decoupled extended supply chain is now increasingly featured in the fashion and apparel industry. A great example of this strategy is found at Lands' End. Lands' End provides custom-tailored clothing for a slight premium over the typical garment. The customer logs on to www.landsend.com and clicks on the type of apparel that he is interested in under "Lands' End Custom Clothing." Items offered include men's dress shirts, jeans, chinos, and corduroy dress pants, as well as women's jeans and chinos.

As an example of how its system works, let's take the case of men's custom dress shirts. The customer first selects the type of solid fabric color and cloth type that he wishes the shirt to be made out of from over thirty different options. He then selects one of five collar types, four cuff styles, pocket or no pocket, and box or shoulder pleats. In the next step, the customer creates his individual fit profile by answering a series of questions that allows Lands' End to mathematically "model" his body shape in a way not possible with standard sizing. Of course at this stage, the customer has to answer as accurately and truthfully as possible, or even the best system can go wrong.

After that, customers go though a series of pictures describing their physique including chest, shoulders, arm size, stomach, and torso length. This may sound complicated, but it is not. In almost the same amount of time it just took us to describe Lands' End system to you, we could have placed an online order for a customized shirt.

In a very few instances, certain body proportions may result in patterns that fall outside of Lands' End production capabilities. Whenever that happens, the company contacts customers by phone or e-mail to politely explain the problem. Assuming that the customer's order is within parameters, delivery takes two to three weeks from order placement. Although not nearly as fast as Dell's typical week turnaround time, it is still impressive considering the product's price and what the customer ultimately receives. Moreover, once a custom item is purchased, the customer does not typically need to update his personal data the next time he shops. In the case of a shirt, the customer only needs to decide on the fabric, cuffs, pockets, and shoulder pleats. The next time around, if he is buying custom pants, then his individual profile is automatically used to help swiftly guide the fitting of that custom product.

Other examples of the decoupled extended supply chain are starting to show up across apparel and fashion. Take the case of Nike iD. Nike now offers a range of over thirty-five custom-designed running and basketball shoes. Similar to Lands' End, you go online to www.nikeid.com and first select the basic shoe type. After that, you select items like upper and lower patterns, sole colors, and shoelaces. Perhaps the ultimate feature is the ability to have your name (or whatever) inscribed on the heel, side, or bottom of the shoe. Nike iD has even proved so popular that as this book goes to press, Nike is offering two styles of shoes in conjunction with Louisiana State University—the reigning college football champion.

Interactive Custom Clothes Company (www.ic3d.com) is a start-up online company that competes with a mass-customization business model, similar to that of Lands' End and Nike, only it specializes in high-fashion jeans and pants. The company is perhaps most famous for its leather pants that can be customized based upon width, length, belt loops, zippers versus buttons, and flashy accessories like rhinestones. The price, once again, is surprisingly affordable, and delivery is typically a few weeks after the order is placed.

Maybe even more interesting are the custom makeups sold by Reflect.com. Long ago, paint companies like Sherwin-Williams discovered the operational benefits of *postponing* the mixing of colors until the customer finally made up her mind at the store on what shade of paint she wanted.[7] By postponing the final differentiation of the product, a paint manufacturer not only has a much easier time of forecasting demand (finite gallons of white paint instead of limitless shades of color), but also gets to carry much less inventory in the process of providing this virtually unlimited choice to customers. In a certain sense, paint is paint, and you can follow the same postponement strategy with either house paint or facial makeup.

Going back to Reflect.com, the company can mix their customer's eye shadow, blush, and lipstick to order and reap exactly the same fundamental benefits that a company like Dell does, only in an entirely different retailing sector. Most important, the same net results happen—namely lower inventory carrying costs along with higher customer satisfaction. In fact, it is hard to think of a retail sector that cannot somehow take advantage of mass customization with postponement. Remember, it is not for all customers—only the ones most willing to pay the highest margins for the best service. Those folks are out there in every market, and the dilemma is to decide if you should be serving them in yours.

This is also exactly what Dell does in the computer business. Yes—sometimes procrastination does pay—especially if it is done in the supply chain. Dell waits until the last possible minute to load company-specific software and place country-dependent power cords and documentation with each PC before the box is closed. This lets Dell's assembly line turn out an almost limitless variety of PCs to satisfy the needs of every customer. As a matter of fact, this strategy allows the single Dell assembly plant in Ireland to serve all of Europe, despite the numerous languages and several different power voltages and plugs. The same holds true for the other two Dell plants—in Texas covering the Americas and in Singapore covering Asia and the Pacific. It's actually pretty amazing when you think about it, and all it takes is online ordering and three strategically located (yet flexible) plants around the world to cause your competitors global heartache, as you steadily win over the most profitable customers in the market.

Diamond.com is another equally intriguing business, especially because at its core is the somewhat mythical managerial practice called "capable to promise." In order to offer a capable-to-promise system, an online retailer needs to be able to show customers *the exact products* it has in stock, and once the customer purchases the product, allocate that specific item to the customer. You sometimes see this when you order online tickets from a company like Ticketron, where you can view the theater or stadium seating chart and then book the exact seats that you want. A few airlines now also offer you the chance to reserve your seat online, but outside of these service examples, it is rarely (if ever) seen in a manufacturing context. That is, however, until Diamond.com came along with its custom-designed rings.

As we all know, every diamond is different in terms of the famous "four Cs" of cut, clarity, color, and carats. Diamond.com shows customers what diamonds it has in stock at the present moment, and then lets them configure a ring (typically an engagement ring) around any specific diamond. You see online what the ring will look like as you swap stones around, and (of course) the price oscillates up and down as you change different stones in your favorite setting. For the typical male customer, it's a great way to, more or less, stay in budget as you try to get the biggest "rock" for your fiancée. Plus, the instant you complete the transaction, the stone that you selected is "subtracted" by the capable-to-promise system so that the next customer never sees that diamond online as one of his options. Of course, there are so many other stones available that the next customer is oblivious to what is going on and doesn't end up disappointed.

Will companies like Interactive Custom Clothes, Diamond.com, and Reflect .com ever put more traditional retailers such as Levi's, Zales, or Revlon out of business? Probably not, but they are most likely making managers at those companies lose a little sleep as they worry about the future. After all, having a competitor's decoupled extended supply chain squarely aimed at your most profitable products and customers is no fun in any business. Just ask any manager at Compaq or IBM about Dell, and listen to what they have to say.

The Decoupled Extended Supply Chain in Other Businesses

Another excellent example of a decoupled extended supply chain is Ranger-Golf.com. It's the same underlying strategy, only now we are talking about postponement and mass customization in terms of grips, shafts (materials and lengths), heads, colors, and weights. We've seen similar Web sites for sporting goods ranging from customized fishing rods to tennis rackets. There are even customized nutritional supplements for sale at companies like Vitamins.com. In fact, take any product category. As a rule of thumb, if certain customers believe that they can get some type of advantage, in terms of how they look, perform, feel, etc., from customized products, then chances are that a decoupled extended supply chain strategy can be exploited by at least one (or more) retailers in that customer segment.

What are the limits to the decoupled extended supply chain strategy? Good question, and when you get a chance, go take a look at Deere.com if you want to see some mind-boggling mass customization possibilities. In the 1980s, John Deere created one of the world's most flexible manufacturing plants at its Waterloo, Iowa, tractor works. Now fast-forward to the present. It seems natural to let farmers—whose soils and crops all vary—configure tractors online exactly as they want them. Although you are not going to charge it on your credit card (and there is no way that Federal Express is going to be able to deliver it to your front door), at Deere.com you can configure a monster, 450-horsepower, four-wheel-drive $200,000 tractor, including everything from tires to satellite systems. You can even choose how many windshield wipers you'll need. Needless to say, if Deere can mass-customize such complicated (and huge) products for farmers in the countryside, surely this strategy can be exploited in almost any urban setting with much less sophisticated products (perhaps like the ones that your company sells).

The Three Roles of Third-Party Delivery Partners

Somewhat assumed in the above discussion has been the major role played by third-party logistics (3PL) providers in the decoupled extended supply chain.

We'll turn to them now for discussion. As pointed out in Figure 2-1, 3PL providers are the direct link to end customers, and they play a huge role in the overall decoupled retailing process. Third-party logistics partners, in particular, bring three key things to the table. The most obvious one is the ability to offer innovative delivery approaches. The second is a little less obvious, and involves the ability to let customers access shipping data and track orders. The final is an ability to simplify the returns process. We'll address each of these roles in turn.

Probably the most fundamental issue regarding delivery in the decoupled extended supply chain is how you get products into customers' hands. As you will soon see, when you read the following three chapters on other popular extended supply chain strategies, it is relatively straightforward for most other home-delivery approaches. With these strategies, customers actually go to the store to either pick products up (Chapter Three), or they choose a day when they are going to be home to receive items (Chapters Four and Five). It is not quite so simple with the decoupled extended supply chain. Few people will cheerfully take a day off from work to wait at home for a book, a golf club, some makeup, or a shirt. And what about high-value items like PCs and dia-mond rings? They're not the right kind of products to drop off at the front door of somebody's house when nobody is home, no matter how safe the neighborhood seems to be. This is where 3PLs come in, and fortunately, they have been very active in terms of coming up with new solutions to the final few feet in that famous "last mile" of home delivery.

Take UPS, for example. Over the past few years, it has been relentlessly (but often silently) casting off its image as lagging in home delivery, and in many ways, it has now become one of the leading Internet carriers. The com-pany handles 55 percent of all online purchases versus Federal Express's 10 percent. United Parcel Service's core strength, without a doubt, is its huge fleet of over 150,000 trucks that allows them to reach practically every business and home in the United States. To its credit, UPS figured out in recent years how to make quick, mid-distance, night deliveries of up to 500 miles away by truck, which is obviously much less expensive than shipping by air. Their reach also increasingly spans the world, thanks to integrated land and air delivery.

In related actions, UPS also recently introduced money-back guarantees for residential shipments in the lower forty-eight states aimed at narrowing the service gap with Federal Express and the U.S. mail. They likewise purchased Mailboxes Etc. and its 3,000 franchised stores to provide (among other reasons) easier package pickups. Security concerns largely go away in a single stroke, thanks to these convenient drop-off and pickup points, plus customers now have a place to bring return items for repackaging and forwarding back to the retailer.

Federal Express has long dominated the overnight business-to-business delivery industry, thanks to its modern fleet of planes and famous hub-and-spoke logistics network radiating out of Memphis, Tennessee. On the other hand, Federal Express has belatedly begun to build its own home-delivery system, and it has struggled to duplicate the ground system that UPS spent almost one hundred years building. Not to be outdone, however, FedEx is in the process of rolling out a program called "Ship & Get" where they are putting package carousels in grocery stores. Customers who are doing their regular grocery shopping can pick up items purchased online at the store. As with Mailboxes Etc., this provides potentially thousands of new drop-off and pickup points that facilitate the final delivery step in decoupled extended supply chains.

But perhaps some of the most interesting recent moves in 3PL are those being made by Deutsche Post. The company has steadily integrated Deutsche Post, DHL, and Postbank into what is now called Deutsche Post World Net (www.dpwn.com). Although critics point out that Deutsche Post World Net is based upon an unfair monopoly (the German mail system), its Web site has linked together millions of consumers and businesses in Europe. In addition to home mail, its vast delivery system also includes retail outlets, delivery bases, and letter boxes, which easily makes the company Europe's leading delivery service provider.[8] In 2003, Deutsche Post also completed the acquisition of the U.S.–based Airborne delivery service, which, with DHL, positions it alongside UPS and Federal Express as a leading logistics company and a major player in the European and U.S. markets for years to come.[9]

Let's interject a few words of caution into the discussion just to balance things out a bit. It is not all positive news regarding decoupled extended supply chains and 3PLs. Relying on third-party partners to deliver your products carries certain risks, and it *has the potential* to lead to problems. Remember the big UPS strike of 1997, and the subsequent one that almost happened in 2002? Don't forget that the Teamsters Union represents labor in many transportation companies in the United States, and that we often see the mail service in countries around the world periodically disrupted by strikes. If you rely on a 3PL, then you are, to a certain degree, vulnerable to any labor-related delivery problems that the third-party partners might have. The same goes for seasonal mailing bottlenecks, such as those occurring around February's Valentine's Day,

April's tax deadline, May's graduations, June's weddings, and the December holidays. At such times your free-flowing, decoupled extended supply chain may become temporary clogged with undelivered packages due to the sheer volume of items being mailed.

As another example of the possible problems lurking in the shadows of the decoupled extended supply chain strategy, 3PLs can raise delivery fees (or modify services) as they see fit, which inadvertently hurts online retailers that are pursuing a decoupled strategy. Such a thing recently happened when most carriers increased the charges for home delivery vis-à-vis business customers during the week. Perhaps even worse, they also dramatically increased the costs for weekend deliveries because of the overtime expense involved, which, of course, potentially harms the overall business proposition of online retailers since that is when many of their best customers are most likely to be home.

Remember, most of these deliveries are not scheduled, so it is hit or miss as to whether or not delivery drivers catch someone at home. In their defense, carriers argue that residential deliveries take more time than business deliveries because private homes are more dispersed, and in many instances, drivers have to return several times if the customer isn't home. The net outcome is that while customers now pay a premium to send packages to someone's home, they are still likely to blame the retailer for delivery problems since the shipment was arranged at the retailer's Web site when the item(s) was or were purchased. And, as more and more packages purchased online flood these transportation networks, the charges to consumers are as likely to rise again as they are to fall.

The second role that 3PLs play in the decoupled extended supply chain is in data management and customer order tracking. Federal Express, UPS, and others pioneered many of these enhanced delivery services, and they have now become standard at almost all 3PLs. When you need to track down a package, you simply log on to the delivery service's Web site, enter the invoice or shipping number, and almost instantaneously see where the package is in the delivery pipeline.

Such tracking technology is now routine, and in our opinion, the interesting managerial issue is not the underlying IT, but where the information is presented. Again, take Dell as an example. Dell carefully integrates the carrier's tracking data into its own Web site, instead of sending the customer from Dell.com over to the 3PL's Web site to locate an item. Why? That's easy—companies like Dell want to offer a *seamless, yet branded* experience to the customer. What do we mean by seamless, yet branded? Simply that every transaction you could conceivably want to do with them—including tracking a delivery—is done thorough Dell.com *and nowhere else*. After all, Dell sold you the PC, and it will provide after-sales service for months, or even years, after you start using it. It makes sense then to have you come back to the company after ordering (but before you take final delivery) to find out where your computer is in the delivery process. This reinforces the relationship that you have with Dell and, in turn, helps it cement its "ownership" over end customers throughout the product's entire life cycle.

The final role of a 3PL concerns returns. Returns management involves moving goods from their final destination backwards up the supply chain in order to recapture the latent value in rejected (or damaged) finished goods, either through repackaging, remanufacturing, refurbishing, or disposal. Don't despair, returns happen even in the best of companies, and when they do, they need to be planned for. At the core of all returns management is giving customers some type of returns authorization, and then arranging to transport the item(s) back to the online retailer. Often, merchandise credit also has to be issued to customers, and in some cases, the condition of the product has to be reevaluated (called disposition) and disposed of, or repackaged and put back into inventory.

The Reverse Logistics Executive Council (RLEC) recently estimated that reverse logistics costs exceeded $35 billion a year for all U.S. companies.[10] And returns are an especially important part of the delivery process for online retailers. According to other estimates from Gartner, product returns cost online retailers $3.2 billion in 2001. Moreover, Jupiter Media predicts that U.S. consumers will make 90 million such returns by 2005, involving almost $6 billion worth of goods.[11]

The best delivery partners have already thought through these returns processes, and it is well worth leveraging their expertise. It probably should be said at this point in the book that we are not getting paid to endorse any particular companies, but some are just better than others are. Take the case of UPS. They have built a strong competence in optimizing the return management process.

Key features of UPS's returns system include a closed-loop return cycle from authorization to credit along with all related transportation and warranty information flows. UPS also offers product testing, repair services, and No Fault Found (NFF) inventory restocking, as well as reboxing, recycling, and disposal of bad items (including regulated substances and products).

Not to be outdone, Federal Express also excels at the returns process through their FedEx Return Manager and FedEx Package Returns Program (PRP). Along these lines, Federal Express recently introduced what it calls "billable stamps." These are preprinted return-shipping labels provided to customers to simplify the returns process. Billing occurs only if and when a label is used. It also offers a related returns service enabling merchants to notify Federal Express that a return shipment is ready for pickup at a customer's location, prints a return label, and provides it to the end customer at the time of pickup. Similarly, Federal Express's Consolidated Return Service is another relatively new service that simplifies the large-volume returns process for online retailers and offers a hassle-free returns process for end customers. Utilizing Federal Express's network of drop-off points, individual returns are consolidated to help online retailers build shipment volume before returning the entire lot. These consolidated shipments are sent to a dedicated returns center hub, where they are opened, sorted, repackaged, and shipped to the final return destination. By consolidating return shipments, and routing to final disposition locations (resale, repair, liquidation, etc.), this service helps nonstore retailers reduce returns handling, overall processing times, and associated costs.

Key Success Levers

This section summarizes the lessons learned for companies interested in featuring a decoupled extended supply chain. The first (and most obvious) key to success is to have an excellent Web site. This is easier said than done, and we can cite case after case of companies vainly searching for that "perfect" online store. Walmart.com itself was even launched and relaunched several times in the past few years before it began to get it right. And if Wal-Mart can stumble in retailing, then anyone can.

The second success lever is to look for products that can be mass customized. A worthwhile exercise is to go through your entire product line and search for items that can be customized *while simultaneously* reviewing your recent customer correspondence, where more variety or choice may have been requested. The most likely product candidates for mass customization are where these two analyses intersect. You can then exploit the decoupled extended supply chain in one of its most potent forms like Dell, Lands' End, and other rising online retailing stars such as FreshDirect have done.

A related lesson learned is to exploit postponement wherever possible as part of your decoupled extended supply chain strategy. Mass customization and postponement can be a devastating "one-two punch" that *can only be done* using the decoupled extended supply chain. Dell used these two techniques against its rivals, and it can no doubt be used in many other businesses. When you can beat your competitors on variety and cost—thanks to the flexibility of mass customization and the favorable economics of postponement—it is just about the pinnacle of all supply chain management.

The final two success levers relate to third-party delivery partners. As suggested throughout this chapter, you need to team with *excellent* 3PL providers. An online retailer "owns the customer," but the delivery service is the only one that "meets the customer." Finally, don't forget about returns. When things don't go right, 3PL providers are often the first to interact with customers who may have been disappointed by the whole experience and are looking to take it out on the retailer in terms of future business. At such times, both retailers and 3PL partners have everything to win or lose. If you don't make a future sale, then they don't make a future delivery.

Action Steps

In this chapter we took a look at one of the most dominant forms of home delivery to so far emerge from the dot-com revolution—the decoupled extended supply chain. Dell and Amazon were pioneers of this form of e-business, but others have adopted and adapted the strategy to their own particular retail sectors. While the decoupled extended supply chain may not be for everybody, you and your colleagues need to carefully evaluate the strategy before dismissing it too quickly in your own particular retailing sector. It is almost guaranteed that the decoupled extended supply chain will be a point of attack on your particular business by either a present-day "weakling" (such as Dell once was) or a new start-up (such as Amazon, FreshDirect, Interactive Custom Clothes, or Reflect.com). Can you afford to let another company seize this proverbial retailing "high ground"? You know what your competitors are going to try to do—offer customized products to the best customers in your sector, and leave you with the lower-margin, standardized business. And if your rival can bring in postponement, then it will catch you (and others slow to react in your retailing sector) in the modern business rendition of the class wartime pincer-movement of a left- and right-hand encircling attack of mass customization and low price.

To get you thinking about what needs to be done next, here are some important actions to consider along with this strategy:

♦ Strive to achieve the perfect online store. Your customers will never actually see your business, except for what they experience online. It has to be as close to faultless as possible, or they may never return for that all-important, second online shopping "trip."

♦ Always double-check to see if it makes sense to offer mass-customized products, along with standardized offerings. Chances are that eventually one or more of your rivals will offer mass-customized products, and you at least want the option to have a first-mover advantage on them.

♦ Wherever possible, exploit postponement as part of the decoupled extended supply chain. This helps ensure that you have the lowest possible inventory-related costs.

♦ Partner with the right third-party logistics providers. They are the critical link between your business and what happens (or doesn't happen) at the customer's front door. Your IT also needs to integrate with theirs in order to offer customers the seamless ability to track packages wherever they are in the delivery process.

♦ Don't forget to think though your *entire* reverse logistics process. Even if margins with a forward-flowing supply chain and home-delivery are excellent, sloppy returns processes will swiftly wipe them out.

Notes

1. "Mighty Amazon," *Fortune* (May 26, 2003), pp. 60–62.
2. Based on information from www.dell.com, University of Virginia Darden Case, G.F. Payne, "Dell Computer: Business to Business Over the Web," (UVA-C-2144), and J. Magretta, "The Power of Virtual Integration: An Interview with Dell Computer's Michael Dell," *Harvard Business Review* (98208).
3. D. Kirkpatrick, "The Online Grocer Version 2.0," *Fortune,* Vol. 145, Iss. 11 (November 25, 2002), pp. 217–218.
4. Ibid.
5. Ibid.
6. Ibid.
7. For more insight into mass customization and postponement strategies in the supply chain see E. Feitzinger and H.L. Lee, "Mass Customization at Hewlett-Packard: The Power of Postponement," *Harvard Business Review.*

8. J. Ewing, "The World's Postman: Europe's Express Deliver King Is Going After the U.S. Market," *Business Week* (September 29, 2003), p. 30.

9. W. Armbruster, "Showdown Time For Express Carriers," *Journal of Commerce* (August 4, 2003), p. 1.

10. A. Zieger, "Reverse Logistics: The New Priority?" *Frontline Solutions* (November 2003), pp. 20–21.

11. T. Kemp, "Next E-Retail Step: Return Analysis—Capturing and Analyzing Detailed Data About Why Merchandise Is Sent Back Can Reduce Returns, Study Says," *Internet Week* (May 21, 2001), p. 11.

CHAPTER 3

Semi-Extended Supply Chains

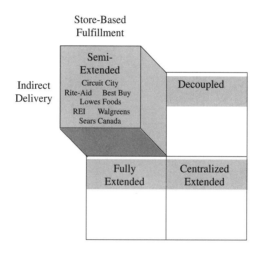

This strategy pairs store-based order fulfillment with indirect delivery. Orders are picked in the store following the receipt of a customer order placed via the company Web site or a telephone. Customers then are asked to pick their orders up at the store via a pickup lane (Lowes Foods) or by stopping in the store (Best Buy, REI). This strategy involves the lowest fixed-cost investment, since retailers primarily utilize existing assets (stores and personnel) with minimal specialized investment. For example, the fixed investment for Lowes Foods involves purchasing a dedicated refrigerator and freezer for storing orders, building a drive-through lane, purchasing hardware for tracking orders, and communicating with customers. The total cost is roughly $20,000 per store.

Advantages, Challenges, and Drawbacks of Semi-Extended Supply Chains

Semi-extended supply chains have numerous advantages. In particular, this approach requires a fairly low capital investment, since it relies on existing stores and does not provide direct delivery to the consumer. Also important to this strategy is the carryover effect it has with in-store sales. By getting customers to the store for a preplanned purchase, there is a good chance for spillover or impulse purchases. Customers may remember something they forgot to order in their preplanning, or they may see a display of some item that captures their attention.

The primary drawback with this approach is low efficiency in picking orders, since existing retail stores are designed with different objectives in mind than distribution centers. Retail stores are often designed to maximize customer exposure to the products on offer and to increase impulse buys. For example, a Best Buy or Circuit City may stock CDs in multiple locations: in an area by themselves for customers browsing for CDs, and next to DVD or CD players so that someone purchasing a new player may also buy a CD. The objective is to increase sales, but this objective conflicts with efficient selection of merchandise when the retailer is picking it for the customer. Another challenge with mixing customers and employees picking orders is that the customers get in the way of the pickers. An employee selecting items for customers who have placed online orders has to yield to customers who may be taking their time browsing the aisles. After all, consider the saying "the customer is king"—this does not fit with running the customer over so that employees may pick items more quickly.

Another major challenge with this strategy involves managing inventory. When customers place an order, they expect it to be in stock. After all, that is the point of ordering ahead. Yet picking orders out of individual stores presents inventory challenges, since most retailers already have problems keeping shelves stocked. In the grocery industry, studies show that a typical store has 5 percent to 8 percent of items out of stock at a given time. Often an item will not be on the shelf but will be in the backroom, since employees have not yet stocked it. If retailers have trouble managing their own inventory, imagine how these challenges are compounded when that item is posted online for ordering. The retailer is essentially promising that the item will be in stock, but unless the IT system is explicitly linked to the Web site for ordering, there are bound to be out-of-stocks. When something is out of stock in a store, customers often will simply choose another size of the same product (say a thirty-two-ounce bottle of catsup rather than a sixteen-ounce), or they will select an alternative product. Customers usually will make such substitutions without giving them a great deal of conscious thought. When ordering is moved online and a "professional" picker is physically selecting the products for the customer, the formerly implicit substitution must now be explicit. In other words, the store employee uses his best judgment (or a predefined rule) to make a substitution. However, since the employee can not get inside the customer's mind, there is no way to handle substitutions flawlessly. We will examine the challenge of substitutions in greater depth in Chapter Eight.

Consider REI Inc., a large retailer of outdoor gear such as canoes, tents, and clothing that has been one of the leaders in this approach. In July 2003, REI first offered customers the ability to order online for in-store pickup. Within just a few weeks, the company found that nearly 30 percent of its online orders were for store pickup. What was the attraction? Large items that came in many sizes or styles (kayaks in particular) were hard to stock at each store, and they were expensive to ship directly to consumers when ordered online or via phone. However, shipping to the store allowed REI to use its existing logistics network and offer customers free delivery. Just as important, once the customer was in the store, there was an excellent opportunity for cross-selling. For example, a customer orders a tent online, but then decides to also purchase a ground cover once in the store. However, because REI sells custom-fitted ground covers to fit specific tent sizes, the customer needs to know the specific model number and dimensions of the tent to get the proper ground cover. REI addressed this problem by having employees use in-store, Web-connected kiosks to access the customer's online order. The key was that the database was connected in real time to REI's distribution center. The end result was surging sales, with August 2003 sales increasing by 50 percent for REI-Outlet.com and 18 percent for REI.com over same-period sales a year earlier.[1]

As illustrated by the REI example, semi-extended supply chains also come with substantial challenges. First, there is added cost for employees to assemble/pick orders off the shelves for customers. Second, conveying accurate inventory information within the company, much less linking this information to customers via the Web, is extremely challenging. Customers are often frustrated when items are out of stock in a store, but if they have specifically ordered them ahead of time for pickup, the stakes are considerably higher. The third major challenge involves the convenience issue—should retailers offer a drive-up window or booth or require customers to come into the store? There are significant ramifications to this choice, since it involves trade-offs between customer convenience levels, company investments, and cross-channel marketing efforts. Consider, for example, a video rental store such as Blockbuster or Hollywood Video. Many have drop-off bins situated in the parking lot that allow customers to drive by and return a video—very convenient. Yet, it seems that most of them do *not* have these bins (they do have a slot in the door or window, but the customer does have to get out of the car). How much of this decision is driven by concerns about locating a drive-up, drop-off box in a parking lot (including costs, operational support, and perhaps local zoning concerns) versus the desire to encourage customers to enter the store? After all, once you are out of the car to drop one video off, it is not much more effort to enter the store and perhaps rent one, or more, additional videos. We suspect that this is the more powerful reason driving the location of drop boxes.

To explore the advantages and challenges of this strategy further, we present two case studies. Lowes Foods in North Carolina is a small (by grocery industry standards) chain that has found numerous ways to differentiate itself from larger competitors, including a fairly extensive online ordering program. Similarly, retail drugstores have been substantially altering their operations over the past decade to fight the pressures brought to bear by customers, insurers, government, and lobbying groups to reduce spiraling drug costs. The ways in which customers order and pick up prescriptions are changing rapidly, and they have the potential to change even more over the next few years.

David vs. Goliath: Lowes Foods Fights the Big Boys Off

Lowes Foods began in 1954 as a single store in Wilkesboro, North Carolina, and has grown to become a major supermarket chain operating in that state and Virginia. The company grew rapidly during the 1960s, 1970s, and early 1980s. Lowes Foods was acquired by Merchants Distributors, Inc. (MDI) in 1984 and began an aggressive expansion program in 1986, opening nineteen stores over the next four years. In 1997, Lowes Foods acquired Byrds Food Stores, located in eastern North Carolina. Today, Lowes

Foods stores number more than one hundred and new stores continue to open throughout North Carolina.[2]

Lowes Foods attempts to differentiate itself by maintaining fresh food, providing high customer service levels, and making the shopping experience easy and convenient. Continuing its focus of making shopping easier for its customers, Lowes Foods started its grocery division "Lowes Foods To Go" (LFTG) in 1997 with phone-in and fax-in orders. In 1998, Lowes Foods added online grocery ordering and later adopted MyWebGrocer as its application service provider (ASP) and IT implementation consultant. Lowes currently operates LFTG in thirty-six of its stores.

The evidence gathered from customers and from interviews with Lowes Foods executives suggests that the service is achieving its objectives. Judging from customer comments, the service of offering increased convenience and service to customers while increasing incremental sales at existing LFTG stores is exceptional. A large number of customers explicitly named their personal shopper, saying things like:

- ◆ Sheila's the best.
- ◆ Sherry usually does my shopping, and she's very good. She (and other clerks, too) will call me if there's a problem or question about my order.
- ◆ Pam is the best. I have been so pleased with her that I brought her flowers—no, not the in-store arrangements that she sees every day, but from a florist. She is worth the extra buck.

Eighteen respondents named their personal shoppers and complimented them on the superior service they provided. This was on a general question that simply asked customers to state what they liked/disliked about the LFTG service. Clearly, some customers are quite enamored of it. Most of us are unlikely to remember a specific employee at Kroger, Wal-Mart, Barnes & Noble, or Best Buy

by name—unless they have achieved the opposite effect and provided truly horrible service.

Figures 3-1 through 3-3 paint a very interesting picture of customer perceptions regarding the online ordering for store pickup
versus traditional, in-store channels for groceries at Lowes Foods.
First, Figure 3-1 shows that traditional customers in physical
stores place a high and roughly equal premium on price and convenience. In contrast, customers of the online channel over-
whelmingly rate convenience as more important than price. The
importance of convenience is rated as 6.76 (on a seven-point
scale), while the importance of price is over 1.5 points lower
(5.12). While it is difficult to state precisely the value of this difference, it clearly implies that customers of the online channel prefer
convenience and, by extension, they are willing to pay some premium in terms of price.

Figures 3-2 and 3-3 provide data regarding the operational challenges of picking groceries for customers, specifically ratings of
service and product quality, assortment, and availability. Figure 3-2
shows that customers rate various aspects of service quality
much better for the online versus in-store channels. In particular,
online customers find employees to be more courteous, responsive, understanding, and available to answer questions. Clearly,
better customer service ought to be a major selling point for companies however, the important issue is achieving this improved
service quality.

There are certainly numerous challenges to executing the service
well: finding and training employees to be pleasant and efficient,
setting up systems that allow interaction with customers without
taking undue amounts of time, minimizing interruptions and errors, etc. However, two things stand out from interviews with executives of Lowes Foods. First, personal shoppers are relentlessly
drilled so they think of the delivery of customer orders at their cars
as a "moment of truth." The five minutes that the customer
spends interacting with the personal shopper to receive paper-

(text continues on page 58)

Figure 3-1. Reasons for selecting Lowes Foods.

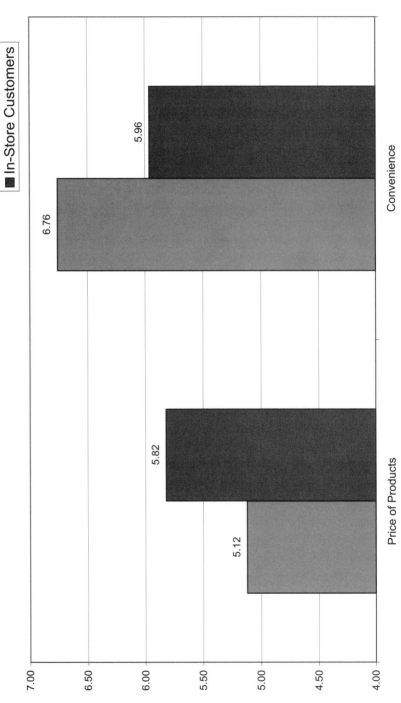

Figure 3-2. Service quality comparison.

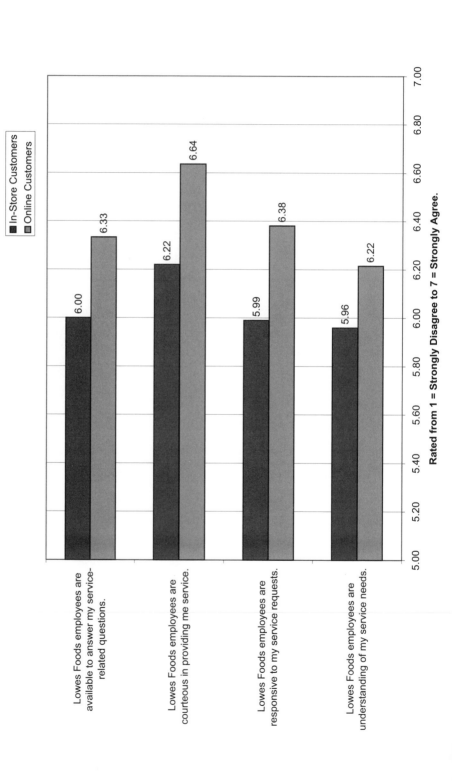

Figure 3-3. Product quality, choice, and availability.

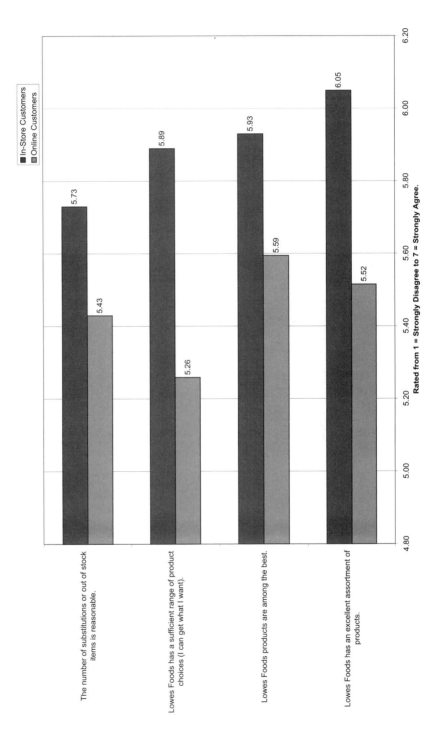

In-Store Customers
Online Customers

The number of substitutions or out of stock items is reasonable. — In-Store: 5.73, Online: 5.43

Lowes Foods has a sufficient range of product choices (I can get what I want). — In-Store: 5.89, Online: 5.26

Lowes Foods products are among the best. — In-Store: 5.93, Online: 5.59

Lowes Foods has an excellent assortment of products. — In-Store: 6.05, Online: 5.52

Rated from 1 = Strongly Disagree to 7 = Strongly Agree.

4.80   5.00   5.20   5.40   5.60   5.80   6.00   6.20

work, review the order, and have the groceries placed into her trunk is the primary, and possibly only, direct, face-to-face interaction with a Lowes Foods employee. The success of these efforts is reflected both in the data shown in Figure 3-2 and in our earlier discussion of the number of customers who *know their personal shopper by name.* Second, personal shoppers are encouraged to get to know their customers and to avoid treating them as just another face. Many of the personal shoppers keep files of 3- by 5-inch cards, noting things like the names, ages, and hobbies of the children of a customer—or the customer himself. The pickup of orders at the store facilitates the process of personal shoppers getting to know their customers, since the same shopper will see each customer repeatedly. This differs substantially from companies that deliver orders, where the shifting of delivery routes leads to a great degree of variation in interactions between customers and drivers/personal shoppers. In addition, Lowes Foods makes a concerted effort to have personal shoppers focus their efforts on customers of LFTG only. They avoid the temptation to use workers for miscellaneous tasks around the store, which, while reducing costs, might also compromise the service and lead to delays.

Unfortunately, while the service quality is a big hit with customers, the ability to supply products of comparable quality, availability, and assortment is a huge challenge, as shown in Figure 3-3. Products out of stock or, in the case of online orders, substitutions, are the inherent weakness of online ordering. Typical grocery stores average 5 percent to 10 percent out-of-stock items.[3] When picking customer orders from a store for pickup, this number should be about the same—so why do online customers rate it so poorly? It is because when someone else picks your order and an item is not included because it is out of stock (or mispicked), or a substitute item is provided, the customer has *given up control.* Consider what you would do if your local supermarket was out of stock of a sixteen-ounce tube of Crest toothpaste. You would likely either get a larger or smaller (eight ounce or thirty-two ounce) size and not think about the difference very much. But what if you order online, and the personal shopper decides that two eight-ounce tubes will be the same as one sixteen-ounce tube? (Suppose you also get the same price: i.e., a sixteen-ounce tube was $2.99, and the eight-ounce tubes were $1.79, but the personal shopper gives you the eight-ounce tubes for $1.49 each.) This should be no big deal to most customers—but to some, it is still a problem. Cases like this (where the customer gets the exact product he wants, but in a different size) can be considered as "near" substitutions. A much harder case is when a store is out of something very specific, such as ribeye steaks. A customer in a store might simply choose a top sirloin instead. However, when stores attempt a "hard" substitution of this type, the customer is much more likely to be dissatisfied. Clearly, Figure 3-3 shows that online customers are substantially less happy about substitutions/out-of-stocks than in-store customers.

Another important supply chain challenge for grocers and other retailers is selecting the proper range of product choices. More products certainly give the customer more choice. However, stocking more products also greatly increases the difficulty of accurately tracking, stocking, and displaying these items. This is particularly challenging in the grocery industry, where an average store carries 35,000 SKUs.[4] Yet, the 5,000 top-selling items account for 80 percent of a retailer's sales. Consumers have been conditioned to expect almost infinite choice in products, yet the average customer's top 150 items (in terms of buying frequency) accounts for over 70 percent of their food purchases.[5] So why do stores stock 35,000 or more items? This is done because customers often remember the one item the store did *not* have, rather than the hundreds or thousands they did have. In addition, U.S. food manufacturers introduce 20,000 or more new products annually, most of which are money losers. Thus, retailers in general and grocers in particular are faced with a conundrum: Stocking a wider variety of items generally increases overall sales, but often comes at the expense of increased stockouts and other inventory management costs. Finally, big-box retailers with superstores that may stock even more items (50,000 or more) generally tout their low costs and their vast choice, but they never mention that customers likely spend large amounts of time getting into, through, and out of the store. A store that is twice as big, and stocks twice as many items, may not take twice as long to shop at, but it certainly takes substantially longer than at a smaller store.

All of the problems/challenges mentioned above are compounded in the online channel because the retailer now takes responsibility for picking items, instead of the customer. Thus, at best, substitutions match what the customer would have done at worst, they are completely wrong. The challenges are clearly highlighted in Figure 3-3, which shows that online customers not only rate substitutions/out-of-stocks as worse than in-store customers, but also rate range of product choice and assortment as worse than in-store customers. Furthermore, online customers rate the products themselves as worse than in-store customers. Why? In theory, the product assortment, quality, and out-of-stocks *should be the same* as if the customer was physically in the store. The problem is that the person doing the selecting is *not* the customer, so the choices made are *not* the same. In a sense, all that a company that picks orders from a store can hope for is to get close to equal ratings. The deficit in customers' minds must be made up elsewhere—through greater convenience and better customer service (as shown in Figure 3-2). This is one of the primary deficiencies of picking from stores: By grafting another layer onto the existing supply chain, there is an increased risk of stockouts, substitutions, and poor product quality, not to mention increased costs. This is the potential advantage for picking out of a distribution center (DC). By removing a layer in the supply chain, these same problems can be improved. Distribution center–based picking is explored in Chapter Two, and more extensively in Chapters Five and Eight.

Despite all of the challenges of picking from a store, the bottom line is that there is a customer segment that greatly values this service. For this group, the improved service quality, increased convenience, and time-saving advantages outweigh the disadvantages. As shown in Figure 3-4, Lowes Foods To Go customers are

Figure 3-4. Customer loyalty.

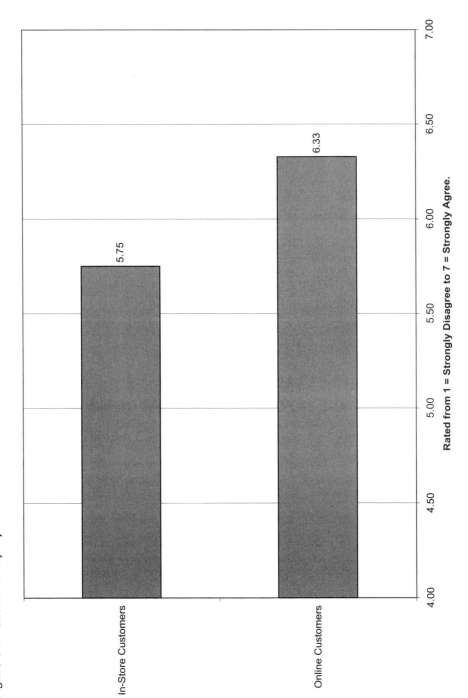

Rated from 1 = Strongly Disagree to 7 = Strongly Agree.

substantially more loyal than in-store customers. Furthermore, the average order for online customers is more than $100, whereas the median in-store sale for all grocery stores is approximately twenty-five dollars.[6]

Retail Pharmacy: Caught in the Middle

A typical retail pharmacy such as Walgreens, Rite Aid, or CVS gets 60 percent to 65 percent of its revenue from prescriptions. This is good in the sense that they are "licensed brokers," and have some degree of protection from market forces. Unfortunately, any protection from market forces comes at a price: Retail pharmacists, for a single prescription, have to deal with (1) the customer or patient who buys the drugs, (2) the insurance company that often pays for most of the cost, (3) the doctor who prescribes the drug, (4) the drug's manufacturer, and (5) the government that oversees all prescription sales. The drug industry receives wide coverage in the media, and the inexorable rise of drug prices as a share of medical expenditures has been well chronicled. Pharmacists are in the difficult position of being caught in the middle: They don't set prices (other than to mark up the price given to them by the manufacturer), and they are told by insurers what they can charge. When there is confusion or misinformation, they are often the party that has to serve as intermediary between the parties (patient and insurer, patient and doctor, insurer and drug company). While their challenges in dealing with the various parties are immense, and obviously important, our focus on extended supply chains means that we are most interested in the relationship between pharmacists and customers.

The relationship between pharmacists and customers is increasingly important. Customers have a hard time talking to insurers, and doctors are spending less and less time with individual patients, so customers tend to look to pharmacists for answers and information. At the same time, pharmacists are swamped with a deluge of prescriptions. The total number of prescriptions filled in 1992 was almost 2 billion (1,947 million), while 3.14 billion prescriptions were filled in 2002—a 61 percent increase in ten years, yet the number of licensed pharmacists remains virtually the same. The 3.14 billion prescriptions in 2002 were filled by 130,802 pharmacists, or approximately 24,000 prescriptions per year per pharmacist. Put another way, that's about twelve prescriptions per hour. Obviously, pharmacists have a lot of help, such as technicians, clerks, and interns to process the work that by law can be handled by nonlicensed pharmacists; however, a pharmacist must be present in a supervisory capacity. In summary, while twelve prescriptions per hour may look efficient, the time spent filling them is only 73.8 percent of the pharmacist's time—"nonrevenue," but necessary, tasks such as administration and regulatory compliance, inventory management, disease management, and other miscellaneous tasks account for the other 26.2 percent.[7] We will examine below how extended supply chains facilitate prescription-filling efficiency and better relationships with customers, but first, let's look at Figure 3-5.

The retail pharmacy industry is changing substantially—both in terms of where prescriptions are filled and how. Figure 3-5 shows that one of the clear losers is the independent drugstore—whose absolute number of prescriptions filled has remained fairly constant, but whose proportion of all prescriptions has fallen drastically from 39.5 percent in 1992 to 23.3 percent in 2001. This business has largely been picked up by three outlets, as shown in Figure 3-6—chain drugstores, supermarkets, and mail order. A comparison of these three outlets illustrates how the extended supply chain changes the pharmacist/customer relationship. First, supermarkets have picked up prescription business because they are convenient and very price-competitive, but only *if* the customer is also shopping for groceries and other items. In contrast, chain drugstores (Walgreens, Rite Aid, CVS, etc.) have also picked up prescriptions, but for different reasons. They are more convenient if a customer is primarily interested in getting only her prescription. They are smaller than large supermarkets, easier to

(text continues on page 66)

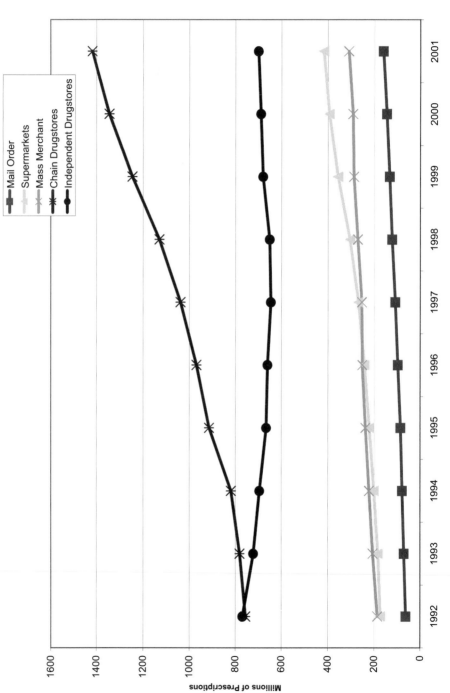

Figure 3-5. Prescriptions filled, by type of store, 1992 to 2001.[8]

Figure 3-6. Percentage of all prescriptions, by type of store.[9]

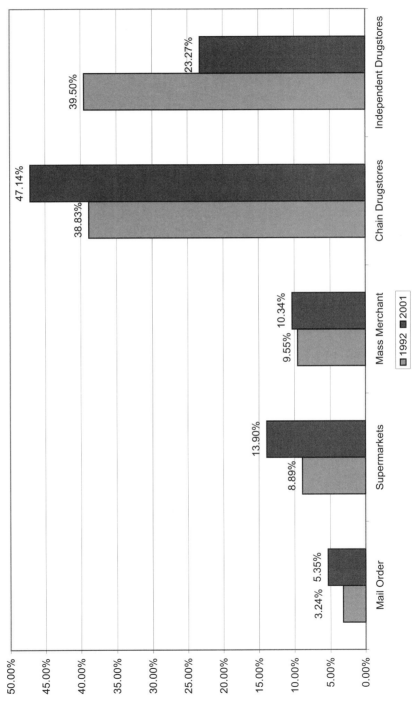

navigate, and have a name brand that is strongly linked with quality service in customers' minds. One reason for the growth of chain drugstores is that they can better afford and manage the huge investments in IT systems to interact with insurers, and they can cut better deals with both insurers and suppliers (drug manufacturers like Merck, Eli Lilly etc.). The other growing channel for prescription drugs, as shown in Figure 3-6, is mail order. Mail or Internet ordering is very attractive to customers who have health conditions or diseases that require long-term care. Prescriptions can be ordered for ninety days at a time versus a maximum of a month in a store. Clearly, this service is very convenient in terms of not having to place orders as often. However, it is also limited by the time delays inherent in mailing a prescription to a central distribution center, and then waiting for the drug to be delivered—*not* an option when the treatment is needed immediately.

The discussion above helps set the stage for an examination of how last-mile supply chains can help connect pharmacists and customers to make stronger relationships. Ordering prescriptions is a challenging transaction because of the need to coordinate information with customers, pharmacists, doctors, and insurance companies. Figure 3-7 shows how customers order and receive their prescriptions, while Figure 3-8 shows how pharmacy staff allocate their time in filling prescription orders. Extending supply chains so customers can order without traveling to the drugstore is beneficial for both parties. First, as anyone who has stood around waiting for the pharmacist to fill a "rush" prescription knows, the process can easily take fifteen or twenty minutes from dropping off the prescription to receiving the filled order. Second, Figure 3-7 shows that the most common drop-off/pickup method for new prescriptions is to go to the pharmacy and wait (A), while the second most common method is to drop off the prescription and pick it up later (B). In total, 58 percent of new prescriptions are in one of these categories—not exactly time-efficient for customers, unless they like making two trips, or browsing through a drugstore. Unfortunately, new prescriptions need to either be dropped off by the customer or called in by the doctor due to

Figure 3-7. Methods of filling prescriptions. [10]

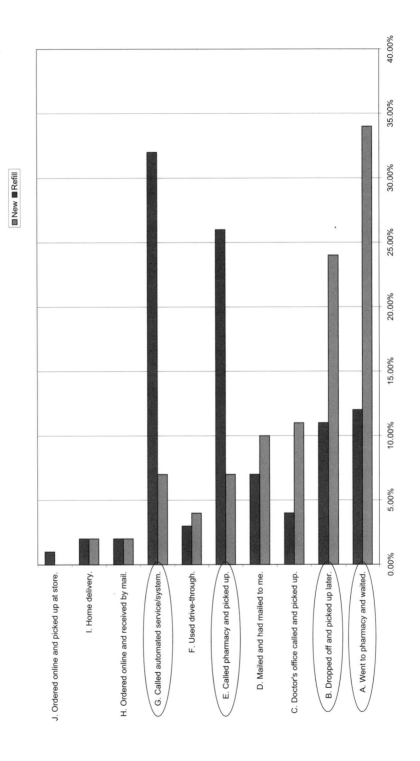

Figure 3-8. Breakdown of activities/time to fill prescription. [11]

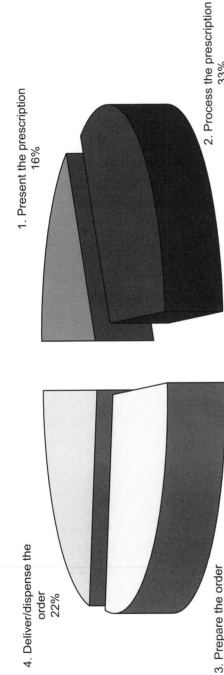

1. Present the prescription
16%

2. Process the prescription
33%

4. Deliver/dispense the order
22%

3. Prepare the order
29%

Steps in Filling a Prescription:

1. Present the prescription: Includes greeting patient, obtaining appropriate data, manually recording information from ID cards.

2. Process the prescription: Includes entering the patient/doctor/drug profile into computer system, complying with third-party requirements, resolving conflicts with PBMs, correcting clinical conflicts.

3. Prepare the order: Includes retrieving drug from storage, counting pills, filling container, preparing/placing label, returning drug to storage, bagging prescriptions.

4. Deliver/dispense order: Includes placing into will-call, retrieving drug from will-call, delivering prescription to patient, counseling patient, cashiering.

government regulations. This is an area where electronic prescription sharing could save time for all involved—doctors, drugstores, and customers—but there are numerous barriers to be surmounted. In contrast, refill prescriptions are substantially simpler, since there is already a prescription on file. Thus, the most common method of ordering refills is by calling an automated service/ system (G equals 32 percent) or by calling the pharmacy and picking up (E equals 26 percent). This approach is convenient for both customers (since it saves them a trip) and for pharmacy staff (since it cuts down on the first step in the prescription filling process, shown in Figure 3-8). If pharmacists can get more customers to order through an automated service/system, then they can potentially save 16 percent of their time. More important, as was mentioned earlier, "rush orders," where a customer drops off a prescription and waits, have a very disruptive effect on the smooth, assembly line-like filling of prescriptions.

Drugstores have made excellent use of automated order-entry systems over the past half dozen years. While specific and public data is difficult to find, it was reported in 2001 that Walgreens handled 400,000 prescription refills daily and that 50 percent of these orders came through their automated voice-response system, while 5,000 (1.25 percent) came from the online pharmacy.[12] If anything, the number of orders placed through automated, voice-response systems and online has quite likely increased substantially for all major chain drugstores. Let us return to Figures 3-7 and 3-8 to illustrate how automated ordering systems can help customers and pharmacists. The circled transactions in Figure 3-7 are the ones where automated ordering systems have the most benefit. Clearly, customers that call the automated service/system (G: 32 percent of all refill orders, but only 7 percent of new orders) avoid making two trips to the store, while saving the pharmacy time in Step 1 (time to fill a prescription, shown in Figure 3-8). The pharmacy can batch-process a series of automated orders with no time-consuming interruptions from customers. For example, a pharmacist or technician may come in in the morning and find a stack of one hundred orders, sorted by time due, or perhaps by type of drug. If the orders are sorted by type of drug, the worker filling the prescription avoids setups. Say that there are fourteen orders for drug A, twelve for drug B, five for drug C. It is more efficient to do all the orders for A, then B, etc., than to constantly switch back and forth between orders.

What about customers who call the pharmacy and then pick up the orders (Method E in Figure 3-7)? Presumably, this occurs in pharmacies that have not invested in, or established, automated systems. The ability to call the pharmacy may save the customer time by not having to make two trips (one to drop off, and one to pick up), but it does not save the pharmacy much time. The pharmacist must interrupt the order he is working on to take the call, then take the prescription details from the customer, and then return to his original task. Clearly, it is beneficial to the pharmacy if customers can be migrated to an automated system—that way the pharmacist does not get interrupted, and the customer "self-sources" by entering her own order information, without requiring the pharmacist to do double duty. For this self-sourcing to work, it must be an attractive option to the customer, and easy to accomplish. We will examine how to make automated order entry easy and attractive in Chapter Nine.

The final two order drop-off options in Figure 3-7 (A and B) represent areas where drugstores can have a big impact by pushing customers to use automated systems. A majority of customers with new prescriptions (58 percent) place their orders in these manners. Unfortunately, the need to present a written prescription represents a huge hurdle when filling new prescriptions, but the industry (doctors, insurance companies, pharmacies) is working hard to develop electronic prescription capabilities, and it could overcome this barrier within a few years. Note that there has been some resistance to electronic prescriptions from doctors, as many do not see an immediate benefit to this technology. However, pressure from the pharmaceutical and insurance industries, as well as consumers, should overcome this.[13]

In the case of refill prescriptions, it is surprising that 23 percent of customers place orders by physically dropping off the prescription, since this requires two trips (or wasted time) while waiting. While it is difficult or impossible to get all customers to accept a new method of ordering, communicating the benefits of automation and designing systems to be as appealing as possible helps encourage technology laggards to adopt such systems. There are huge benefits to the drugstore as the percentage of orders that must be manually input by the pharmacy (Methods A, B, C, E, and F in Figure 3-7 account for 80 percent of new prescriptions and 56 percent of refills) drops. As time is freed up within pharmacies, it can be used either to cut costs, or to offer new services, such as patient counseling or home delivery of prescriptions. There is a great deal of potential for home delivery with customers who have trouble getting to stores to pick up prescriptions. Offering home delivery of prescriptions would move a drugstore from a partially extended supply chain to a fully extended one. Obviously, the challenges associated with increasing reach need to be carefully balanced relative to the potential advantages as seen by customers.

Success Levers

To be successful with this strategy, companies must carefully think through several design decisions on how to coordinate their channels. The following list highlights some of the key concerns.

Balancing Convenience and Fulfillment Cost

Ordering online offers customers increased convenience. However, the key question is how much this convenience will cost companies in terms of actual dollars and changes to their current fulfillment systems. With these considerations in mind, there are two key decisions that must be made: (1) how to connect with customers for pickup of orders and (2) what range of products to offer for sale online. Let's examine each decision separately.

Companies have a variety of choices on how to get orders to customers for pickup. For the customer, the easiest option is to have the pickup service outside the store with a dedicated service lane, such as that offered by Lowes Foods, or the drive-up service offered by most fast-food restaurants. But this approach has two negatives: It requires the company to invest in more resources, and it keeps the customer from entering the store, preventing any impulse purchases. This works well for a retailer like Lowes Foods, since the consumer is generally making a large purchase (average order over $100), and he is attracted by the convenience of the drive-up service. Customers who remember one or two additional items they need may likely park their cars and run quickly into the store. As stated above, this approach requires more resources, both a dedicated drive-through lane and appropriate electronic equipment, and employees who must be available to take orders out to customer cars. In addition, there will be many situations where personal shoppers will have to interrupt an activity (such as order picking) to deliver merchandise outside to a customer. Thus, it is critical to define procedures for how this will occur and to develop standards for what constitutes acceptable service. For example, should a personal shopper immediately interrupt an in-store task to take an order out to a customer, or should there be secondary shoppers who can handle this task in a pinch? Similarly, what should be the standard for performance—should a drive-up customer be served within one minute? Three minutes? Five minutes? All of these decisions have implications for how the processes are defined and executed.

Alternatively, an organization such as Blockbuster provides a less convenient service for the consumer (a drop-off window that the customer must get out of her car for). Yet this is operationally much easier for Blockbuster to handle, since the videos are in the store and can be collected quite easily. This approach also encourages customers to enter the store to browse for another video or game. The final alternative is to have the pickup location inside the store, such as in the case with Best Buy, Rite Aid, or Circuit City. This is the least convenient option for customers, but it could be mitigated somewhat by having special parking spots for pickup orders, like many carry-out restaurants do. This is the easiest operational option for the retailer, since the customer pickup location can be combined with a service desk, or an alternative area. The key here is to set the service up so that the customer feels he is getting more personal attention—faster service, name recognition, or counseling on his purchase—than a walk-in customer to the store. Thus, online customers should have a separate line for completing their purchases.

Let us offer a final thought on pickup options: They should not be static; they should evolve over time. Consider one of the most successful companies of the last fifty years—McDonald's. The first McDonald's was in San Bernardino, California, and it was run by the McDonald brothers. It was a drive-in restaurant typical of the 1940s and early 1950s—customers pulled into a parking space and a carhop came, took your order, and delivered it when ready. The McDonald brothers revolutionized the business by firing all their carhops, drastically reducing their menu size from fifty to ten items, and only offering a single walk-up window. When Ray Kroc bought the rights to the McDonald's system, his first restaurant in Des Plaines, Illinois, did not have any indoor seating—all orders were placed at a walk-up window. One of the first things that Kroc discovered was that a walk-up window in Illinois could get a bit cold—so an early decision was made to cover it in Plexiglas. As McDonald's evolved, it added indoor seating so that by the 1970s most of its business was for customers who entered the restaurant and either ate in or carried out. Starting in the late 1970s, drive-up service became increasingly popular, so most of the restaurants added a drive-in window, which required changes in store layout.[14] As the percentage of drive-in business increased (it is now well over 50 percent of an average restaurant's volume), McDonald's first added a separate ordering station (those radios that are so hard to hear through). The company then added a second window so that the first could take payment, and the second could deliver the food. Clearly, delivery methods can (and should) change over time and different business climates.

The second major consideration when balancing convenience and fulfillment cost is to decide which products will be offered online and which will be offered only in stores. While it is tempting to sell everything that can be found in stores, it is also quite challenging for a number of reasons. First, different stores stock different items, and creating a Web site to track these differences is daunting, to say the least. Second, not all items offer an appropriate value-to-picking difficulty ratio to make them profitable. Best Buy is happy to pull a $1,000 wide-screen television out of inventory for customer pickup, but is much less enthusiastic about pulling a four-dollar box of writable CDs. Obviously, stores can simplify the Web-ordering process by only offering a limited selection of products online, but there are consequences to doing this. First, stores must be aware of the risk of upsetting customers and giving false impressions that the two channels are identical, when they are not. Second, pricing must be identical. Customers quite often are outraged if they find different prices online versus those in the store, and no explanation that it costs more to pick/deliver these products will satisfy them. Thus, there is incentive for stores to offer online primarily products with higher profit margins (not the loss leaders so common in physical stores) and to make additional money to cover picking/delivery via other methods—delivery charges, subscription fees, or minimum-order sizes.

Cross-Selling

Getting customers to the store (either inside or outside) to pick up an order is one thing, but getting them to buy some additional products or services is another. The trick is to balance two things: convenience for the customer and additional product promotions. First and foremost, retailers must make customer pickups easy and more convenient for those who place their orders ahead of time. This involves developing separate processes for customers to pick up orders—such as the dedicated drive-through lane used by Lowes Foods, or the dedicated pickup counter for online orders in a Best Buy. Many pharmacies have now installed drive-up windows for both dropping off and picking up prescriptions. It is a good assumption that 70 percent to 80 percent of orders for pickup will not involve customers making further purchases, so the goal is to make things as quick and easy as possible. However, some percentage of customers will browse for further items while making their pickups, or remember something they forgot to put in their initial order. Many others will not make additional purchases, but will be more likely to return to the store at a later date if they perceive the pickup service as valuable and smooth—thus creating a valuable halo effect.

So what are methods of creating cross-selling opportunities? One method is to actively suggest additional products. This works well when customers are buying fairly expensive, special-purpose equipment. This also works well in a Best Buy or Home Depot where customers may think of or see additional items that may enhance their original purchase. Suggestions for additional products can also be made at the point of original purchase—online. Amazon has created a wonderful Web site that tracks customers' past purchases, suggests other products the customer may be interested in, and provides reviews from other customers. This type of community building can have an immense effect on customer loyalty. Customers see the business as more than just a place out to make a quick buck. Another example of a Web site that is useful in educating customers on products and encouraging further purchases is that of FreshDirect. This New York based online grocer focuses on fresh foods—produce, meats, seafood, and cheeses—and offers information on what makes superior products.

Another key method of creating cross-selling opportunities is really very simple—make the direct customers feel special. Greet them by name. Remember personal details or problems on past orders. If the customer is making the pickup via a drive-through lane, also provide a dedicated parking space for him to use if he remembers an item he forgot to include on his order. OK, so doing these things is not necessarily easy, but the advantage of the semi-extended channel is that you have well-defined contact points with the customer (at the time of order, at the time of pickup, and if anything goes wrong with the order). Since there are few points of contact relative to a typical customer, they can be controlled and managed more carefully. The trick is to make these few interactions go smoothly and to focus on creating a bond with the customer— particularly since this is likely to be an ongoing relationship in which the retailer will have access to a lot of data on the customer's purchase patterns.

Information Accuracy and Ease

A critical component of any direct-to-consumer supply chain is getting the correct information and making the transaction as easy as possible for the customer. Consider the case of ordering groceries online—the first few orders for new customers are actually *much harder* and psychologically different than simply going to the store. Food is a very visual and tangible product, and ordering it online is difficult. The average first order time for groceries is over seventy-five minutes—not very convenient, particularly considering that customers are likely guessing at many of the products. Most of us can readily visualize many of the products we buy—say, a sixty-four-ounce box of cornflakes—but when presented with a choice online of either a forty-eight-ounce or sixty-four-ounce box, the difference is not very intuitive. Yet, despite the difficulties, there are ways to overcome these barriers—the average order time for customers who have placed five or more orders is under thirty minutes, and many customers place their weekly grocery order in under fifteen minutes.

So what are the keys to making the ordering process as easy to use as possible? First, balance the information content and presentation with a reasonable amount of choices—do not overwhelm the customer. Amazon's entry pages are generally fairly simple—showing only a few best-selling items and offering links to key product categories. Many grocers offer customers a "starting list" of the thirty to fifty most commonly purchased items, or offer to scan in your first order for you from a receipt from a visit to the store—even a competitor's store. Second, minimize and simplify the information-entry process for customers. Amazon patented its "one-click" ordering system, but most major Web sites now have fairly simple-to-use methods for customers to use existing accounts, once they have placed their first order. Customers should also be given access to past orders in order to modify and update them. This is why the ordering time, or learning curve, for customers of online grocers drops so quickly.

Lands' End is a good example of a company that makes the repeat-ordering process easy and appropriate for custom chinos. Once you have placed one order, the next order simply involves making modifications to the first. The company explicitly makes the customer confirm four or five key dimensions for each pants order—both to give him an opportunity to improve fit and to encourage him to consider factors that may have changed the fit that are beyond Lands Ends' control—i.e., weight loss or gain.

Finally, the ordering system should be linked as directly as possible to the inventory or manufacturing system. Generally, it is better to let a customer know at the time of the order if an item is out of stock than to come back later with this unfortunate news. If an item is out of stock, but a similar size is available, offer that option. For example, if a sixty-four-ounce box of Kellogg's Frosted Flakes is out of stock, most customers will not mind if two thirty-two-ounce boxes are substituted at the same price. While it is clearly better for customers if the ordering and inventory systems are tightly linked, this often presents a serious challenge due to different software systems. Therefore, companies must carefully think through how these linkages are created and, if not created, how they can be worked around. For example, if a product is out of stock, or will be substituted, then the customer should be notified in a clear manner and given a choice to decline. Even better, many companies are now asking customers to provide guidelines for what to do if an item is out of stock—i.e., does the customer want a substitution or just want that item omitted, or does she want to be directly contacted, etc.

There are many issues associated with information accuracy and ease. We have tried to convey some of the main ones here, and we will provide more detailed information in Chapter Nine.

Channel Integration

Multiple channels of selling usually lead to increased sales, but without careful integration, they can create customer backlash. In Chapter One, we discussed several examples of delivery and return problems that companies had during the 1997 to 2001 period. Pets.com managed to deliver a total of $13.4 million in goods that were sold for only $5.8 million—not a good performance in anyone's book. Similarly, eToys proved to be the anti-Santa in 1998, leaving 10 percent of its customers with no presents for Christmas. Delivering products in a timely manner is clearly critical, and offering customer pickup as in the semi-extended strategy helps substantially. A key issue is product returns. Jupiter Research Inc. found in a recent survey that 17 percent of consumers who shop online have purchased in stores instead of on the Web because the online returns process can be too difficult. Further, 36 percent of online shoppers said they would be influenced to shop more online if offered free returns.[15]

In theory, easier returns ought to be one of the major benefits of ordering for pickup at the store, right? Well, it should be, but many companies simply don't integrate their channels sufficiently to make this process smooth. A survey conducted by The E-Tailing Group Inc. found substantial problems with in-store returns. The E-Tailing Group shopped twenty-five merchants of back-to-school products and attempted to return products to sixteen that had return-to-store policies. In 44 percent of the returns, the store manager had to be summoned to override the system, as Internet and store order numbers or procedures were not compatible. Most of the problems were due to the lack of clear data—the employees couldn't make sense of the online order. This included, for example, packing slips and invoices that did not provide pertinent information for store associates to process the return, such as taxes paid on the purchase, credit card used, and Internet order number.[16] These types of disconnects between online operations and in-store personnel can not only damage the organization's perception for online customers, but can easily spill over to in-store customers.

Action Steps

This chapter has profiled two excellent examples of the semi-extended supply chain strategy. Both Lowes Foods and numerous pharmacies have utilized on-line/phone-ordering systems to allow customers to place orders in advance for pickup in their local store. These companies and many others have been able to increase customer loyalty, increase incremental sales, and capture customers from competitors. We have also reviewed some of the main success levers for making this strategy work effectively. The most important lesson is that this strategy must have effective, multiple-channel integration, since the goal is to increase total sales through online and in-store channels. Therefore, customers must see that the two are seamlessly integrated, and they must also clearly recognize the benefits of online ordering versus in-store shopping.

The following list of steps provides a starting point for implementing this strategy:

- Define what customer pickup of orders in a store offers in terms of convenience, saving time, and better service.

- Evaluate how offering customer pickup can be done from an operational point of view, without compromising customer benefits or leading to unsupportable costs.

- Do *not* treat customers as afterthoughts—customer pickup must be seamlessly integrated with traditional channels.

- Focus on providing accurate and useful information to customers via the ordering system. Customers can no longer physically handle the product, so information *must* be accurate.

- Identify opportunities for cross-selling and for paring the number of SKUs offered online.

Notes

1. Information drawn from "In-Store Pick-Up Is a Hit with REI's Online Customers," *Internet Retailer* (September 3, 2003), see www.internetretailer.com.

2. Information drawn from corporate Web site (see www.Lowesfoods.com).

3. Extensive information on out-of-stock rates and causes is available from the report titled "Retail Out of Stocks: A Worldwide Examination of Extent, Causes, and Consumer Responses," 2002." This joint study was sponsored by the Grocery Manufacturers Association, Food Marketing Institute, and the CIES—Food Business Forum. The report is available from the CIES Web site at www.ciesnet.com.

4. Information drawn from the Food Marketing Institute Web site, see www.fmi.org for 2002 supermarket facts.

5. Glen Terbeek, "A Gentry Agenda: Selling Food in a Frictionless Marketplace," Breakaway Strategies Inc. (1999).

6. Online sales figure is drawn from the research study conducted by the authors, whereas the in-store figure is taken from the Food Marketing Institute Web site, see www.fmi.org for 2002 supermarket facts.

7. Arthur Andersen, *Pharmacy Activity Cost and Productivity Study* (1999), as posted by National Association of Chain Drugstores, see www.nacds.org.

8. National Association of Chain Drugstores, see www.nacd.org.

9. Ibid.

10. Source: WilsonRx Pharmacy Survey, Wilson Health Information, LLC (New Hope, PA: 2002), for more information contact info@WilsonRx.com or see www.WilsonRx.com.

11. Arthur Andersen, *Pharmacy Activity Cost and Productivity Study,* as posted by National Association of Chain Drugstores, see www.nacd.org.

12. Liz Parks, "Drug Chains Push Ahead with Automated Dispensing," *Drug Store News*, Vol. 23, No. 3 (March 5, 2001), pp. 68–72.

13. An excellent overview of e-prescribing barriers and potential benefits is provided in Tyler Chin, Tyler, "Five Obstacles to E-Prescribing," *American Medical News*, Vol. 46, No. 18. (May 12, 2003), pp. 17–18.

14. An excellent reference on McDonald's corporate history is provided by John F. Love, *McDonald's: Behind the Arches*, revised ed. (New York: Bantam Books, 1995).

15. Paul Demery, "Eye on Returns," *Internet Retailer* (September 1, 2003), see www .internetretailer.com.

16. "Return to Store Should Be Easy, But Often Isn't, a New Study Reports," *Internet Retailer* (August 26, 2003), see www.internet retailer.com.

CHAPTER 4

Fully Extended Supply Chains

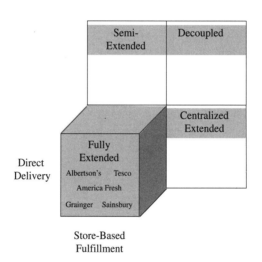

Next to the decoupled supply chain strategy of Chapter Two, perhaps the most famous of home-delivery approaches is the fully extended one. Let's get this point out in the open right now. Famous does not necessarily mean the best. The fully extended strategy just happened to be the strategy that so many companies (such as Tesco) adopted in the "heady" dot-com days when anybody with an Internet idea and a slick business plan could make a killing in the stock market. Having said that, the fully extended supply chain strategy lives on today (although the financial markets no longer fawn all over it), and it is more than worthy of a full chapter in this book.

What Is the Fully Extended Strategy?

The fully extended supply chain strategy means what it says. A retailer's supply chain is *continuously* linked from the supply side all the way to the customer's front door. Is this a new strategy? No, not at all. A hundred years ago many grocers followed this same strategy. A customer dropped off a grocery list, a clerk (typically, either a relative of the owner or an apprentice) picked the items for you, and then a delivery boy brought the groceries around to the customer's house and collected the money.

Conceptually, this first-generation model of the grocery business looked like Figure 4-1. The most expensive part of this four-step process was delivering the groceries (approximately 56 percent of the total labor cost), closely followed by the picking costs (roughly 37 percent of the total labor cost).

Perhaps most important, the margins were high enough to cover these home-delivery costs. In other words, the cost of delivering to a person's home was passed on to the customer. And, it all worked. Customers who shopped at these stores expected to pay a little more for each item because of the extra service they received in the bundling and delivering of their groceries. If someone didn't want to pay this premium (indeed, many recent immigrant and working-class families of that era could not afford this service), there were always sidewalk peddlers and the weekly farmers markets where these people could go and buy lower-cost items to carry home.

Then along came those paper bags and Piggly Wiggly's revolutionary second-generation model where customers come to the store and pick their own groceries, then the grocer bags them, and the customer carries them home. as summarized in Figure 4-2. In less than a generation, the dominant grocery model changed forever. In other words, a more profitable way of doing business obliterated a less-efficient strategy. Of course, the key to Piggly Wiggly's new model was having customers come and do all the labor that was traditionally performed by clerks and delivery boys. Referring back to Figure 4-1, a link in the supply chain is removed (home delivery), and the labor costs to the grocery operator collapse to next to nothing except for the time of the checkout teller and the grocery bagger. In constant 2003 dollars, what once cost the grocery retailer over thirteen dollars per order now costs less than a dollar. (Of course, in a macro, "societal sense," these costs did not vanish—they were just shifted from retailers to consumers.)

Unfortunately for modern retailers today, along with this new, open-aisle

Figure 4-1. The labor economics of first-generation groceries.

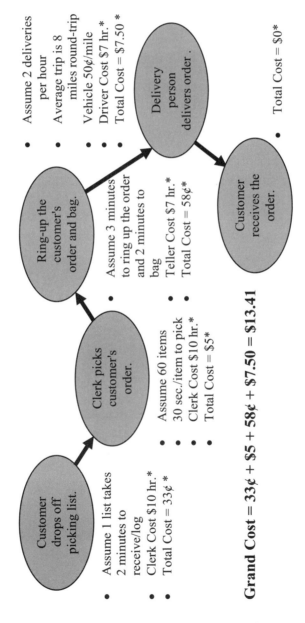

Customer drops off picking list.

- Assume 1 list takes 2 minutes to receive/log
- Clerk Cost $10 hr.*
- Total Cost = 33¢ *

Clerk picks customer's order.

- Assume 60 items
- 30 sec./item to pick
- Clerk Cost $10 hr.*
- Total Cost = $5*

Ring-up the customer's order and bag.

- Assume 3 minutes to ring up the order and 2 minutes to bag
- Teller Cost $7 hr.*
- Total Cost = 58¢*

Delivery person delivers order.

- Assume 2 deliveries per hour
- Average trip is 8 miles round-trip
- Vehicle 50¢/mile
- Driver Cost $7 hr.*
- Total Cost = $7.50 *

Customer receives the order.

- Total Cost = $0*

Grand Cost = 33¢ + $5 + 58¢ + $7.50 = $13.41

*Note: Example shown is in 2003 dollars.

Figure 4-2. The labor economics of second-generation groceries.

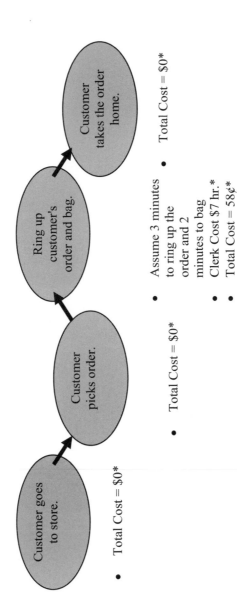

- Customer goes to store.
  - Total Cost = $0*

- Customer picks order.
  - Total Cost = $0*

- Ring up customer's order and bag.
  - Assume 3 minutes to ring up the order and 2 minutes to bag.
  - Clerk Cost $7 hr.*
  - Total Cost = 58¢*

- Customer takes the order home.
  - Total Cost = $0*

Grand Total Cost = 58¢

Note: Example shown is in 2003 dollars.

concept of groceries, pioneered by Piggly Wiggly and soon copied by everyone else, came lower selling prices. Notice that up to now nothing has been said about the upstream side of supply chains, inventory costs, and the overhead expenses for buildings and utilities. They remained unchanged. When key variable costs like inventory and fixed costs don't change—and only revenue does—then, of course, profit has to shrink. And this is what the second generation of grocery retailing did—customers expected to pay a little less, other expenses (besides labor) did not change, hence, profits dropped.

The second generation of groceries is still with us today, but all the innovations adopted by the industry across the years have only served to cut margins more and more. Use a new computer system to better forecast and reduce costs. Your competitors copy you, and one rival cuts the price to customers to build market share. Soon, everybody else has to match that price to stay competitive. Now customers always expect to pay that new, low price. Use bar codes to save some labor costs. Again, your competitors copy you, and one rival cuts the price to customers to build market share. Everybody else has to match that price to stay competitive. Now customers always expect to pay that new, low, low price. Use *a scanner* to reduce labor costs even more. Well, you get the picture. It never really ends. Each innovation eventually leads to lower (and lower) prices.

In hindsight, then, it is strange that Wall Street and the venture capital community made such an uproar over Internet-based, home-delivery services such as Webvan, Peapod, and Streamline just a few years ago. Once again, referring back to Figure 4-1, these so-called revolutionary business models were only putting costs back into the supply chain, not taking them out. Does this mean that the fully extended supply chain will never work? The answer is a "maybe," and the secret is in the customer. Recall from the above that first-generation grocers knew all too well that there were two types of customers. Those who will pay for a service, and those who will not. If you wanted the service, you dropped your list off at a grocery store, the items were delivered to you, *and you paid for it.* If you didn't, you went to a market, did it yourself, and pocketed the savings.

The Economics of the Fully Extended Strategy

As just suggested, the economics of the fully extended strategy pivot off of different customer types. While there are almost an infinite number of people, they more or less boil down to two types of grocery customers. Those who will either directly (or indirectly) pay for the convenience of extra services—like home delivery—and those who will not. Let's first discuss the customer who will not pay for extra service, because after this discussion, there is not much need to come back to them later in this book.

There are a variety of reasons why some customers will not pay for extra service, but it mostly revolves around time and money. Some people have a lot of money, but they also have a lot of extra time. Although they can afford to pay for an extra service, on average, they are not likely to. The same goes for people in the diametrically opposite financial position of not having a lot of money, but having a lot of extra time. And of course, if time and money are an issue, then someone, on average, is not likely to be a major user of home-delivery services. So at the end of the day, home delivery is pretty much common-sense targeting of customers.

This leads us to the ideal customer segment to target. These are, of course, people willing and able to pay for the service (typically five to ten dollars) who are pressed for time. If a good home-delivery service can save several hours out of a hectic week, then the time savings can easily offset the extra expense to *some* customers.

Going back to the characteristics of the grocery industry, this typically means that the best targets are women. Working women are good, and working women with small children are even better. This type of customer has a lot going against them in terms of discretionary time. They are typically holding down a job (besides that of "mom"), have one or more kids to care for, and face a relatively large grocery shopping trip every week. This customer is going to pay for a little extra help, and in fact probably already does so in other aspects of her life. No doubt her sanity already depends on dry cleaning, McDonald's, and possibly a home-cleaning service to help balance out the ceaseless workload. Paying a few extra dollars per week for help with the groceries is a bargain.

Do men also make up the possible pool of home-delivery customers? Of course they do, but they are not as likely to be feeling the time pressures their spouses do. At this point in our argument, some data will help to back up these statements. At one of the many grocers that participated in the study behind this book, we randomly surveyed 500 of their online home-delivery customers and found the following data, represented in Figure 4-2. Not only did women vastly outnumber men in terms of home-delivery customers—83 percent to 17 percent—but 90 percent of those surveyed who were titled "Dr." were female.

This illustrates the high proportion of professional women who value and use this service.

Of course, the burning question at this point is, how many customers are likely to pay for home delivery? In basic implementation theory, a good rule of thumb is that 15 percent of people will like a new idea and be open to change. Seventy percent will be indifferent to it, but largely disinclined to change, and 15 percent will unconditionally hate change, no matter how good the idea is. According to these figures, you should expect that no more than 15 percent of your customers are ever going to try home delivery. Refining these numbers a little bit more based on our experience, we anticipate that companies will be able to eventually convert between 3 percent to 5 percent of their customers into consistent home-delivery customers and the remaining 10 percent to 12 percent into occasional users. Don't be too depressed at this point. Remember that you probably have thousands of individual customers, so 3 percent to 5 percent of them is not a trivial number, plus chances are that this represents many of your best customers who could easily defect to a rival if you don't satisfy them. Let's go to the worst case—when wholesale defections occur and the math gets ugly. Imagine if your chief competitor converts its best 3 percent to 5 percent of customers to an extended supply chain, and picks up most of your best clients too—they are really going to be doing well. Of course, if you turn the tables on your rivals by better exploiting an extended supply chain than they do, then it is the competition that will be singing the blues when it comes time to look at the end-of-the quarter sales numbers. Moving on to focus on these online customers, the next obvious question is, how often do they shop using the Internet? At the same company referenced in Figure 4-3, our research discovered the following data, shown in Figure 4-4. As you can see, almost 68 percent of the sample had shopped more than three times at the service, and 40 percent of the same would be classified as very loyal, having shopped more than seven times with this service.

Figure 4-3. Genders of the typical home-delivery customer.

Person's Salutation	Total People	Comments
Ms.	47	
Mrs.	340	
Miss	17	
Dr.	10	9 of 10 Drs. were women
Mr.	86	

Percentage Women = 83%   Percentage Men = 17%

Figure 4-4. Online shopping frequency.

Number of Orders Placed	# Customers Contacted	# Responses	Response Rate
1	120	76	63.33%
2	38	29	76.32%
3–6	139	97	69.78%
7 or more	203	154	75.86%
Missing		17	
Total Sample	500	373	74.6%

What is the point to all this online home delivery? More important, what are these customers looking for from a good home-delivery service that will let businesses revert to the "ancient," first-generation model of grocery retail?

Figure 4-5 clearly shows that convenience wins hands-down. On a one-to-seven scale, it averaged 6.44, and the standard deviation was the tightest at 0.88. This shows strong agreement among the respondents that they are using home delivery because it makes their lives simpler, and remember that over 80 percent of the respondents are women. Order accuracy was right behind convenience. Why? Because these customers don't want to have to swing by a grocery store later in the week to pick up the missing eggs, bar of soap, or whatever else got accidentally left off the Internet order. It defeats the point of having home delivery in the first place if you still have to fight your way in and out of a grocery store later during the week to buy several omitted items.

Remember our earlier point about cost? Notice that the price of products

Figure 4-5. Why people use online home-delivery services (survey questions).

"How important were the following in your decision to use Alpha's (we disguised the name of the company) online ordering system?"

(1 = Not Important 4 = Somewhat Important 7 = Very Important)

	Mean	St. Dev.
Price of Products	4.19	1.49
Convenience	6.44	0.88
Ordering Speed (time to place an order)	5.89	1.10
Availability of Delivery Slots	6.05	1.02
Hour-Delivery Slot (vs. 2 hours)	5.81	1.49
Free Delivery	6.07	1.30
Order Accuracy	6.28	0.99
Security of Ocado's Web Site	5.98	1.41

has the lowest overall average (4.19), and one of the highest standard deviations (1.49). This means that opinions vary somewhat between the respondents, but on average, everyone considers price to be least important. In fact, if you stare at Figure 4-5 for a few moments, you can almost hear these women saying between the lines, "Our lives are crazy, and all we want is a convenient online service that doesn't screw it up. We really don't care too much about the final cost." If you are a professional woman with kids reading this book, you are probably saying, "Amen to that." And if you are a married man reading this, you are probably fidgeting in your chair and quietly thinking, "Wow, that sounds an awful lot like what my spouse would say, too."

This is only the beginning. Across the data behind this book we have consistently found different types of online customers. These are summarized in Figure 4-6. Before explaining what Figure 4-6 means, however, we need to describe how this analysis was done. Marketers have long used a relatively simple statistical technique called "cluster analysis" to break data up into a number of groups depending on some characteristics. Cluster analysis conceptually works rather like the way we used to choose teams when we were kids in gym class. One captain might think that the biggest kids were the best, while another might prefer all the fastest kids. As the two captains took turns choosing from all the rest of the kids standing there, the biggest kids soon ended up on one team and the fastest on the other. Small, slow kids would not get picked by either captain and eventually ended up on a third team. Cluster analysis conceptually does the same, only with data and often on more than two selection criteria. We took the eight criteria in Figure 4-5—price of products, con-

Figure 4-6. Why people use online home-delivery services (results).

	Delivery-Insensitive	Internet Acceptors	Demanders	Price-Insensitive	F-Value
Price of Products	**5.17**	3.65	4.28	3.00	20.72★★
Convenience	**6.36**	**6.56**	**6.51**	5.92	4.16★★
Ordering Speed	5.83	**5.85**	**6.02**	5.35	3.23★
Delivery Slots	5.47	**6.08**	**6.26**	5.62	11.59★★
Hour-Delivery Slot	3.76	6.01	**6.46**	4.88	95.53★★
Free Delivery	**6.29**	5.96	**6.49**	2.88	122.0★★
Order Accuracy	**6.40**	5.62	**6.60**	5.61	27.23★★
Web Site Security	6.22	3.91	**6.70**	6.15	184.55★★
Total	58	79	198	26	361
Percentage	**16.07%**	**21.88%**	**54.85%**	**7.20%**	

venience, ordering speed, delivery slots, hour-delivery slot, free delivery, order accuracy, and Web site security—and used these as the selection criteria in cluster analysis. Low and behold, there were four groups "hiding" in the data.

In Figure 4-6, the smallest group was price-insensitive (7.2 percent). These people really couldn't have cared less about the price of products, and were mostly concerned with Web site security and convenience. The third smallest group (16 percent) were delivery-insensitive—kind of like the price-insensitive folks—except now these customers were not too fussed about having relatively tight one- versus two-hour delivery slots when they needed to be home to receive the groceries. The second-biggest group is called the Internet acceptors. The Internet has been around now for almost half a generation, and these are the types of customers that have no problem shopping online. Notice that they are the least troubled by Web site security. These technologically savvy customers know that with modern encryption codes, and the fact that the Internet breaks messages up into thousands of packets and then routes them every which way around the worldwide Web before they are reassembled at the final destination, the odds of someone else intercepting your credit card number are nil. (It is funny that people are so suspicious of the Internet's security—they forget that it was originally designed in the 1960s to be the final form of reliable communication after an all-out nuclear war.)

The final, and largest, group (55 percent) are the demanders. This is kind of good news/bad news. The majority of online customers are alike (the good news), but they really want an awful lot from a home-delivery service (the bad news). In fact, they just about demand that everything be exactly correct, except for the price of the products. For the rest of this chapter, and the following Chapter Five on the centralized extended supply chain, keep these four groups in mind in the discussion of strategies. In particular, keep the demanders toward the front of your thoughts. If you can only please one group, you have got to keep them happy with your own online home-delivery strategy.

Let's go back and look at a little more data just to reinforce the above. You might be saying about now (and rightly so) that all of the above data was collected by looking at the customers of just one company. Don't worry, this data was checked by looking at information that was collected across numerous companies. Figure 4-7 compares the customer types for two such companies. For reasons of confidentiality, we can't disclose their names because they are bitter head-to-head rivals in the same market.

What can be said about these two companies is as follows. Alpha is the

Figure 4-7. Customer types in two different companies.

	Delivery-Insensitive	Internet Acceptors	Demanders	Price-Insensitive	n
Company Alpha					
Total	58	79	198	26	361
Percentage	**16.07%**	**21.88%**	**54.85%**	**7.20%**	
Company Beta					
Total	140	98	378	251	867
Percentage	**16.15%**	**11.30%**	**43.60%**	**28.95%**	

company used in Figures 4-3 to 4-6, when we analyzed their 500 online customers. Alpha is also much younger than Beta, has more managers in almost every function (marketing, customer service, operations, etc.) that seem to be technologically adept, and has never had traditional, in-store customers before they started selling groceries online. Perhaps most important to this story, Alpha has been very aggressive in wooing and winning customers from rivals who are not only already very comfortable shopping online, but also dissatisfied with the overall level of service that they receive from the more established players in the market. Hence, they have almost double the percent of Internet acceptors as Beta (21.88 versus 11.30 percent), and predictably, the percentage of the picky demanders at Alpha in comparison to Beta was also higher (54.85 versus 43.60 percent).

Beta, in opposition, traces its roots in the traditional grocery business back for generations, and it has been trying to aggressively convert its traditional shoppers into home-delivery customers. This is most likely why almost 29 percent of Beta's online customers are price-insensitive. They don't care too much about the costs of home delivery and were successfully "shifted" from being loyal, in-store customers to faithful home-delivery clients. Alpha, on the other hand, has relatively few price-insensitive customers. Although still a preliminary finding, this suggests that price-insensitive customers tend not to shop around too much on the Internet. If they like the company that they are presently shopping in-store with, then they will gladly shift over to take advantage of a decent home delivery. After all, they know the company's products and are comfortable with what the brand stands for—now it is just a little easier to shop with them from home.

The final point to make with our data is as follows. Even though there are four home-delivery types of customers, they are not all equal. Some more bad news here—the demanders tend to be the most lucrative customers, as seen in Figure 4-8 for Alpha's customers. Once again, don't get too bogged down with the statistics. Significance (abbreviated Signf. in Figure 4-8) just means that the smaller the number, the less likely the probability of it being due to random "dumb luck," instead of something that is really going on in the data. On the other hand, anything significant at or below 0.01 makes statistical types really sit up and take notice because it means that the odds of something being real, and not due to some "fluke," are greater than 99 percent. If you bet a thousand dollars on a game, then you will win ninety-nine out of one hundred times. Who wouldn't take those odds every time?

As you can see in Figure 4-8, the demanders order more than twice as often as the price-insensitive group and, in terms of total revenue, are almost four times as valuable ($795 versus $211) to a retailer. Along the same lines, the delivery-insensitive and Internet acceptors are about equal in terms of relative value to a home-delivery service. A company can't overlook them, but they are just not quite as exceptional in terms of shopping frequency and total order sizes as the demanders.

All this data nicely sets the stage for what must be done—craft the right strategy and implement an online home-delivery service that is just what the demanders want. Hit the bull's-eye with the demanders, and you will no doubt keep the other three groups happy. And, equally important, you will really take your competition by complete surprise. Badly miss the bull's-eye with the *demanders*, however, and . . . well, by following this book it won't happen, so let's skip these negative remarks. OK, so now that what has to be done is

Figure 4-8. Customer types in two head-to-head rivals.

	Delivery-Insensitive	Internet Acceptors	Demanders	Price-Insensitive	Signf.
Total Number of Orders (Pre- + Post-Survey)	10.44	10.73	12.92	5.85	0.006
Number of Post-Survey Orders	3.78	3.75	5.16	1.54	0.007
Total Value of Orders	$573	$597	$795	$211	0.005
Average Value of Order	$98	$109	$101	$90	0.191

understood, let's get into some industry specifics and look at companies that are already grappling with these important issues.

Some Industry Examples

Although it is debatable who first pioneered the fully extended supply chain model, many people attribute it to the UK grocer Tesco in the very late 1990s.[1] It is a well-known story, but it is still worth recapping for the insight it gives to much of today's grocery home-delivery services. Europeans watched with amusement the early phases of "dot-communism" in the United States up until 1998, and then, all of a sudden, the world's financial markets started to take many of these Internet companies seriously and placed wild valuations on businesses such as E-Steel, Priceline, and Webvan. Now it wasn't nearly so funny to the Europeans to be so far behind their U.S. cousins in terms of the Internet, and the UK's historically aggressive grocery retailer, Tesco, was one of the first major foreign companies to jump into the fray with its own online home-delivery model. In short, Tesco.com was born in the crazy gold-rush days of the Internet boom. Experienced managers all know what often happens when any project is conceived and executed in the midst of pandemonium and confusion—for better or worse, it is rushed into action despite limited time for strategic thinking and perfecting processes.

Fortunately, Tesco.com got it right, and for a while, it basked in the same type of financial market praise and adulation as many of Wall Street's Web darlings in the United States. Go back and look at the popular press of the day, and you will see Tesco.com prominently splashed across the headlines of many leading business magazines. How did Tesco get it right? Well, as you can probably guess, they cobbled the late twentieth century's Internet together with the late nineteenth century's first-generation grocery model. You couldn't find a more exquisite blend of the old and the new as you refer back to Figure 4-1 and compare it with the updated Internet version, shown in Figure 4-9.

Remember the point discussed earlier in this chapter concerning the first- versus second-generation groceries? Even using the Internet, and by automating the information flows for order receipt and invoicing, Tesco.com' s home-delivery model could never be lower-cost than having its in-store customers do most of the work. Having said that, taking about a dollar out of the old first-generation extended supply chain cost was still an accomplishment to be proud of. A model that had not been refined for almost a century suddenly had ap-

Figure 4-9. The early fully extended supply chain model.

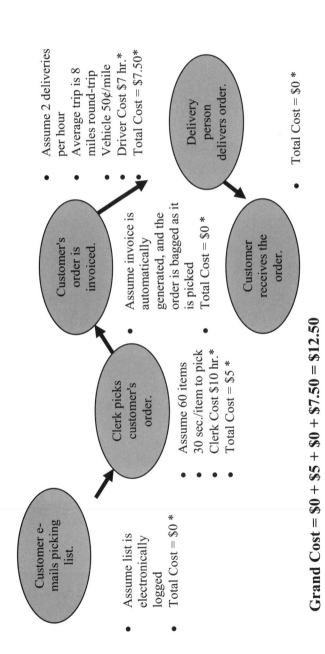

- Customer e-mails picking list.
  - Assume list is electronically logged
  - Total Cost = $0 *

- Clerk picks customer's order.
  - Assume 60 items
  - 30 sec./item to pick
  - Clerk Cost $10 hr.*
  - Total Cost = $5 *

- Customer's order is invoiced.
  - Assume invoice is automatically generated, and the order is bagged as it is picked
  - Total Cost = $0 *

- Delivery person delivers order.
  - Assume 2 deliveries per hour
  - Average trip is 8 miles round-trip
  - Vehicle 50¢/mile
  - Driver Cost $7 hr. *
  - Total Cost = $7.50*

- Customer receives the order.
  - Total Cost = $0 *

Grand Cost = $0 + $5 + $0 + $7.50 = $12.50

Note: Example shown is in 2003 dollars.

proximately another 7 percent of its costs erased overnight thanks to the Internet.

Right about now you are probably grinning and thinking to yourself—finally, we know the truth about why all those dot-com home-delivery services reported steady losses during their often short lifetimes. They just pretended the long-term market share was all that mattered and to hell with something like short-term profitability. Of course, the fully extended supply chain was never going to do everything that the dot-commers promised, such as offering the same (or better) in-store variety at lower cost. Money can't (and won't ever) be made by applying the basic, fully extended supply chain to everybody. Or, in other words, the fully extended supply chain is mass merchandising, only it is not for the masses. While the service may not apply to many, there are always going to be some customers for whom this type of business makes perfect sense.

Taking This Model to Its Ultimate Form: Sainsbury's and Albertson's

Since the dot-com era, retailers have seen the basic fully extended supply chain model refined and perfected. In the course of doing research for this book, we have had the chance to talk to dozens of managers about their own variations of the fully extended supply chain. Two good examples of this "best of breed" are found at the UK–based Sainsbury's and the U.S.–based Albertson's. Both are the second-largest grocery retailers in their respective countries, and together they operate hundreds of traditional grocery stores. Although Sainsbury's markets are over 5,000 miles away from Albertson's, their strategies have closely evolved, despite the relative isolation. Strategy types would call Sainsbury's and Albertson's "fast followers" in the sense that they trailed companies like Tesco and Peapod into Internet-based home-delivery business. Of course, following a pioneer often means that you don't get lost in the wilderness (or shot full of arrows), so when Sainsbury's and Albertson's finally entered the home-delivery market, they did it right.

Let's spend a few paragraphs describing their operations. Figure 4-10 captures their refinements today over the first fully extended supply chains, circa the year 2000. Obviously, you can't improve on the zero costs of steps one and three, so the focus at companies like Sainsbury's and Albertson's has been on steps two and four. Both companies have automated picking wherever possible.

Powerful IT systems (see Chapter Nine for more details) are used to generate picking lists in a logical flow around the store. When necessary, they can also list aisles and even shelf locations on the picking list. When you hear the phrase "picking lists," however, don't think of stacks of paper. These lists are downloaded into handheld remote scanners, and these scanners are what the clerks use to guide their picking. It is as simple as it sounds. Starting in the very back of the store, pickers place some empty totes, or bags, in a shopping cart (or a custom-designed trolley, in the case of Sainsbury's). Then they proceed out into the store with their handheld remotes. The handheld remotes tell pickers what the desired items are, the quantities, and their locations. As each item is picked off the shelf, its bar code is scanned, and if there is a problem, the system beeps to let the picker know it is the wrong item. During one amusing demonstration at Albertson's, we were shown how the handheld remote beeps louder and louder if the picker keeps trying to read an incorrect item until, by the third try, it is practically shrieking at the operator to "give it up—you have got the wrong item."

In both stores, pickers wear uniforms and "shop" right alongside regular customers. Because pickers do this over and over, they can get their per-item pick rates down into the twenty- to twenty-five-second range. (This may seem like a short period, but just try sitting still for twenty-five seconds right now. You soon realize that it is more than enough time to walk ten or fifteen feet down an aisle, pick up the next item off the shelf, zap it with the handheld remote, and put it in a bag in the cart.) Accordingly, Figure 4-10 shows step two taking only twenty-five seconds instead of the thirty seconds in Figure 4-9, which reduces the picking costs from roughly five dollars to $4.17. In other words, there is approximately a 17 percent savings due to the famous "learning curve" (doing the same activities over and over as volumes rise).

In some cases, pickers average twenty seconds per item, which works out to $3.33 per order. According to experience, this has to be about the theoretical minimum cycle time for this step in the process. It is interesting to note, however, the hard trade-offs that have to be made to consistently achieve this kind of speed. In order to race through a store and pick sixty items with an average pace of twenty seconds per item (i.e., do an *entire* grocery shop in twenty minutes), you can't really stop and talk to regular in-store customers who are going to ask questions. (For example, "Excuse me, can you help me find the pimento olives that were on sale last week? I like the kind in the red and blue bottle, not the yellow cans, and definitely not the ones in spicy olive oil.") This

Figure 4-10. The "perfected" fully extended supply chain model.

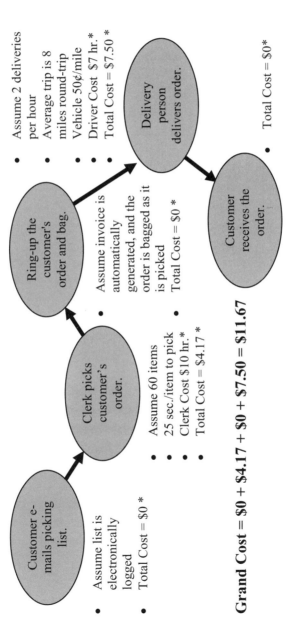

Customer e-mails picking list.
- Assume list is electronically logged
- Total Cost = $0 *

Clerk picks customer's order.
- Assume 60 items
- 25 sec./item to pick
- Clerk Cost $10 hr.*
- Total Cost = $4.17 *

Ring-up the customer's order and bag.
- Assume invoice is automatically generated, and the order is bagged as it is picked
- Total Cost = $0 *

Delivery person delivers order.
- Assume 2 deliveries per hour
- Average trip is 8 miles round-trip
- Vehicle 50¢/mile
- Driver Cost $7 hr. *
- Total Cost = $7.50 *

Customer receives the order.
- Total Cost = $0*

Grand Cost = $0 + $4.17 + $0 + $7.50 = $11.67

Note: Example shown is in 2003 dollars.

is a real problem, because, remember, pickers wear company uniforms, and when a customer asks an in-store employee for help, he doesn't really know (or care) if an employee is on a mission to pick items in twenty seconds or less. He just wants a little help, and it really annoys him when pickers don't stop (as we observed on several occasions). In one case, when we were just shopping in a store as regular customers, the manager intervened and explained that the "rude employee" was only someone trying to do his job for Internet shoppers. The situation went from bad to worse as the customer incorrectly jumped to the conclusion that online customers were more important than traditional, in-store shoppers. Pretty soon, everybody in that aisle was in on the discussion, and all thought that the manager and picker were wrong.

Innovations on the fourth step, the home delivery part of the fully extended supply chain, have been more elusive. Variability kills the efficiency of any operation, and of course, nothing is more variable than traffic and different delivery locations. In the best cases, companies achieve three deliveries per hour. More common are two deliveries per hour, but there again, this mostly depends on how dense the local populations are than any home-delivery inno-vations.

Let's do the math to think through this point. Assume that houses are four miles apart, and it takes eight minutes to unload an order (a typical order is about four plastic totes, or roughly seven to eight bags), reconcile any substitu-tions or deletions, and to briefly chat with the customer. It probably also takes a further two minutes to get back into the van and get rolling again to the next delivery. In most residential areas, drivers can only legally go about thirty miles per hour, plus they are going to hit at least one or two stop signs, some yields or merges, red lights, construction, or traffic, and this can all easily soak up another five or so minutes. Don't forget that drivers often get a briefing before they hit the road and are commonly entitled to two, fifteen-minute breaks in a standard shift, and that in order to stop working after eight hours they have to start heading back after about seven-and-a-half hours. This means there are at least seventy minutes of downtime for a typical eight-hour shift that has to be spread across all the deliveries in that period. According to these approxima-tions, it is going to take roughly twenty-three minutes to deliver an order (four miles multiplied by two minutes per mile equals eight minutes, plus eight minutes to greet the customer and unload the van, plus two minutes to get rolling again, plus five minutes for random traffic events, *plus* a percentage of the downtime). This would be about seven minutes, on average, if the van makes ten deliveries per shift (a typical delivery van holds about fifteen orders), and that is divided into the seventy minutes downtime.

Hence, it takes roughly thirty minutes per delivery if the houses are around four miles apart. If they are further apart—say eight miles—you are looking at about thirty-eight minutes, and, of course, if they are only a mile apart, then twenty-four minutes. Or under different circumstances, if there is more traffic (ten versus five minutes), or you can make fourteen deliveries a day (now the seventy minutes downtime averages out to five minutes per delivery), the range could be anywhere from nineteen minutes (best case, one mile apart, fourteen orders on a van, and normal traffic) to forty-three minutes (worst case, eight miles apart, ten orders on a van, plus bad traffic).

The point is that it is hard to innovate in such circumstances. The number of loads on a van and their destinations are largely governed by the "luck" of who ordered what on any particular day. Plus, local traffic depends on countless factors, ranging from time of day to weather and accidents. In short, deliveries are pretty much capped at around a maximum of two per hour, except under all but the most favorable of conditions.

Now we are starting to get somewhere. If you charge your customers ten dollars for home delivery, and it is costing you less than twelve for the entire process, then it starts to make sense. You may still be losing around two dollars on each order, but if you are incurring this cost to keep some of your most profitable customers loyal—women spending over $100 every week as they shop for their entire families—then it may well be worth it. Particularly when the "lifetime value" of a customer is taken into consideration. In ten years, the numbers from such a person are fifty-two weeks times ten years times 0.02 gross margin, or $52,000 (revenue) and $1,040 (profit), respectively. Home delivery costs fifty-two weeks times ten years times two dollars, or the same $1,040. An even draw—except recall that these tend to be higher-income families than on average, which often means higher-margin purchases, in addition to the lower-margin staples of bread, milk, and vegetables. Indeed, even if these customers just purchased natural bread, branded milk, and organic vegetables—that all carry a higher profit margin—you are now making money. And, of course, these types of customers also tend to order everything else from higher-margin deli cheeses to steaks and wines.

At this point, in terms of profitability, it really does starts to look like a "no-brainer" to offer an efficient home-delivery service. Not to keep panicking you, but if you don't offer such a service to your best customers, what makes you so sure that your competitors won't?

The Extended Supply Chain in Action at Other Companies

One of the themes of this book is that home delivery can potentially apply to every form of retailing. Let's take a look at a few examples that are about as far as you can get from the traditional grocery business to reinforce this point. A good example in industrial product retailing is W. W. Grainger. During your career, if you have ever rotated through the production, maintenance, ware-housing, or logistics parts of a business on the way to your present position, then you no doubt know about Grainger's famous "blue-collar" catalog of everything from uniforms and safety glasses to hand tools. Grainger has dominated this particular retail catalog business for decades by offering over 80,000 different types of products in more than 350 retail branches across the United States. In 1995, it made sense for Grainger to move its traditional business online using the extended supply chain. And today, Grainger's customers can shop online for more than 220,000 products that are available from 8,000 different suppliers (talk about SKU proliferation) for delivery to their places of work.[2,3]

Grainger conducts, on average, more than 130,000 transactions a day for a total of more than two million customers per year.[4] Even at this volume, the average invoice per customer is under $150.[5]

Perhaps even more important, when you compare Grainger's business to that of Tesco's in their *pre-Internet* forms, Grainger had extra costs for step one (pick-list processing in Figure 4-9), simply because many customers placed orders by either mail or phone. This, of course, meant that Grainger had to staff expensive call centers and mailrooms, whereas Tesco's customers always came into their stores bringing their own shopping list. The extended supply chain let Grainger achieve immediate cost reductions in these labor-intensive customer-service areas.

You might be thinking, however, that there are major differences between Grainger and Tesco, in terms of volumes and margins. Tesco's grocery business is built around large customer orders (i.e., high volumes) at low margins versus Grainger's much lower average order sizes (and frequencies) at higher profit margins. Don't worry, the extended supply chain works just as well in either of these contexts. In groceries, because of the large order sizes, a picker can typically only select one order at a time, which means a relatively high per-order labor cost. This is no problem. Since these customers usually place large orders *every week,* a grocery will, in the long run, make money even though it takes twenty to thirty minutes to put each individual order together.

At a company like Grainger, the economics are different. Now customers are placing smaller orders less frequently. This means that a picker can typically pick for more than one customer's order at a time, which maximizes picking productivity in terms of number of orders per hour. At the same time, although these customers won't typically be repeat customers every week, the products that they are buying have a much higher profit margin, which generally means greater income, even though the order size is smaller. Figure 4-11 helps portray this point with a hypothetical set of order sizes and profit margins. As Grainger illustrates, it does not really matter what type of product you sell, only that you have customers who are willing to pay for the convenience of the extended supply chain.

Key Success Levers

There are a variety of key lessons learned concerning fully extended supply chains. Going back to the points made earlier about Piggly Wiggly's revolutionary second-generation model—*no home-delivery process is ever going cost less than the second-generation, open-shelf method of retail.* That fact probably comes as a big disappointment. After all, the consultants, venture capitalists, and know-it-all dot-com entrepreneurs told everybody it would work (of course, most of their stocks are now worthless). What is more, you may have bought our book because you thought that somehow someone could defy the basic tenets of finance, accounting, and operations to make it work. Believe us, we have stud-

Figure 4-11. Economics of different order sizes and margins.

	Order Size	Average Cost	Profit Margin	Total Profit	Orders Picked/Hr.	Total Profit
Very Large Order	70	$70[1]	0.02	$1.40	2[2]	$2.80
Large Order	50	$50	0.04	$2.00	3	$6.00
Medium Order	25	$25	0.10	$2.50	5	$12.50
Small Order	15	$15	0.20	$3.00	9	$27.00

[1] Assume every item costs $1.00.
[2] Assume thirty minutes to pick a seventy-item order, hence two orders per hour. Similarly, about three fifty-item orders can be picked in sixty minutes and so on for twenty-five- and fifteen-item orders.

ied this home-delivery model to death, and you simply cannot add labor to a process (any process) and an extra step (in this case the delivery step) and somehow "magically" make it cheaper than one where the customer does almost everything himself. Self-service gas is always cheaper than full-service, as is street parking in comparison to valet, and home perms versus going to the beauty parlor. The same goes for second- versus first-generation grocery retail.

This brings up the second success lever concerning the fully extended supply chain, namely that *some customers will always be willing to pay for extra service*. For some reason today, many managers (and consultants and Wall Street analysts) seemed to have forgotten this most basic of facts, and incorrectly, they tend to lump all retail customers together. This is wrong, and the key to the extended supply chain is to first segment your customers. Once you understand the economics of these two different types of customers, you can then move on to the important task of putting together a winning home-delivery strategy.

A related line of reasoning holds for our third critical success lever. *On average, 80 percent of your home delivery customers are likely to be women* (and many of them will work outside the home). While men make up the possible pool of home-delivery customers, they are more than likely a distinct minority (at least in terms of targeted customers for the fully extended supply chain). As noted above, they are not as likely to be feeling the pressure of not enough time to get everything done as their spouses are, and therefore, it follows that the typical fully extended supply chain should be focused toward women.

It is time, then, to shift gears a little and go from talking about what success levers you can use to address the question, should you do it? In other words, does it make sense for your business to adopt a fully extended supply chain strategy? The checklist in Figure 4-12 is designed to help you make this call. As seen in the checklist, there are six preconditions for when the fully extended supply chain strategy makes the most sense.

Figure 4-12. Preconditions for the fully extended supply chain.

	Yes	No
Can we wait to deploy home delivery?	——	——
Can we afford to build a dedicated warehouse(s)?	——	——
Can we get planning approval for such warehouse(s)?	——	——
Is the population density in our target markets high?	——	——
Can our management run both in-store and warehouse operations?	——	——
Will our IT handle both in-store and warehouse operations?	——	——

If you answered "no" to each of the questions in Figure 4-12, then the conditions are most likely not right for a fully extended supply chain versus the centralized strategy discussed in the next chapter. If you need to rapidly deploy home delivery, then the fully extended supply chain is the way to go. As noted earlier in the discussion around Tesco.com, rapid deployment is what led such dot-com pioneers to figuratively "pull out of mothballs" the first-generation, in-store model of grocery picking and quickly throw it back into battle. Similarly, for issues two and three in Figure 4-12, if a company can't afford to build a dedicated warehouse for picking, or the local opposition to building a large facility and the inevitably heavier traffic are large, then the in-store approach is best.

Finally, you need to honestly appraise your management team and your company's IT. There is no need to be ashamed—some managerial teams can run traditional stores, and some are warehouse specialists. The odds of a company being good at both are really small. Likewise, the kinds of IT systems best able to handle traditional retail stores versus warehouses are very different. As already suggested in Figures 4-9 and 4-10, IT plays a strong role in automating online, home-delivery processes. If your IT is not up to it, then it will no doubt be a disaster in waiting to go ahead and press forward.

Up to now, this book has shared our insight into the critical success levers of the fully extended supply chain, but what happens if you are not the first in your business to adopt it? How will your competition attack you? How should you counterattack?

First, in terms of the competition, if they beat you to the fully extended supply chain (and they have read this book), they are going to know to segment and target the "best customer" (those time-pressed moms again). Chances are that they will target *your best customers* with printed ads and radio where these people congregate—at work, schools, and along commute routes. They will especially be trying to hook these customers with free offers for three tries. As discussed in terms of tapping customers' latent needs in Chapter Seven, if you can get these customers to use a good service for *just three tries*, the odds of converting them into consistent online shoppers go up dramatically. If you can recall, by about the third time you first used an ATM machine, a cell phone, or pumped your own gas, you were probably firmly hooked on the new service. The same goes for wooing online home-delivery customers.

Finally, your rival(s) will, in all likelihood, try and make the service as convenient as possible by offering either one- or two-hour delivery windows with multiple time slots available during the week. Once again, this is to give these cherished time-pressed customers a variety of options in terms of when they need to be home to receive their orders.

If your competitors are competing against you using home delivery, there are strategies to counterattack. As discussed in more detail in Chapter Nine, the fully extended supply chain's greatest weakness is a lack of integration between the dot-com and in-store IT systems. To paraphrase the old saying "what you see is not always what you get," items on the typical Internet home-delivery Web site are (at least with the technology available when this book went to press) *never exactly* what may be available in the local store. You have probably seen this phenomenon yourself—go into a store of a chain on one side of town and you have no trouble finding an item. Drop by a different store of the same chain, and you can't find the item because they never carry it, or it is sold out.

In the home-delivery world this is known as a substitution. It is perhaps the most "feared" word in the entire fully extended supply chain. It means that when a customer ordered something online, it was not available at the store on the day that it was picked, and therefore, something may have been substituted for it (or it was just left out of the order). Substitutions take many forms—a different brand is swapped in, two small cans instead of one big jar, branded over generic products, or even something as simple as red versus green apples. Sure, one or two substitutions in sixty to ninety items may be no big deal, but our research has seen evidence that they often run as high as 12 percent to 15 percent at many stores. At that rate, substitutions really start to matter. Imagine if a customer has ordered eighty items, but ten to twelve of these are substituted for. What if these items were the only foods that her choosy kids will eat, that are included on her husband's low-fat diet, or that are called for in a special recipe for a big party on Friday? The mom-with-no-time now has to drop everything and go to the store to buy them. Will she go to the same store that just hit her with a dozen or so substitutes? Not likely!

If your rival is offering a home-delivery service, then you can try to capitalize off of these substitutions. You should first focus on making your substitution rates as low as possible, and then making much of your competition's own problems. In fact, this leads to another critical success lever—*the most important thing to* minimize *in home delivery is substitutions.*

Moreover, there are a few related tips to offer. In-store picking has to usually take place during regular store hours. The late night hours, when it might seem like you could do a lot of picking, are typically reserved for restocking shelves. Plus, chilled and frozen items typically can't be picked much more than seven to eight hours before they are delivered. Therefore, pickers will be out there "mixing it up" with regular customers. Try to make sure that these pickers don't obstruct regular shoppers with giant carts jamming the aisles, or you could inadvertently lose in-store shoppers as you win online ones.

The final two critical success levers are subtle, but equally important. As a rule of thumb, a typical store is capacity-restricted to about 800 to 900 orders per week. There is typically neither enough room in the back storage room(s) to stage that many full orders, nor the surplus loading docks from which to launch a fleet of delivery vans. Bluntly, most modern retail stores in the United States and Europe were built sometime before the 1990s without anyone even remotely dreaming that they would ever want to someday deliver home groceries out of them. Going back to your competition, this means that even if they operate a very "tight" home-delivery service out of their store, they may not be able to serve the entire community. Your nearby store can also help satisfy this demand.

Chances are that as the demand for home delivery grows in the years to come, even yours and your rival's stores will not be able to satisfy all the demand for it. In other words, don't race to be first in every neighborhood just because your rival(s) may be launching their service ahead of you in that area. Just make sure that when you do launch, it is the very best service operation possible.

Action Steps

This book will return to the likely evolution of this strategy in the final chapter. To summarize, this is one of the oldest (of the still young) dot-com home-delivery models, and when targeted at the right customers, remains among the best. Expect it to be around for a good many years to come, and depending on your own particular business, if you are not already trying it, it may be the right one for you to think about implementing it in the near future. And, if this is the right strategy for your business to consider adopting, then you need to carefully consider the following actions.

- ◆ Don't oversell the extended supply chain strategy to top management or investors. By its very nature, it can never beat the low-cost position of traditional, second-generation retailing, where the customers come to stores and do all the picking.

◆ There will always be some customers interested in premium services, including Internet-based home delivery. They all want convenience and order accuracy, so make sure that your fully extended supply excels at these two things.

◆ Craft the right strategy and implement an online home-delivery service that is just what the demanders want. While there are four types of online customers, if you can satisfy the demanders, you will also please the other three groups.

◆ Wherever possible, perfect and automate in-store picking. This is where you can typically save the most money in a fully extended supply chain.

◆ The most important thing to *minimize* in online home delivery is substitutions.

◆ Put into place a plan before your in-store picking capacity is entirely used up. As a rule, a typical store is capacity-restricted to about 800 to 900 orders per week, and when you bump up against this ceiling you may upset both your online customers and your traditional in-store customers (who now have to contend with all those extra pickers).

Notes

1. J. Curtis, "The Dot-Com Decade 1992–2002," *Marketing* (July 11, 2002), pp. 22–23.
2. D. Buss, "The New Deal," *Sales and Marketing Management* (June 2002), pp. 154–159.
3. M. Johnson, P. Green, G. Platt, A. Rombel, and A. Williams, "The World's Best Companies 2002," *Global Finance* (November 2002), pp. 26–44.
4. Buss, op. cit.
5. Ibid.

CHAPTER 5

Centralized Extended Supply Chains

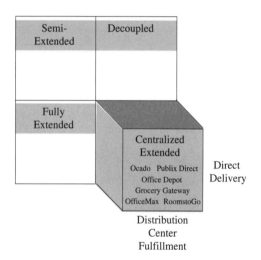

This strategy has three major advantages over strategies utilizing store-based order fulfillment. First, it eliminates a link in the supply chain by removing stores—a strategy that Dell has proven for computers. Besides the inventory aggregation advantages discussed earlier, this can be a substantial benefit in industries where freshness counts. In particular, this strategy is attractive for groceries because it gets perishable products to customers faster than traditional supply chains. The data from our study of online grocers indicates that customers consider their products to be both substantially fresher and of better quality than products they themselves select when shopping in stores. This often surprises customers because they rarely think about the numerous hands through which every item they buy passes—both before it gets to the store and once it is on the shelf. The failure of Webvan scared off many businesses because of its high visibility, yet this strategy is viable when it is carefully examined. While the net-profit margin in groceries is one percent, the gross-profit margin is around 30 percent. By removing stores from the supply chain, this strategy utilizes the 30 percent margin to deliver directly to customers' homes, rather than cover the costs of building, outfitting, and running stores. Webvan failed not because it was a bad strategy, but because it was poorly executed, poorly marketed (they promised groceries at lower or similar costs to traditional stores, when they should have marketed the increased value of home delivery), and poorly timed—the market simply was not ready yet.

The second major advantage, and the one that sets it apart from the decoupled extended strategy, is direct delivery. For customers who truly value convenience, having a product delivered to their home or office quickly (within a day or two) and reliably (when promised) is a very enticing proposition. You've probably had at least one delivery or repair in your life not occur when you were told, or at a convenient time. Often, when we purchase a piece of furniture or a large appliance, we are told that "deliveries in your area are on Tuesdays," and if you ask what time the delivery will be, the response will be "sometime on Tuesday." Often, we feel lucky if we can get the time narrowed down to morning or afternoon. After taking the morning off from work or other activities and having the delivery actually occur at 3:15 P.M., customers are often frustrated, to say the least. Direct delivery from a centralized DC can do better with two conditions: (1) that customers are willing to pay extra for the improved service, and (2) that the company can balance customer convenience (shorter, more precise delivery windows are good for customers) with delivery cost and difficulty (shorter windows are more expensive to support and more difficult to accurately fulfill). For example, Ocado offers one-hour delivery slots versus the prevailing industry standard of two hours for the majority of home-delivery grocers. The key question here is whether the added convenience for customers outweighs the increased difficulty of meeting one-hour delivery windows rather than two-hour windows.

The third major advantage of this strategy is that working from a distribution center rather than a store allows aggregated inventory—simultaneously making it possible to hold less inventory while having both an extended range of products and greater in-stock availability. The picking or selection of products is also more efficient since the DC is laid out and designed for the efficiency of employees, rather than to appeal aesthetically to customers and increase sales. Typical picking productivity in a DC versus a store ranges from two to six times. A final major advantage is the ability to turn inventory more quickly—a particularly valuable feature for providers of fresh products or products with short life cycles or perishability.

Unfortunately, centralized extended supply chains also come with substantial challenges. First, there is a high fixed cost of investment to build and outfit a DC. Second, the cost of delivery is quite high since everything needs to be delivered to the customer, and the distances to customers are higher than from a network of smaller stores. The need to deliver everything also creates a long lead time—typically from one day to as much as a week. The final major challenge is creating customer awareness—for companies that do not have existing stores or brands it is difficult to make vivid impressions on customers. As much as Dell is known worldwide as the leading computer manufacturer today, it is easy to forget that Dell started from very humble beginnings and faced a long uphill battle to develop brand awareness.

The remainder of this chapter offers two detailed profiles of companies that are excelling using the centralized extended strategy. First, Office Depot is one of the largest retailers via the Web with approximately $2.5 billion per year in sales. While they have existing stores, their direct fulfillment is done primarily out of their DCs. Second, Ocado is an example of a start-up company that is working hard to build brand awareness and change how customers shop for groceries. We will examine each of these to show how their techniques can be applied to a variety of different businesses. We then close the chapter with a discussion of key success levers.

Office Depot—Quietly Leading the Way

While companies such as Amazon, eBay, Webvan, and Kozmo were toasted in the popular press as the prototype of the "new economy" companies in the late 1990s, Office Depot quietly went about developing the Internet as a sales channel. Office Depot is a leading retailer of office supplies, with 1,045 office supply stores in forty-four states and twelve countries. Sales in 2002 were $11.4 billion with profits of $500 million. Office Depot is widely considered to be the leader in both office supply retailing in general and online office supplies in particular.[1] What few people realize is that a large percentage of its profits are from its Business Services Group (BSG), and increasingly, its online channels. The BSG provides direct delivery of office supplies to business customers. As shown in Figure 5-1, BSG accounts for a substantial portion of Office Depot's overall sales, but, more important, it also accounts for a large percentage of profits, as shown in Figure 5-2. Note that Office Depot offers accounting figures for three reportable segments (North American retail, Business Services Group, and international) and that sales figures for online operations represent sales within both BSG and international. Figure 5-1 clearly shows that online sales have been increasing more rapidly than other methods. Figure 5-2 indicates that profits within the BSG group have been increasing rapidly, we believe, in part, because of the shift to Internet-based ordering.

Office Depot has also developed the Internet as a critical sales channel, and it has become one of the recognized leaders in Internet retailing. The company first started selling online in 1995 by developing customized Web sites for large Fortune 500 corporate clients, and then expanded its offerings via OfficeDepot.com to the public in 1998. As Figure 5-1 clearly illustrates, the company's Internet sales have grown extremely rapidly. In effect, the Internet portion of sales within the BSG group is the only growing area of Office Depot in the last couple of years. Most important, Office Depot makes a profit on Internet sales, unlike many of the last-mile retailers that sprang to life in the late 1990s.[2]

Fundamentally, Office Depot latched onto two key concepts regarding last-mile supply chains earlier than most competitors. First, it realized that the supply chain was of critical importance— the orders were not going to pick and deliver themselves. Second, Office Depot also recognized that the Internet offered ways to streamline the sales process, but that this new ordering method had to be carefully designed in order to gain customer acceptance.

Figure 5-1. Office Depot sales by segment.

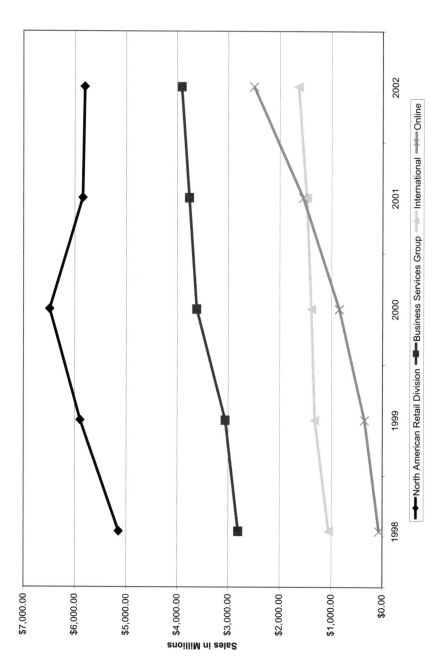

◆— North American Retail Division ■— Business Services Group — International ✕— Online

*Data drawn from Office Depot Annual Reports 2000 to 2002.

Figure 5-2. Office Depot profits by segment.

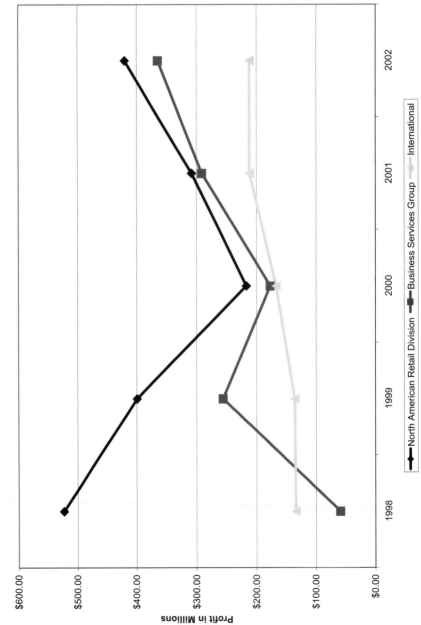

*Data drawn from Office Depot Annual Reports 2000 to 2002.

The emphasis on managing the extended supply chain can clearly be seen in Office Depot's annual reports and on its Web site. As of March 29, 2003, its supply chain for delivering customer orders consisted of: twenty-four domestic delivery centers, thirteen regional call centers, over 1,900 trucks, and 2,400 drivers. This network of resources was first developed for the Business Services Group in the early 1990s, when orders were placed by mail, phone, or fax. As Office Depot developed the Internet as a sales channel, this network formed the backbone to which Web site development and marketing were added. Careful management of these resources was critical in order to balance efficiency (cost of delivery) with customer convenience. One major advantage that Office Depot has capitalized on is that delivering to businesses is significantly easier than delivering to home customers since, for the most part, businesses are open regular hours and have employees ready to receive orders at any time during the day. Thus, deliveries can be scheduled to minimize the distance traveled, rather than to meet a prespecified delivery window. The difference in drop density is substantial. Office Depot averages between thirty-five and forty-five deliveries per driver per day, as compared to a goal of fifteen to seventeen for home-delivery grocers, such as Ocado.[3] This dramatic difference is due to a number of factors, but a primary cause is the ability to deliver with far fewer time constraints. Clearly, there is also a substantial impact on the costs of delivery.

The second major insight that Office Depot capitalized on involved the streamlining of transaction costs. Prior to the shift in orders to the Internet, the BSG group took orders via telephone, fax, or mail, which worked well but fundamentally involved a substantial degree of double-processing—i.e., customers had to fill out their orders and transmit them, then Office Depot employees had to enter the order, clarify any mistakes or miscommunications, and transmit the order to the fulfillment center. This double-processing is costly for both Office Depot and the customer, and it offers many opportunities for mistakes. The Internet provides an opportunity for customers to self-source—i.e., to enter their own order without direct interaction with an Office Depot employee. When done properly, this can be very convenient for customers and also represents a substantial savings for the company.[4] Monica Luechtefeld, executive vice president, e-commerce, estimates that online orders represent a cost savings of approximately one percent of sales—quite a substantial amount in a low-margin business, such as the retailing of commodity office products. Applying this estimate to the $2.5 billion in online sales reported for 2002 suggests that moving transactions to the Web has saved approximately $20 million per year. However, this savings is only realizable when the volume of Internet orders reaches a critical mass of customers. If an organization only collects 5 percent of its orders online and the other 95 percent over the telephone, the need for call centers has not been greatly changed, nor has the cost of developing and maintaining a customer-friendly Web site been adequately defrayed. Thus, Office Depot has realized greater benefits in 2001 and 2002 as the percentage of Internet orders within the BSG has approached and passed 50 percent. When this happens, the allocation of resources changes substantially. For example, call centers will still be needed, but the number of calls/customers will be much lower, since customers will no longer place routine calls to order and will only call on an exception basis. Therefore, fewer call centers should be able to handle more customers.[5] The sharp increase in profits attributed to the BSG group in 2000 through 2002 (as shown in Figure 5-2) is likely a result of the shift in ordering patterns to the Internet.

Cisco Systems offers an excellent illustration of the advantages of shifting transactions to the Internet. By encouraging customers to use the Web to place orders and ask questions, Cisco was able to have 80 percent of customer questions answered online, with 55 percent of all sales orders passing through their system without being touched by a single person. As a result, Cisco had 1999 sales that were more than six times their 1994 sales level, yet their technical support staff was only double the 1994 level—an increase in productivity of 3:1.[6]

The key to effective self-sourcing is ensuring that there are bene-fits for both the company and the customer. So, what do custom-ers think of OfficeDepot.com? Over $2 billion in orders per year suggests that they like it, but why? Drawing from our study of over 400 customers of OfficeDepot.com in 2000, Figure 5-3 shows customers in three groups based on increasing number of orders placed online. Each of the five questions asked customers to rate how ordering online improved various aspects of the ordering ex-perience. Figure 5-3 illustrates two primary things. First, custom-ers generally felt that ordering online improved all the aspects of ordering (the mean response for all five questions is greater than 4.0—rated as a moderate improvement). Second, more experi-enced and loyal customers (those with seven or more orders) rated each question substantially higher. In particular, experienced customers rate the time to place an order, the thoroughness of order documentation, and the ease of interpretation of documen-tation as much higher than newer customers. This illustrates the importance of learning curves—customers will improve in their ability to use the ordering system over repeated orders, but com-panies such as Office Depot must also work to find ways to speed up and simplify this learning process.

Customers were also asked whether the online ordering system improved various aspects of purchasing, as shown in Figure 5-4 and Figure 5-5. The responses indicate that customers generally perceived fairly small improvements in the cost of both the activi-ties associated with purchasing and the cost of training new per-sonnel. However, the responses regarding the accuracy of billing and the availability of supplies/materials were dramatically higher. The study results generally indicate that online purchasing helps companies track orders, expenditures, and receipts more pre-cisely, rather than directly lowering the cost of materials or the cost of labor to purchase supplies. In other words, online purchas-ing helps lend a degree of certainty regarding what has been or-dered, what is in stock, and what is incoming. Most of the readers of this book can appreciate this since it is likely that they have run short of paper, toner for a printer, computer disks, envelopes, or

(text continues on page 119)

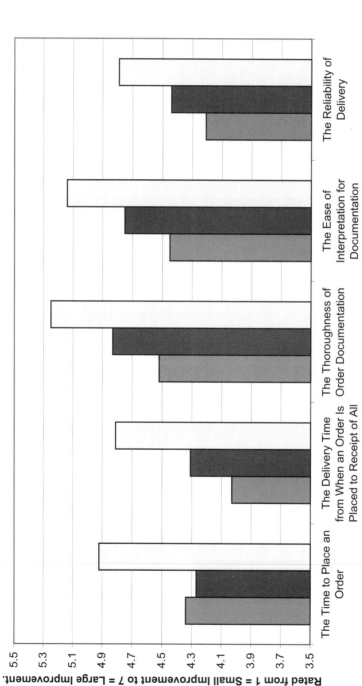

Figure 5-3. Comparison of order frequency and improvement in ordering for Office Depot customers.

Please rate the degree of improvement when the following tasks/events are conducted using the internet for purchasing products through Office Depot in comparison to traditional methods (order by phone, fax, or mail).

■ 1 or 2 orders ■ 3 - 6 orders □ 7 or more orders

Rated from 1 = Small Improvement to 7 = Large Improvement.

The Time to Place an Order
The Delivery Time from When an Order Is Placed to Receipt of All Items
The Thoroughness of Order Documentation
The Ease of Interpretation for Documentation
The Reliability of Delivery

Figure 5-4. Customer perceptions of online ordering at OfficeDepot.com.

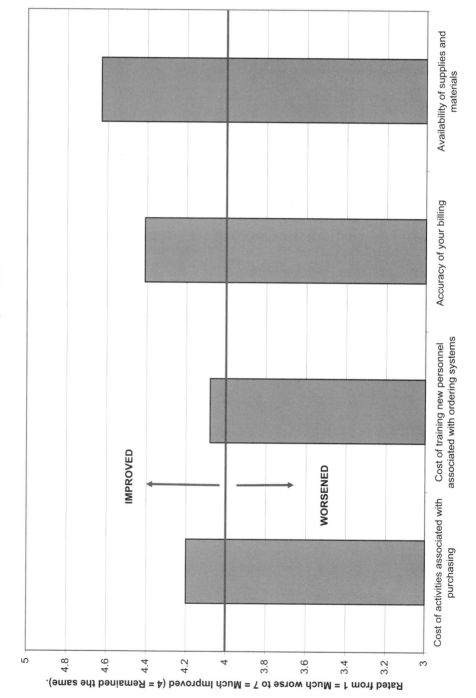

Figure 5-5. OfficeDepot.com customers, comparing purchase channel with purchase size.

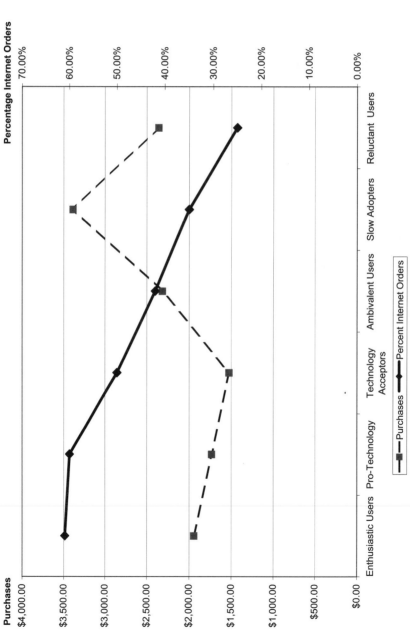

Drawn from J. R. Olson and K. K. Boyer with John Olson, "Factors Influencing the Utilization of Internet Purchasing in Small Firms," *Journal of Operations Management*, vol. 21, no. 2, 2003, pp. 225–246.

some other "essential" office supply, which, although not expensive, presents an inconvenience when not available.

We close our discussion of Office Depot with a selection of anonymous quotes from customers that completed our survey. It is important to note that almost all of the 400-plus customers who filled out the survey took the opportunity to write additional comments beyond the specific questions that we asked them to rate on a one to seven scale. The vast majority of these comments were positive, while a substantial minority (roughly 5 percent to 10 percent) were fairly negative. This is not necessarily a bad thing; after all, Abraham Lincoln once said, "You can please some of the people all of the time, and all of the people some of the time, but you can't please all of the people all of the time."

Selected Comments from OfficeDepot.com Customers

- I love the convenience of not leaving my desk to place an order; it avoids extra distractions, and it is easier to keep a record of items ordered, expected delivery, etc.
- I liked the tracking system of my past orders. I tend to order repetitive items, and it gave me a fast way to reorder, not to mention budget-tracking information.
- I can find things on the Web site that I can't find in the stores. I can order online when I am "on hold," doing research on behalf of my clients.
- I like the option of ordering online and not having to be put on hold or having difficulty trying to get a knowledgeable person on the phone.
- I have always been able to connect immediately. At times when I placed orders by phone, I would have to call several times to get through to an operator.
- I hate the Web site, you need to give information like what is your third cousin's sister's wife's son's name to order!

Ocado—Changing The Habits Of A Lifetime

Ocado was formed by three ex–Goldman Sachs directors (Jonathan Faiman, Jason Gissing, and Tim Steiner) in early 2000, and was originally named Last Mile Solutions. Financed by a £46 million investment and 40 percent ownership stake by Waitrose, Ocado has taken a deliberate and carefully planned approach to developing its business, under co–managing directors Nigel Robertson and Roger Whiteside and logistics director Robert Gorrie. This approach is in stark contrast with the shoot-for-the-stars approach taken by many of the failed Internet grocers such as Webvan and HomeGrocer. Ocado spent the better part of two years developing and planning all aspects of its business with a core group of fifteen to twenty employees. This planning phase was followed by a phased rollout of service, starting north of London and working down toward central London between March and December of 2002. This approach is based on recognition that the idea of mass-market home delivery requires new techniques on the part of both companies and customers. Nigel Robertson states, "It makes sense to learn all the problems in the early days, before we commit advanced resources to the operation. And believe me, there will be a learning process to go through. We don't have any doubt of that."[7] Equally important to the long-term success is the understanding that customers need to be nurtured and guided to learn a new (and hopefully easier) way of shopping for groceries, or, as Nigel Robertson states: "We are working to change the habits of a lifetime."

About twenty miles north of central London, in the town of Hatfield, Hertfordshire, England, a 300,000-square-foot distribution center is in its second year of operation. This distribution center is the center of Ocado's operations—built to handle orders placed over the Internet for home delivery to customers in the London metropolitan area. The ultimate capacity of the distribution center is equivalent to the sales volume of approximately twenty stores.

So why does Ocado think that it can do better than failed grocers such as Webvan and HomeGrocer? First, a purpose-built facility with no stores to support effectively (at least in theory) removes a link in the supply chain. If Ocado can make the DC–based picking approach work, then it can remove the costs of running stores, which typically run 20 percent to 25 percent of sales. These cost savings can be used to offset the costs of picking and delivering the orders. More important, removing a step in the supply chain facilitates quicker inventory turns and fresher produce, meats, and dairy. Second, Ocado believes that it has learned valuable lessons from the efforts of its predecessors. In particular, Nigel Robertson states, "Our Hatfield facility is built on a larger scale [to approximate the size of a typical DC that supplies about twenty stores]. So it's much easier for us to deal with 'peakiness' and maintain availability. Also we're completely focused on home deliveries—they're not an add-on to a retail operation [as with Asda]."[8]

In particular, there are three major differences between Ocado's approach and that used by predecessors. First, Ocado is taking time to allow learning to take place. The first picking operation was a largely manual process setup in a warehouse in Hemel, Hempstead. This allowed Ocado to learn and refine its processes before committing to a more automated approach at its Hatfield purpose-built facility. In addition, Ocado is rolling out this new and yet to be proven approach at a single facility, while Webvan ignored time-tested principles by trying to do something new not in one or two places, but in eight or more at a time. As everyone at Ocado readily admits, "This is a new business, we try our best to get a good answer, but we are under no illusions that everything will work perfectly out of the box—so we are always ready to adapt and revise." Second, Ocado has designed the Hatfield facility so that it can be opened up in three phases:

◆   Phase One involves constructing the entire footprint of the facility (all walls and roofing), but only two out of three bays of the facility are finished (i.e., concrete flooring poured and all utilities hooked up). During Phase One, all orders will be picked using an automated trolley system running through bay one (which has all of the refrigeration equipment necessary) and outgoing orders will be packed in bay two and inbound orders received.

◆ Phase Two involves finishing out bay three (i.e., pouring flooring and installing utilities etc.). Then packing is moved to bay three, and orders will be delivered via a trolley on the outside of bay two. Then, bay two will be installed with the automated cranes and trolley system necessary to operate at higher volumes.

◆ When sufficient volume is reached (approximately 10,000 orders on peak days), the final layout will consist of picking refrigerated and frozen orders in bay one, picking of ambient orders in bay two, and packing of outgoing orders and receiving of inbound orders in bay three.

The ultimate capacity of the Hatfield facility will be 20,000 orders on a peak day. (We estimate that Ocado's goal is to achieve picking rates of above 200 items/employee per hour.) According to Robert Gorrie, logistics director, "This phased approach reduces our initial investment in Phase One by 40 percent, primarily through the savings in not having to buy all of the equipment for the final state immediately. In the long run, it costs a bit more, but it conserves resources in the short run while we are building the business."

As of early September 2003, Ocado was in Phase One of its rollout, and it was doing quite well in attracting customers to the service, while trying to scale up picking operations in a manner that provided continued excellent service and high quality. Figure 5-6 shows a comparison of Ocado customer responses to a series of questions on how online shopping compares to in-store shopping. Customers were asked to rate five questions on a scale ranging from one, equaling much *better* than shopping in a traditional store, to seven, equaling much *worse* than shopping in a traditional store, with the neutral midpoint being four, equaling about the same as shopping in a traditional store. Figure 5-6 divides customers into three groups: new customers (have only placed one

Figure 5-6. Rating Ocado's home delivery vs. in-store shopping.

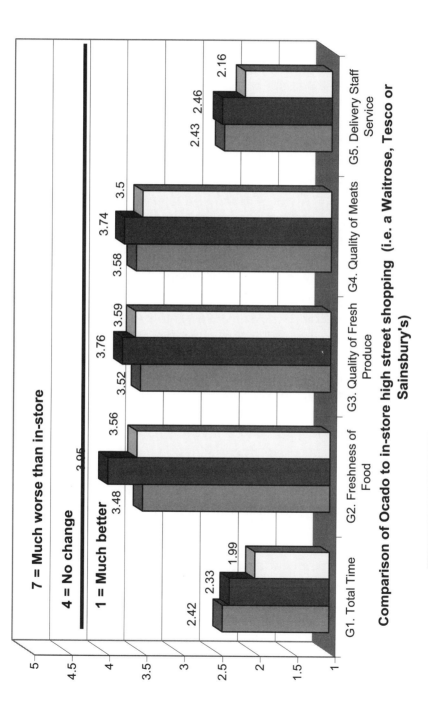

7 = Much worse than in-store

4 = No change

1 = Much better

Comparison of Ocado to in-store high street shopping (i.e. a Waitrose, Tesco or Sainsbury's)

■ New Customer ■ Return Customer ☐ Loyal Customer

G1. Total Time — 2.42, 2.33, 1.99

G2. Freshness of Food — 3.48, 3.56

G3. Quality of Fresh Produce — 3.52, 3.76, 3.59

G4. Quality of Meats — 3.58, 3.74, 3.5

G5. Delivery Staff Service — 2.43, 2.46, 2.16

3.05

or two orders), repeat customers (have placed three to six orders), and loyal customers (seven or more orders). Three things are clearly shown in Figure 5-6. First, most customers rate all aspects of shopping online better than in traditional stores—particularly the savings in time and the service provided by the delivery staff. Second, there is a pronounced learning effect—more experienced customers appreciate the time savings and service substantially more than new customers. Third, customers of Ocado rate the freshness and quality of produce and meats as better than in traditional stores. This data was collected prior to the rollout of the purpose-built facility, and when Ocado was still handling a fairly small volume of orders. As volume increases past the 10,000-order-per-week mark, the freshness should increase further.

Another key component of Ocado's strategy is providing superior service quality. Figure 5-7 shows customer responses to four questions regarding whether Ocado employees were understanding of customer needs, responsive to service requests, accessible to answer questions, and easy to communicate with. The responses show a clear pattern of improvement as customers gained familiarity with Ocado's service. The ratings for new (customers who have placed one or two orders) and return (three to six orders) are all fairly good, with averages around 5.8 with seven being the best possible. However, loyal customers who have purchased seven or more times have substantially higher ratings, all of which are higher than 6.2. This underscores the importance of two things. First, the importance of working carefully with new customers to develop a level of trust and a comfort level with online ordering of groceries. Second, it is critical to manage points of customer contact with customers carefully—primarily the actual delivery, the online ordering system, and any calls on the customer service line. The goal is to make the customer feel special and valued. As shown in Figure 5-7, Ocado appears to be doing a good job accomplishing these goals.

Figure 5-7. Service quality ratings by Ocado customers.

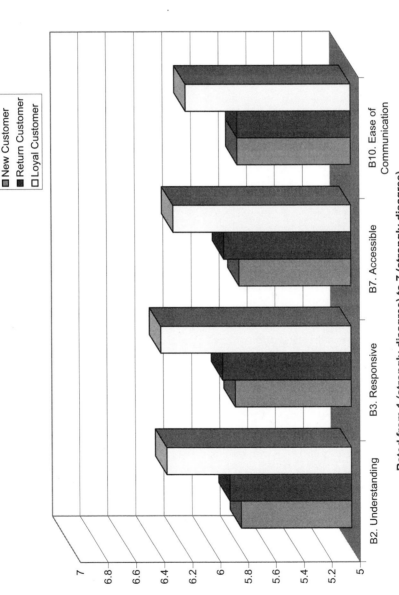

Success Levers

There are several success levers that can be applied to centralized extended supply chains.

Convenience, Convenience, Convenience

The real estate slogan that selling a house is about location, location, location is familiar to anyone who has ever bought, sold, or rented a house. Likewise, retailers hoping to sell items for home delivery ought to continually remind themselves that this service is all about convenience. Customers do not order for home or business delivery to get lower prices (although this would certainly be nice), but to ease some aspect of their lives. Parents with two small children order groceries to *avoid* dragging these children through the store with the attending chorus of "can we buy this," or "he hit me." Office workers order supplies online to avoid having to leave work, fight traffic, and waste valuable work time. Customers order furniture from Rooms to Go, rather than by mail order, because part of the service includes carrying their new bed into their house, rather than having it dropped unceremoniously (for later assembly) on the doorstep by a UPS driver.

While it is obvious that convenience is the major driver of home-delivery sales, choosing the proper amount of convenience is a bit more challenging. Should grocery deliveries offer a thirty-minute reserved window, a one-hour window, a two-hour window, or a longer window? Should deliveries from Office Depot be offered to any location on any day of the week, or should they be more limited to prespecified days? How should shortages or substitutions be handled—should the customer simply be told, "Sorry, we were out of that item," or should there be some type of discount or rain check? Too often, the answers to these questions reveal a poor match between marketing and supply chain objectives. There is a strong tendency to overpromise and underdeliver, but unlike traditional retailers that focus primarily on low cost (i.e., Wal-Mart or Home Depot), extended supply chain retailers cannot afford to leave many customers unsatisfied. Of course, there will always be some problems (late deliveries, substitutes, damaged goods), but the trick is to provide a high enough service level that the customer is generally amazed and is much more accepting in those less-frequent situations where something goes awry. In short, the goal is to serve the target market and forget about those customers who do not value convenience sufficiently (i.e., those unwilling to pay some type of premium for it). Last-mile retailers must seek to capitalize on the greater loyalty of convenience-oriented customers by either getting more frequent orders and/or getting larger orders with higher margins.

Relationships

Creating a two-way relationship with customers in the centralized extended supply chain is perhaps the biggest challenge—and opportunity. Because the company does not have physical stores (unless it uses a hybrid strategy such as Office Depot), developing name recognition with customers is challenging. Companies must think through their marketing campaigns and physical assets very carefully. For example, the delivery trucks and drivers are perhaps the most visible asset of a company. Therefore, creating a visually striking and memorable design for trucks and uniforms is important. Ocado has done this with a fresh theme—all of its trucks are painted to look like a close-up of a particular fruit or vegetable (including limes, cabbages, oranges, etc.). Similarly, the uniform and the presentation of the driver who contacts the customer must be consistent, friendly, and professional. Thus, companies such as Ocado, Office Depot, Grocery Gateway, etc., all have carefully designed training programs to help drivers not just with normal deliveries, but to teach them how to handle exceptional circumstances such as an upset customer, missing items, damaged items, etc. As shown in Figure 5-7, it often takes several transactions for customers to develop a comfort level due to the disconnected nature of buying online from a remote location, but repeat customers do develop strong feelings of loyalty when companies manage the key interactions effectively.

Consider two of the leading firms that follow the decoupled strategy (Chapter Two)—Amazon and Dell. Neither of these firms has ever had physical stores, or direct delivery interaction with customers (both contract with outside vendors such as Federal Express or United Parcel Service). Yet, these two firms have incredible retention rates for keeping customers committed. Much of their ability to build customer relationships is based on their Web sites, their call centers, and their marketing programs. The important lesson is that companies that have little direct contact with customers can form strong relationships. In the centralized strategy discussed in this chapter, the companies have an added opportunity to bond with customers—the actual delivery. Clearly, making sure deliveries go as planned—on time, with the correct items and with pleasant interactions between employees and customers—is a critical component for success.

We will further examine ways to support and build customer relationships in Chapters Six through Nine. For now, we close with a general comparison of the two basic strategies for picking customer orders: in-store picking (either via semi-extended or extended supply chain) and DC–based (either via decoupled extended or centralized extended supply chain). Figure 5-8 shows average responses to the question, with four groupings of customers:

Ordering groceries online is more attractive than going to the store (rated from 1 = strongly disagree to 7 = strongly agree).

❑ **Group 1:** New customers of grocers that pick orders in store
❑ **Group 2:** Loyal customers of grocers that pick orders in store
❑ **Group 3:** New customers of DC–based picking grocers
❑ **Group 4:** Loyal customers of DC–based picking grocers

This comparison includes three different companies that pick from a DC and two companies that pick exclusively from existing stores. For in-store operations, there is very little improvement between new and loyal customers (in other words, the customers do not perceive the experience as improving substantially). However, for DC–based operations, there is a large improvement between new and loyal customers. This illustrates the need to carefully educate, develop, and build relationships with newer customers when using a centralized DC. While the customer ratings are lower in both cases for DC–based picking, the improvement is substantial as customers gain experience. This suggests that this approach may be better for customers in the long run, if companies can perfect their operational processes and capture a sufficient base of loyal customers. While we cannot reveal individual company results for this question, at least one of the DC–based grocers has ratings that exceed those for all the in-store picking companies.

Availability and Freshness

One of the biggest advantages of delivering from a DC versus from stores is the ability to aggregate inventory in one location rather than several. This greatly increases the ability to smooth fluctuations in demand and to track inventory

Figure 5-8. Comparison of store pick vs. DC pick overall attractiveness.

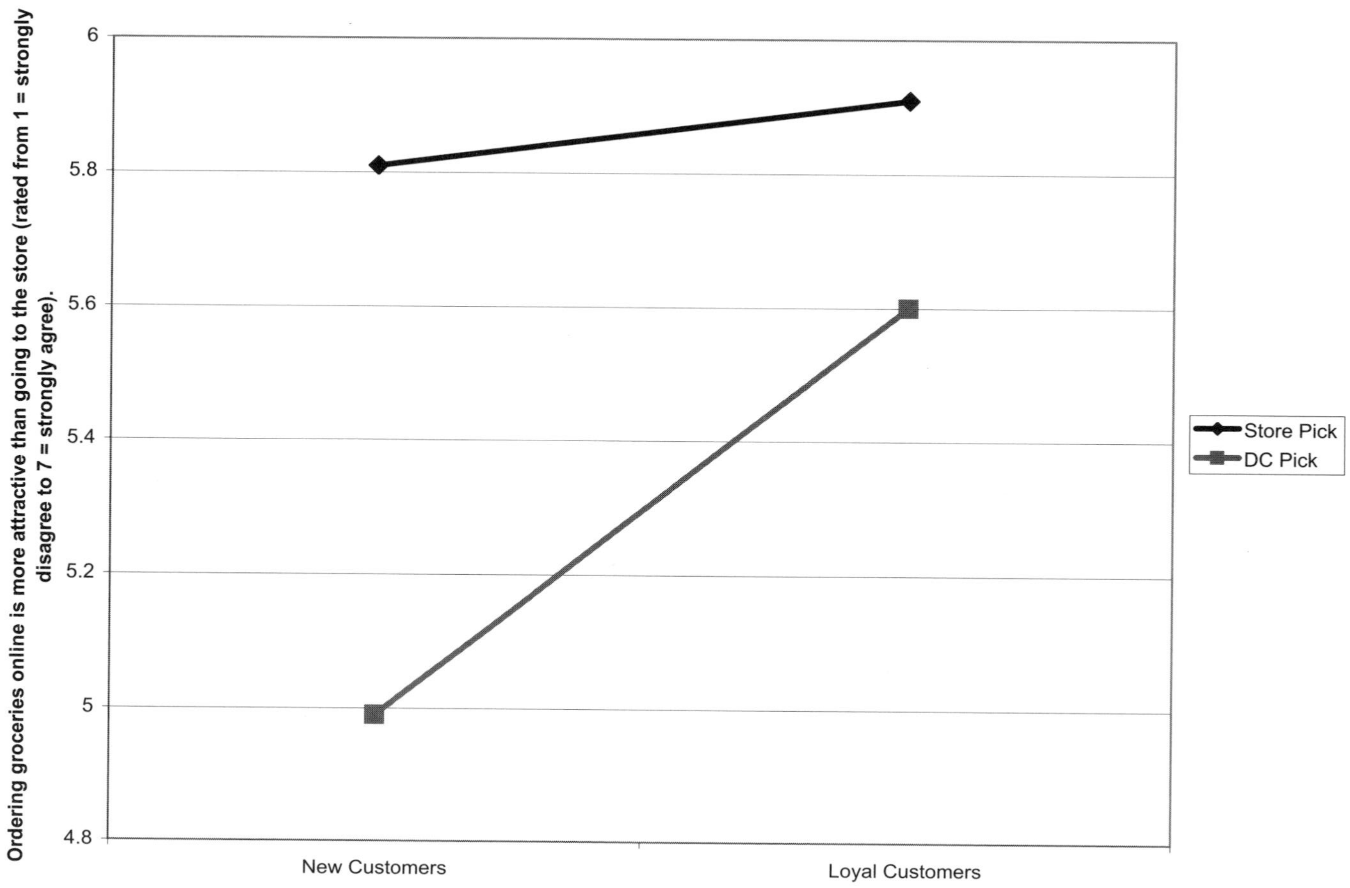
Ordering groceries online is more attractive than going to the store (rated from 1 = strongly disagree to 7 = strongly agree).
6
5.8
5.6
5.4
5.2
5
4.8
New Customers
Loyal Customers
Store Pick
DC Pick

availability. In retail environments, customers cannot touch merchandise in a DC, and what they can't touch they can't eat, misplace, or steal. This is particularly important in the grocery industry, where shrinkage is a substantial problem—the average for all stores was 1.14 percent of annual sales, or a total of $2.5 billion in the United States in 2002.[9] Clearly, customers are not the sole cause of shrinkage or unsaleables, but they are one of the major causes, so delivering out of a DC should offer improvements.

In the grocery industry, delivering to customers directly from the DC should offer improved freshness. Most customers do not spend much, if any, time thinking about the journey that a head of lettuce takes from the field that it is grown in to their cart at the supermarket. This may be a good thing, since it involves handling by numerous people and transportation in several different trucks. For our purposes, we assume that the steps taken by the head of lettuce are identical up until they reach the DC. Traditional stores receive their items for sale from a DC—either an independent distributor or a company-owned DC in the case of large chains. Home-delivered groceries from an Ocado, Grocery Gateway, or FreshDirect also get picked at a DC, but rather than being sent to a store, where they are handled again (often multiple times), the orders are sent directly to the customer.

Action Steps

This chapter has profiled two excellent examples of the centralized extended supply chain strategy. Office Depot has turned its direct-to-consumer group into a very profitable business unit within their company—by far. Its strategy has been to build on the core distribution capabilities that were in existence through its Business Services Group, while adding Internet ordering as a mechanism for streamlining customer transactions. Figures 5-1 and 5-2 aptly illustrate that while this business unit is a minority of Office Depot's sales, it is the key driver of both growth and profits. In contrast, Ocado was described as a company facing a substantially different challenge—namely, establishing a brand in the minds of consumers without having physical stores, and developing a radically new business model for grocery shopping. While its efforts are still in the early stages, there are preliminary signs of success—customers love the service, and sales have been steadily increasing. Much like FreshDirect, Ocado is building a strong customer base and approaching the break-even point financially. While there are certainly hurdles to be overcome, we believe that these companies offer a uniquely differentiated product/service bundle that will soon create separation from more traditional companies that focus primarily on low costs.

The keys to being successful with a centralized extended supply chain are deceptively simple on the surface, yet quite challenging in practice.

- ◆ Focus marketing on convenience and added value. Increase service at the point of customer interaction: delivery and customer support.

- ◆ Avoid leaping before looking. Carefully develop a plan for building out distribution centers in stages to avoid overbuilding before the market develops.

- ◆ Do not let marketing run the show. Markets must be built with operational constraints in mind.

- ◆ Capitalize on the opportunity to provide better customer service through better in-stock rates and/or extended choice of products.

- ◆ Choose delivery windows with a careful balancing of customer desires and operational constraints.

- ◆ Focus on high-density market growth.

- ◆ Build relationships with customers through personalized interaction at key contact points.

Notes

1. R. Gulati and J. Garino, "Get the Right Mix of Bricks & Clicks," *Harvard Business Review* (May–June 2000), pp. 107–114; M. Warner, D. Roth, E. Schonfeld, and M. Gunther, "Ten Companies that Get It," *Fortune* (1999), 140(9), pp. 1,154.

2. Financial figures are drawn from Office Depot's 1999 to 2002 annual reports. From these sources, it is impossible to determine the amount of profit earned on Internet sales since that is not explicitly reported.

3. Author estimate based on 2002 BSG group sales of $3.9 billion, employment of 2,400 drivers (assumed to be full-time) and an estimated average order size of $167. Sales and driver data drawn from Office Depot's 2002 Annual Report; average order size is author's estimate.

4. For more discussion of the advantages of self-sourcing, see K. K. Boyer, "E-Operations: A Guide to How the Internet Streamlines Operations," *Business Horizons,* Vol. 44, No. 1 (January–February 2001), pp. 47–54.

5. "NWA's Livonia Calling Center to Close," *Detroit Free Press* (September 26, 2003), p. C1.

6. Ibid., p. 49.

7. "Ocado's Online Grocery Gambit Goes Live," *E.Logistics Magazine* (February 2002).

8. "Ocado Moves into Full Launch Mode," *E.Logistics Magazine* (February 2002).

9. *Unsaleables Update*, Vol. 3, No. 1 (Winter, 2003), newsletter published by the Food Marketing Institute.

PART III

TRANSFORMING THE SUPPLY CHAIN

CHAPTER 6

Strategy—Meshing Operational and Marketing Goals

The relationship between an organization's operations and its marketing activities has always been a critical element to achieve desired success. Interestingly, operations and marketing often are at odds with each other in terms of the focus of the organization and the degrees to which one drives the success versus the other. For example, given limited resources, where should the focus be? Operations? Marketing? Judging by the title of this chapter, our argument is obviously both. Integration is the key. And, although this integration is perhaps intuitive to some, many (if not most) organizations are skewed toward either operations or marketing in implementing their strategies. Previously, we discussed online groceries in some basic detail. The following example specifically illustrates the "meshing" that is needed between operational and marketing strategies to succeed in the online grocery industry.

Online Groceries as a Case Example

Groceries are typically viewed as the most universal commodity in the marketplace. As a result, cost efficiency and effectiveness become key success factors for grocery organizations. Specifically, customers' demands and the competition's eagerness to satisfy those demands often lead supermarkets to go to great lengths to develop new technologies and methods of streamlining both their supply chain operations and their marketing efforts. Of course, the grocery products are also important, but by and large, most products can be found in most stores. So, instead, streamlining is seen as a way to cut costs in the high-intensive, low-margin grocery business.

For example, on the operations side, in 1974 supermarkets introduced the first application of bar coding and UPC coding for inventory and transaction purposes (at the Marsh Supermarket in Troy, Ohio, on June 26, 1974). Without the introduction of this new technology in supermarkets, prices were estimated to have risen twice as fast without the use of the UPC symbol. And, by some estimates, this technology has been twenty times more valuable than its developers originally projected. Today, there are over five billion scans per day using the UPC code.[1]

Direct product profitability (DPP) is the extension of the bar-coding technology. The DPP is used to track scanning data by brand, category, and other measures to gather information on coupon use, the effects of promotions, and shelf displays. The use of DPP has led to greater integration and coordination between marketing research and sales.[2] Presumably, the operations function has something to learn from the DPP data too. One example can be found in the latest batch of online grocery organizations and how they operate.

Recently, a great deal of interest has been placed on the use of the Internet as a technological tool to improve the value-added benefits offered to customers in the entire grocery supply chain. The Internet has been positioned, in this case, as a way to link customers with grocery stores from their homes, offices, and other remote places that have access to a computer and an Internet connection. This gives grocery organizations a chance to better integrate the value-added elements, as perceived by customers, in the supply chain. If designed appropriately, an opportunity exists for all the new (and established) online grocers to closely link marketing, sales, operations, purchasing, and logistics.

At the same time, as Webvan and other online grocers discovered the hard way, numerous challenges and drawbacks to online groceries also (still) exist. From the operations side, an argument can be made that delivering groceries to customers presents severe logistical difficulties. Companies such as Tesco, Ocado, or Peapod seek to deliver groceries within a specified delivery window. Marketing professionals thrive on the short windows—the tighter the window, the more consumers like the service. But obviously tight windows make deliveries difficult—and the operations people crazy. Now we have a mismatch between the goals of operations and marketing . . . and trouble is born.

This last mile to the customers proved to be a crucial barrier that had to be overcome to make online groceries a viable business model. Webvan could not make their processes cost-competitive compared with traditional grocers (e.g., Kroger, Meijer, Safeway). Webvan tried to build market share by offering groceries delivered to a customer's door in a specified thirty-minute window at prices comparable to what consumers got by doing the shopping themselves. This sounds great from a marketing perspective, but Webvan's operations (read "process" here) were simply unable to meet this logistical challenge. Of course, in hindsight, Webvan may have been more successful by providing groceries at low cost while delivering in a less timely fashion (i.e., two-hour delivery windows) as opposed to within a tight window (half-hour delivery windows). The market would not have been as large as with the more convenient windows, but there are consumers who would pay more for the higher convenience relative to traditional shipping in the store. Without these adjustments to the business model, Webvan went bankrupt—falling from a high market value of $7.9 billion to the $2.7 million that Louis Borders sold his 45 million shares for (at six cents per share) in July 2001.[3]

In contrast to Webvan, Tesco, Britain's leading grocer, has implemented a very different process for providing online ordering of groceries. First, Tesco markets online groceries as a convenience, not as a low-price option—charging customers an eight-dollar delivery charge, in addition to the retail cost of groceries. Second, Tesco has kept the operations of grocery delivery comparatively simple by using existing assets, rather than building high-tech warehouses. Online orders are filled by Tesco employees at the nearest Tesco store, then picked up and delivered via van. This approach works much better for lower volumes of business, albeit at a high cost per order. Compare Tesco's approach to that of Webvan. Webvan had high fixed investment and a low variable cost. Webvan, thus, counted on a very high volume to be financially viable. The net result is that Tesco had sales of $336 million in 2000, making it the world's largest online grocery.[4] Revenues increased to $450 million in 2001, with operating profits of ~$22 million while estimates for 2002 are that Tesco.com will crack the $600 million level.[5,6] Recognizing that the potential market reach for Internet grocery sales was fairly small (Internet sales are still only 1.5 percent of total revenue), and the associated operational challenges, allowed Tesco to develop an appropriate Internet strategy, rather than shooting for the stars and flaming out as Webvan did together with many of the first-batch Internet grocers.

With a few notable exceptions, what these Internet grocers overlooked or miscalculated was that the marketing strategy of low prices needs to be matched with an operations strategy that actually achieves low costs. The online grocery companies that have achieved some success (e.g., Tesco, Sainsbury's, and Albertson's) take an alternative approach of marketing their services to customers as a convenience-added option that will cost customers more, but which can then be supported by using the extra funds to support operations aimed at providing convenient and timely delivery.

Meshing Operations and Marketing

What are the critical elements in operations that drive strategy? What are the critical elements in marketing that drive strategy? Figure 6-1 illustrates the "Hexagon of Operations and Marketing Integration," outlining the factors we think are the critical elements in (supply chain) strategy.[7]

Figure 6-1. The hexagon of operations and marketing integration.

At the conceptual level, marketing has contributed more rigorously and effectively to the right side of the hexagon (i.e., competitor orientation, customer orientation, and value chain coordination). Operations professionals (read supply chain) have contributed more specifically to the left side of the hexagon (i.e., logistics management, operations management, and supply management). To facilitate benchmarking of the six elements of the hexagon, at the cultural level of organizations, in this chapter we have included perceptual questions to assess each construct. However, prior to introducing the measures, we define and discuss the logic of each construct:

- *Customer Orientation.* A customer orientation is viewed as the sufficient understanding of an organization's target customers to be able to create superior value for them continuously. A customer orientation requires that an organization understands a customer's entire value chain, as it is today and as it will evolve over time.[8]

- *Competitor Orientation.* Competitor orientation refers to the organization understanding the short-term strengths and weaknesses of current competitors, as well as the long-term capabilities and strategies of both key current competitors and potential future entrants into the field.[9]

- *Value Chain Coordination.* This refers to the coordinated utilization of resources at each sequential step, as well as between each step of the value-chain process. Coordination drives the effective and efficient integration of marketing and operations goals and their accompanying strategies, tactics, and implementation mechanisms.[10]

- *Logistics Management.* As viewed by the Council of Logistics Management (CLM), logistics involves planning, implementation, and controlling the efficient and effective flow and storage of goods, services, and information from the point of origin to consumption in order to meet customers' needs and wants.[11]

- *Supply Management.* Supply management (e.g., purchasing, procurement, sourcing) in its broadest form refers to the processes that enable the progress of value from raw material to final user and back to redesign and final disposition.[12]

- *Operations Management.* A general definition of operations management (OM) holds that OM is the design, operation, and improvement of the production system that creates the organization's primary products, services, and accompanying information. The production system typically includes the 4Ps of people, plants, parts, and processes.

As defined and operationalized, these metrics can be used by organizations to identify the degree to which one element of the hexagon is emphasized more than another element. Logically, over time, each element of the hexagon should be emphasized equally for most organizations in most industries. Clearly, however, certain organizations that stress one or a few of the elements in their basic operation (i.e., their reason for being in business) should focus on those particular element(s). For example, Federal Express typically stresses "logistics management" and "value-chain coordination," while Dell is likely to focus more efforts on "customer orientation" and "operations management." That said, both Federal Express and Dell also rely, over time, on all six elements of the hexagon to drive success.

Each factor has been found, statistically, to be reliable and valid in a general marketing/operations context. Although one should always incorporate contingencies in any study design, we suggest that the metrics offered in this chapter can serve as a great starting point for an organization's benchmark assessments, as well as their assessments of degrees of focus on a specific element in the hexagon. Ideally, as we stated above, a relatively equal emphasis should exist over time (allowing, however, for core competencies to flourish in perhaps one to two of the categories). Perhaps most significantly, this means that, for example, the degree of customer orientation and the degree of operations management orientation should be even with each other in an organization's efforts to span the last mile to customers.

Perceptual Measures for the Element in the Hexagon

This section provides a set of sixty questions (ten for each element of the hexagon—customer orientation, competitor orientation, coordination, logistics management, operations management, and supply management). These questions have been designed to be comparable across the six elements of the hexagon, as well as be comparable across organizations at various points in time. As such, a company can track its relative emphasis on a particular marketing (i.e., competitor orientation, customer orientation, and value-chain coordination) or operations (i.e., logistics management, operations management, and supply management) aspect over time.

Usually, organizations use a seven-point Likert-type scale ranging from "strongly disagree" to "strongly agree" when using the metrics in a benchmark assessment, with the middle rating listed as "Neither Agree nor Disagree." These questions can be given to a variety of respondents within an organization to compare both the organization's relative emphasis on elements of the hexagon and the relative emphasis of individual respondents. The scores can be computed as a sum within each element—e.g., if using a one-to-seven scale, scores for each element will range from 10 to 70 (i.e., a low of 10 equals ten responses of 1, while the highest possible response is 70, which is ten responses of 7). Another approach entails forced rankings. This involves allocating a fixed number of points to be allocated across all questions. For example, each respondent could be given 240 points to allocate across all 60 questions (an average of four points per question). This approach "forces" respondents to choose what they consider to be really important, not just rate everything the same. Spreadsheets provide a good tool for collecting such forced ratings.

Strongly Disagree	Disagree	Disagree Somewhat	Neither Disagree Nor Agree	Agree Somewhat	Agree	Strongly Agree
1	2	3	4	5	6	7

Customer Orientation

Customer orientation is considered one of the crucial components in an organization's efforts to achieve efficient and effective value-chain practices. Often, customer orientation has been viewed as within the domain of marketing. The questions below address the degree to which your organization has a customer orientation.

♦ We believe that it is important to constantly monitor our commitment to serving customer needs as a part of our value-chain activities.

♦ We believe that it is important to communicate information about customer experiences across all units as a part of our value-chain activities.

♦ We believe that it is important to develop value-chain strategies based on our understanding of customers' needs.

◆ We believe that it is important to measure customer satisfaction systematically and frequently as a part of our value-chain activities.

◆ We believe that it is important to disseminate data on customer satisfaction at all levels on a regular basis as a part of our value-chain activities.

◆ We believe that it is important to help our customers, as a part of our value-chain activities, be prepared for developments in their markets.

◆ We believe that it is important to try to discover the additional needs of our customers, as a part of our value-chain activities, of which they may be unaware.

◆ We believe that it is important to seek opportunities, as a part of our value-chain activities, in areas where customers have difficulty expressing their needs.

◆ We believe that it is important to try to recognize customer needs, as a part of our value-chain activities, before the majority of the market recognizes them.

◆ We believe that it is important to extrapolate key trends, as a part of our value-chain activities, to understand what customers will need in the future.

Competitor Orientation

Competitor orientation is considered one of the crucial components in an organization's efforts to achieve efficient and effective value-chain management practices. Typically, competitor orientation has also been viewed as within the domain of marketing. However, the last decade has seen competitor orientation often being viewed as a separate function within organizations, as well as a separate phenomenon to study within business schools. The questions below address the degree to which your organization has a competitor orientation.

◆ We believe that it is important to constantly monitor our commitment to understanding competitors as a part of our value-chain activities.

◆ We believe that it is important to communicate information about competitors across all units as a part of our value-chain activities.

◆ We believe that it is important to develop value-chain strategies based on our understanding of competitors.

◆ We believe that it is important to assess competitors systematically and frequently as a part of our value-chain activities.

◆ We believe that it is important to disseminate data on competitors at all levels on a regular basis as a part of our supply-chain activities.

◆ We believe that it is important to understand our competitors, as a part of our value-chain activities, to be prepared for developments in our markets.

◆ We believe that it is important to try to discover additional actions of our competitors, as a part of our value-chain activities, of which we may be unaware.

◆ We believe that it is important to seek opportunities, as a part of our value-chain activities, in areas where our competitors have difficulty delivering to customers

◆ We believe that it is important to try to recognize competitor actions, as a part of our value-chain activities, before the majority of the market recognizes them.

◆ We believe that it is important to extrapolate key trends, as a part of our value-chain activities, to understand what competitors may do in the future.

Value-Chain Coordination

Value-chain coordination deals with the organization's coordination between functions and activities in the supply chain (e.g., customer orientation, competitor orientation, logistics management, operations management, and supply management). It has, too, been viewed as part of marketing's domain. Obviously, however, coordination is a broader phenomenon. Coordination is considered one of the crucial components in an organization's efforts to achieve efficient and effective value-chain management practices. The questions below address the degree to which your organization has coordination among its value-chain functions.

◆ We believe that it is important to constantly monitor our coordination of value-chain functions.

◆ We believe that it is important to coordinate information about our value-chain activities across all units.

- We believe that it is important to coordinate strategies based on understanding of our value-chain activities.
- We believe that it is important to coordinate our value-chain activities systematically and frequently.
- We believe that it is important to coordinate data on our value-chain activities at all levels on a regular basis.
- We believe that it is important to coordinate our value-chain activities to be prepared for developments in our markets.
- We believe that it is important to coordinate our value-chain activities to try to discover additional possibilities of which we may be unaware.
- We believe that it is important to coordinate opportunities in areas where our value-chain function has difficulty delivering for us.
- We believe that it is important to try to coordinate value-chain possibilities before the majority of the market recognizes them.
- We believe that it is important to extrapolate key trends to coordinate what value-chain activities we may need in the future.

Logistics Orientation

Logistics is considered one of the crucial components in an organization's efforts to achieve efficient and effective value chain management practices, and it was viewed as coming under the umbrella of marketing. Recently, logistics has been more attached to the operations side of the hexagon. The history and recent developments in logistics makes it a great bridge between marketing and operations management. The questions below address the degree to which your organization has a logistics orientation.

- We believe that it is important to constantly monitor our commitment to understanding our logistics activities as a part of our value-chain activities.
- We believe that it is important to communicate information about our logistics activities across all units as a part of our value-chain activities.
- We believe that it is important to develop value-chain strategies based on our understanding of our logistics activities.
- We believe that it is important to assess our logistics activities systematically and frequently as a part of our value-chain activities.

◆ We believe that it is important to disseminate data on our logistics activities at all levels on a regular basis as a part of our value-chain activities.

◆ We believe that it is important to understand our logistics activities, as a part of our value-chain activities, to be prepared for developments in our markets.

◆ We believe that it is important to try to discover additional logistics possibilities, as a part of our value-chain activities, of which we may be unaware.

◆ We believe that it is important to seek opportunities, as a part of our value-chain activities, in areas where our current logistics function has difficulty delivering to customers.

◆ We believe that it is important to try to recognize logistics possibilities, as a part of our value-chain activities, before the majority of the market recognizes them.

◆ We believe that it is important to extrapolate key trends, as a part of our value-chain activities, to understand what logistics activities we may need in the future.

Operations Management Orientation

Operations management is considered one of the crucial components in an organization's efforts to achieve efficient and effective value chain management practices. The questions below address the degree to which your organization has an operations orientation.

◆ We believe that it is important to constantly monitor our commitment to understanding our operations management activities as a part of our value-chain activities.

◆ We believe that it is important to communicate information about our operations management activities across all units as a part of our value-chain activities.

◆ We believe that it is important to develop value-chain strategies based on our understanding of our operations management activities.

◆ We believe that it is important to assess our operations management activities systematically and frequently as a part of our value-chain activities.

◆ We believe that it is important to disseminate data on our operations management activities at all levels on a regular basis as a part of our value-chain activities.

◆ We believe that it is important to understand our operations management activities, as a part of our value-chain activities, to be prepared for developments in our markets.

◆ We believe that it is important to try to discover additional operations management possibilities, as a part of our value-chain activities, of which we may be unaware.

◆ We believe that it is important to seek opportunities, as a part of our value-chain activities, in areas where our current operations management function has difficulty delivering for us.

◆ We believe that it is important to try to recognize, as a part of our value-chain activities, operations management possibilities before the majority of the market recognizes them.

◆ We believe that it is important to extrapolate key trends, as a part of our value-chain activities, to understand what operations management activities we may need in the future.

Supply Management Orientation

Supply management is considered one of the crucial components in an organization's efforts to achieve efficient and effective value-chain management practices. Supply management (often called procurement, purchasing, or sourcing) has been viewed as within the domain of operations management. However, the marketing function also addresses supply management issues when it focuses on organizational buyer behavior. As such, similar to logistics, supply management can serve as a great bridge between marketing and operations strategies. The questions below address the degree to which your organization has a supply management orientation.

◆ We believe that it is important to constantly monitor our commitment to understanding suppliers as a part of our value-chain activities.

◆ We believe that it is important to communicate information about suppliers across all units as a part of our value-chain activities.

◆ We believe that it is important to develop value-chain strategies based on our understanding of suppliers.

◆ We believe that it is important to assess suppliers systematically and frequently as a part of our value-chain activities.

◆ We believe that it is important to disseminate data on suppliers at all levels on a regular basis as a part of our value-chain activities.

◆ We believe that it is important to understand our suppliers, as a part of our value-chain activities, to be prepared for developments in our markets.

◆ We believe that it is important to try to discover additional actions of our suppliers, as a part of our value-chain activities, of which we may be unaware.

◆ We believe that it is important to seek opportunities, as a part of our value-chain activities, in areas where our suppliers have difficulty delivering to us.

◆ We believe that it is important to try to recognize supplier actions, as a part of our value-chain activities, before the majority of the market recognizes them.

◆ We believe that it is important to extrapolate key trends, as a part of our value-chain activities, to understand what suppliers may do in the future.

The battery of questions above can help an organization assess its current marketing and operations integration and provide benchmark guidelines on "where to go from here." Two examples—Dell and the online grocery industry—provide great illustrations on the meshing that needs to be done to accomplish an organization's goals effectively. Meshing of marketing and operations strategies is clearly the path to success.

Example 1: Meshing Marketing and Operations Effectively at Dell.[13]

To illustrate some of the logic and linkages between marketing (in this case, we will focus on product development) and operations (with a particular emphasis on the overall supply chain), we use Dell. Dell is an example of an organization that works with marketplace shifts and interactions between product development management (PDM) and supply chain management (SCM) processes to create its long-term advantage vis-à-vis competitors (current as well as potential entrants into the marketplace).

As is well known in business circles, Dell does not take possession of processors until they are wheeled off the trailer at the dock. This allows Dell to put the latest processors into computers that are built-to-order for their customers. In the keep-inventory mentality typified by most of Dell's competitors, the typical competitors have to wait much longer until an existing supply of processors are used before moving on to the next technology in processors. This customization at Dell is also a function of managing and integrating all value-chain elements to facilitate not only design and development but also the production and delivery of those solutions. This is possible by having "relationship-based intimacy" in the value chain—a set of ongoing, tightly bonded relationships both internal and external to the organization, but specifically with external suppliers of next-generation knowledge, materials, parts, and components. Dell is a company that has a close relationship with its suppliers of processors, drives, software, and peripherals, including its competitor IBM. At the same time, Dell often takes part in networked rivalry by leading and participating in multiple value-chain networks to spawn, nurture, and integrate the development of products, knowledge, and efficiencies that would otherwise be impossible. Finally, Dell has a unique ability to leverage technology across market segments. An instance of this is Dell's use of standardized core components across product lines. While each line of desktop and portable computers has a particular usage context and customer segment, the ability to leverage technology and knowledge across segments allows efficiencies that would otherwise not be possible. Both Dell's own technology and knowledge and those of the value-chain partners are always examined by Dell for these opportunities.

Example 2: Meshing Marketing and Operations Effectively in Online Groceries

As we have illustrated throughout this book, a new market such as online ordering of groceries for home delivery (or pickup) places great pressure on the integration of marketing and operations. The need to drive markets from a marketing perspective, while simultaneously keeping a tight rein on operational costs and challenges, puts a great deal of pressure on this market (see Chapter Seven for more on driving markets).

As viewed by the operations professional, one of the biggest concerns with online ordering and home delivery of groceries is that it represents a fundamental shift from consumers selecting their own groceries to companies providing a shopping service for consumers, based on consumer orders. From a corporate point of view, this represents an increased challenge for operations, since the company is essentially taking back work that had previously been self-sourced by the customer. Fortunately, there is building evidence that home-delivery grocers are able to achieve efficiencies in picking customer orders.[14] Unfortunately, from an operations standpoint, a major hurdle is getting the customer's initial order. Studies have shown that the first order a customer places averages between seventy-five and eighty minutes, while the average order time decreases to twenty-five to thirty minutes by the time the customer places her fifth order.[15] Now let us turn to the marketing professional.

As viewed by a marketing professional, one of the biggest challenges in online groceries is convincing customers that the products they buy are of at least comparable quality to what they would select if they were shopping in a traditional store. If I pick out my own apples in the store, I have a chance to evaluate each of them. If I order online, someone else will pick my apples out for me. From the customer's perspective, the bottom line is whether I can trust "that other person" to be as good about picking out my produce as I am. Only very trusting shoppers would have complete confidence in someone else. So, what should a marketing professional do? First, in the case of packaged goods, which are primarily commodities and differ very little within a specific item, this is not as great a concern. However, there is a large degree of concern for customers when buying produce, meats, and other fresh items. Interestingly, one argument is that the groceries coming from a centralized distribution center (i.e., Ocado, FreshDirect, GroceryGateway etc.) are fresher because they actually get to customers quicker, with fewer handling steps in the process (i.e., some intermediaries are cut out of the supply chain). And, in the case of grocers that pick customer items directly from existing stores, the groceries can be argued to be equally fresh, given they are handled by only one person (whether it's the person packing the groceries or the customer). Remember, there is evidence that customers can be educated, and, once they understand the processes involved, they do accept that groceries delivered to their homes are as fresh, and in some cases fresher, than those in the store.[16] How would the "perfect" manager see this, i.e., the manager with an equal mind for marketing and operations?

This perfectly integrated marketing/operations manager would first start by admitting that integrating marketing and operations is a challenge in any business, since a natural tension exists between the two functional areas. At best, the tension between these two functions results in a dampening of marketing's tendency to overpromise to customers and a push on operations to move beyond an internal focus on reducing costs without a clear vision of end consumer needs. At worst, the tension leads to a rift between the two functions that prohibits any integration of goals, and leaves consumers poorly served. Even without tension between the two functions, organizations often end up being at least skewed toward one of the functions, based on the organizational leaders' professional backgrounds and/or mind-sets.[17] On the positive side, however, this integrated manager knows that evidence exists that companies that manage the marketing and operations integration will tend to outperform companies in which a rift exists.[18]

Guidelines for Managers

The strategy process is most often modeled as a higher-order phenomenon in which functional strategies, such as operations and marketing, are driven by a higher-level corporate or business strategy. A key element of this strategic framework also involves coordinating functional-level strategies to work in concert (hopefully, in a synergistic manner) to implement strategy effectively and efficiently, rather than locally optimizing outcomes for individual functions, business units, plants, or stores. One of the primary challenges in implementing effective strategy involves achieving fit or consensus within an organization—both between corporate and functional strategies, and between various functional strategies. This is particularly critical across functions in our mind. Top-down strategies can always be controlled by top-level managers. Strategy alignment across functions is harder to synchronize. In spanning the last mile to the customer, we often find that marketing and operations clash in their roles, and in the interpretation of what needs to be done. Clearly, however, marketing and operations issues should be tackled jointly by marketing and operations.

The result is that while this integration concept is sound, and perhaps obvious at a conceptual level, actual implementation is typically very difficult. It often creates an internal selling climate, whereby employees from one function have to justify their reasons for wanting more of the resources versus giving more resources to the other function. As we have illustrated in several places in this chapter (and throughout the book), the failed Internet grocers provide an excellent example of a fundamental failure of the strategy process to match marketing with operations. Of course, the classic illustration in online groceries has become Webvan. Webvan marketed groceries at low prices, which were competitive with traditional bricks-and-mortar stores (partly by waiving shipping fees) in order to grow its business quickly. Most likely, Webvan felt a need and external pressure to satisfy the huge investments and valuations placed on it by investors. Yet, as we now know, it proved difficult, if not impossible, to actually deliver groceries at a cost that would allow for a profit, given Webvan's business model. In our analysis, Webvan failed to adequately match its marketing and operations goals and strategies with a corresponding efficient and effective implementation.

Interestingly, using the rationale by Christensen and Bower, the power of the dominant grocery customers (i.e., those who go to the traditional store to shop) contributes to the failure of many organizations in the Internet grocery industry.[19] Specifically, many grocery stores devote so much attention to traditional customers (who are already considered as established in high-margin segments) that they may miss out on opportunities that emerge in low-margin niche markets. Intuitively, online ordering of groceries provides a value-added service to customers, similar to home pizza delivery and next-day, at-home service of computers. However, to date, most grocery stores have failed in their attempts to be profitable in the online ordering segment, mainly due to a lack of focus on behaviors that target a customer's latent needs (needs that the customer cannot directly express without being exposed to the product/service in question).

Action Steps

This chapter has outlined two successful examples of meshing, marketing, and operations effectively. The following are some suggested steps to success for implementing strategies.

Benchmark the organization's operations and marketing efforts (for example, using the hexagon metrics provided in this chapter). Use internal guidelines and historical records to define what constitutes poor, good, and excellent scores.

- ◆ Based on the benchmark results, align the organization's *operations* objectives, centered on logistics management, operations management, and supply management.
- ◆ Based on the benchmark results, align the organization's *marketing* objectives, centered on customer orientation, competitor orientation, and value-chain coordination.
- ◆ Mesh the operations and marketing objectives. Develop a process that allows for rigorous evaluation of operations objectives by marketing people and marketing objectives by operations people.
- ◆ Develop strategies that are integrative in nature, i.e., strategies that reap the best long-term advantages from operations and marketing activities (rarely will the organization achieve maximum efficiency and effectiveness in one area; some give and take is typically needed from both operations and marketing).

- ◆ Conduct internal benchmark assessment regularly. (We suggest yearly.)
- ◆ Conduct external benchmark assessments regularly (i.e., benchmark other organizations). (We suggest every two to three years.)
- ◆ With the benchmark assessments, revise operations and marketing objectives, and implement new or revised strategies, as necessary. Given contingencies in the marketplace for most organizations, revisions will be needed regularly.

Notes

1. Anonymous, "Universal Product Code Turns 25," *Industrial Distribution*, Vol. 88, No. 10 (October 1999), p. A7.
2. T.C. Taylor, "The Great Scanner Face-Off," *Sales and Marketing Management* (1986), 137 (4), 43.
3. T. Rizzo, "The Death of Webvan," *Internet World* (August 1, 2001), pp. 4–5.
4. R. Tomlinson, "A British E-Grocer Takes on Amazon," *Fortune* (June 12, 2000), pp. 246–255. J. Hall, "British Supermarket Giant Cooks Up Plans to Go Global—Tesco's Move to Duplicate High Growth at Home Comes with Big Risks," *The Wall Street Journal* (July 5, 2001), p. A9.
5. A. Reinhardt, "Tesco Bets Small—and Wins Big," *Business Week* (October 1, 2001), pp. EB26–32.
6. "A Universal Requirement," *Grocer Today* (November 11, 2002).
7. G.T.M. Hult, "Global Supply Chain Management: An Integration of Scholarly Thoughts," *Industrial Marketing Management* (2004), 33 (1), pp. 3–5.
8. John Narver and Stanley Slater, "The Effect of a Market Orientation on Business Profitability," *Journal of Marketing* (October 1990), 54, pp. 20–35.
9. Ibid.
10. Ibid.
11. Council of Logistics Management (2003), see www.clm1.org.
12. Institute of Supply Management (2003), see www.ism.ws/ISMMembership/Files/NISCIJuly2000paper.pdf.
13. This example is based on G.T.M. Hult, "From the Special Issue Editors: A Research Agenda for the Nexus of Product Development and Supply Chain Management Processes," *Journal of Product Innovation Management* (2003), 20 (5), pp. 333–336.
14. Reinhardt, 2001. M. Spindler, "Grocers Find Profitable Growth in the Darndest Places," *MyWebGrocer Press Release* (June 10, 2002).
15. Caroline Ellis, "Lessons from Online Groceries," *Sloan Management Review* (2003, 44 (2), p.8.

16. Ibid.

17. Actually we are hoping that this book presents a fair assessment of both marketing and operations, and their respective importance and drawbacks. We have taken utmost care to present the issues as constructively as possible, given that two of us are operations professionals and one of us is a marketing professional!

18. David A. Collier, "A Service Quality Process Map for Credit Card Processing," *Decision Sciences* (1991), 22 (2), p.15.

19. C.M. Christensen and J.L. Bower, "Customer Power, Strategic Investment, and the Failure of Leading Firms," *Strategic Management Journal* (1996), 17, pp.197–218.

CHAPTER 7

Marketing—Tapping Customers' Latent Desires

For decades, companies have struggled to design their strategies and structures to be market-oriented.[1] Lately, listening to the customer has taken precedence over believing in your vision and the product designs you create. In either case, though, the central element has been to deliver on the needs and wants of customers, based on given environmental factors, established company structures, and companies' strategic capabilities. The goal has been to beat the competition by delivering appropriate solutions to customers' needs and wants.

Beating the competition is still the goal. But the approach to accomplishing it has been drastically altered by many organizations. Delivering on the needs and wants of customers has taken on a much broader form. Now, latent needs (i.e., needs that the customer may not be consciously aware he has) are a part of the assortment, and driving markets has become the efficient way of operating. In particular, the online grocery industry (with its modest successes five to seven years ago, and its dramatic failures three to four years ago) has realized that its original business models did not work. A wealth of successful examples of companies driving markets and being proactive exist—this chapter will highlight a few of them as illustrations of how organizations can drive markets to successfully span the last mile to customers.

Four key concepts are of critical, strategic importance in the new era of e-business, fast cycle times, globalization, and spanning the last mile to customers. These are: expressed customer need, latent customer need, responsive market orientation, and proactive market orientation, as illustrated in Figure 7-1.

A successful, spanning-the-last-mile organization needs to have strategies, structures, and implementation mechanisms in place to reap sustainable advantages in the marketplace. The most direct route to achieve desired benefits is to align the appropriate market focus with the corresponding customer need. (See Figure 7-2.) In a nutshell, a market-oriented firm attempts to find and satisfy customers' expressed needs via responsive actions. And a market-oriented firm attempts to satisfy customers' latent needs via proactive actions. This requires a "total market orientation, where responsive and proactive actions are taken in coordinated sequences."[2]

Of course, nothing is as easy as aligning one with the other. Other alternatives also exist. Clearly, organizations can be proactive and go after a need that the customers have already expressed. The proactive element is then tied to the firm's first-mover advantage in the marketplace. Unfortunately, first movers are not gaining the momentum and benefits today that they may have gained a decade ago, especially in the international marketplace. Likewise, a firm can be reactive but still strike gold in that this reactive market-orientation behavior also ends up satisfying some latent needs of customers.

The most critical aspect of total market orientation is centered on the word "total." While a firm needs to satisfy their existing customers' expressed needs to continue their ongoing relationship with them, these same organizations also need to discover their existing (and potential) customers' latent needs. The latter is an important part of avoiding being complacent. Complacency may

Figure 7-1. Four key concepts in the new era of e-business, fast cycle times, and spanning the last mile to customers.

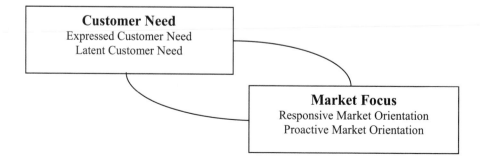

Figure 7-2. Aligning appropriate market focus with corresponding customer need.

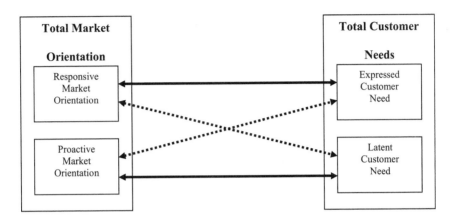

An expressed need refers to a need that the customer is aware of and can articulate. For expressed needs, the customer perceives some sort of desired solution. A responsive market orientation is typically used to attempt to understand and satisfy customers' expressed needs.

A latent need refers to a need of which the customer is unaware. A latent need encompasses a potential for satisfaction. A proactive market orientation is typically used to attempt to understand and satisfy customers' latent needs (via, for example, observation).

mean that today's superior customer benefits become tomorrow's obsolete products. The right combination of responsive and proactive market orientation is therefore critical to *sustainable* success.

Tidbits about the Marketplace[3]

An estimated 40 percent of the products that are sold today will have disappeared from the market ten years from now.	Forty-two percent of the sales growth expected for the next five years will come from products first introduced in that period.

Forty-six percent of the products that will be sold in the next ten years are as yet unknown.

Given the pressures in the marketplace, as illustrated by the tidbits above, organizations need to be able to readily identify opportunities and threats while realizing their own potential and drawbacks. It gets easier though, since most of the products and services that organizations need to create are not really that "new." Only 15 percent of all new products (up from 10 percent a couple of decades ago) are predicted to be "new-to-the-world" products.

New Products Needed[4]

> Fifteen percent will be "new-to-the-world products"—products that will create an entirely new market.

> Thirty-eight percent will be "new product lines"— new products that for the first time allow a company to enter an established market.

> Eighteen percent will be "line extensions"—new products that supplement a company's established product lines.

> Twenty-eight percent will be "product modifications"— new products that provide improved performance or greater perceived value.

The problem is that organizations often do not know where their focus lies and where to go next. The early entries into the online grocery industry (e.g., Webvan) were supported by heavy monetary investment and other resources, and they were flawed in their evaluation of the "taste buds" of customers and unable to develop efficient and effective approaches to operating their businesses.

For example, a recent study found that many organizations appear to only pay lip service to the concept of being customer-oriented.[5] When asked directly, 74 percent of all organizations indicated that they are customer-oriented rather than competitor-oriented. When asked indirectly, with a more sophisticated measurement instrument, 76 percent of the organizations indicated that they are more competitor-oriented than customer-oriented. If organizations cannot even figure out if they are customer- or competitor-oriented, how can they decide whether to be responsive to expressed customer needs or to respond to latent customer needs?

Interestingly, among the organizations with a high percentage of "new-to-the-world products," 90 percent are equally customer- and competitor-oriented. These organizations also tend to be better at driving markets, while being "market driven" in their approach to satisfying current customers, gaining market share, and achieving sustainable success. Having mechanisms in place to do both things represents the key to having a total-market orientation. While scores of writings in magazines, journals, and books have dealt with being market driven and adopting responsive market-orientation approaches, few have addressed the concept of driving markets and adopting proactive market-orientation elements. The rest of this chapter will focus on these issues as a means to be effective in spanning the last mile to the customer.

Driving Markets

Being proactive and driving markets come with major risks as well as potential rewards. As in any stock purchase, where the option is to buy the less-risky, blue-chip stock, or the more-risky, "new-IPO-on-the-block," being market-oriented versus driving markets is a decision that organizations should carefully evaluate and perhaps take. That said, the most efficient business models are those that seek to impose the organization's logic on the marketplace (i.e., drive markets).

This "driving markets" model requires a change in the *market structure* and/or *customers' behaviors,* rather than a change in the organization.[6] Whether the market structure is changed and/or customers' behaviors are changed, the organization's actions are proactive in scope. Responsive strategies (also called reactive strategies) do not work to drive markets. Interestingly, online grocery firms such as Webvan actually tried to change both the market structure and customers' behaviors, without necessarily realizing the implications of such actions. One can argue that they instead drove their market into the ground. The risk-reward equation did not work out to their advantage. Why?

We now must include another qualifier: Organizations need to drive markets via proactive market-orientation actions that attack a latent need of customers *and do so within a well-defined strategy based on sound business principles.* The latter (italicized) portion of the previous statement got lost in Webvan's business model. What got lost in Webvan's operations and business model? A number of books and articles have addressed Webvan's demise. We clearly do not want to add lengthy thoughts to this issue besides what we already covered throughout the book. However, it brings up a point, namely, that "market orientation, whether reactive or proactive, is a process that, in principle, *always* begins with identifying/discovering target customers' needs and only then developing the customer benefits to satisfy them."[7] Focusing on the product (or overall offering) first does not draw on market-orientation principles, and it is not advisable.

So, how do we shape the market structure and market behavior? What are some organizational successes?

Shaping the Market Structure

Three generic approaches have been identified that would allow an organization to drive the structure of the market in which it operates. (See Figure 7-3.)

Figure 7-3. Three ways to shape market structure.

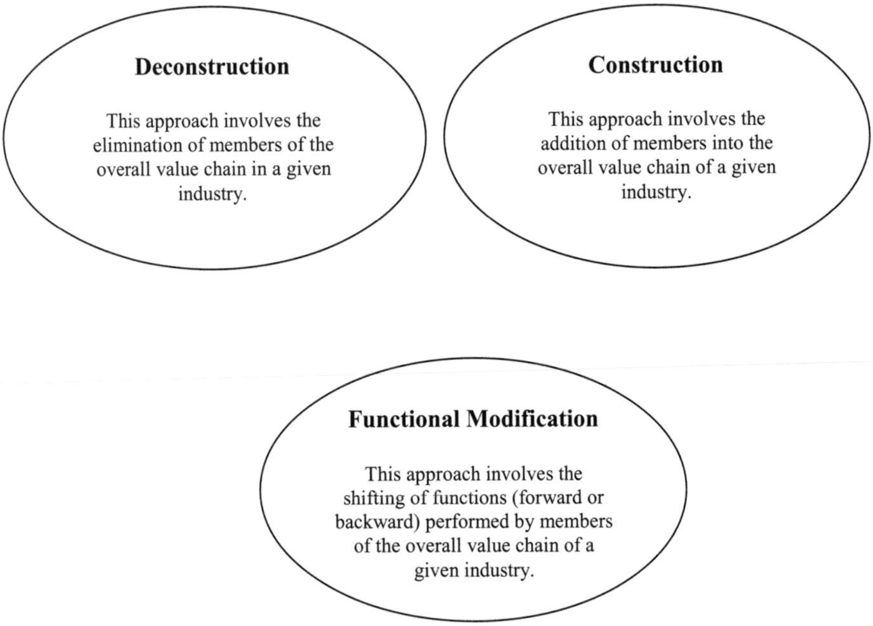

Deconstruction

This approach involves the elimination of members of the overall value chain in a given industry.

Construction

This approach involves the addition of members into the overall value chain of a given industry.

Functional Modification

This approach involves the shifting of functions (forward or backward) performed by members of the overall value chain of a given industry.

Based on work by Jaworski, Kohli, and Sahay, these three strategies can be labeled and described as the deconstructive, constructive, and functional modification approaches.[8]

Examples of a Deconstructive Approach to Shaping the Market Structure

Two examples—involving Dell Computer Corporation and Intel Corporation—provide great illustrations of how firms directly, or indirectly, deconstructed their marketplace structure in efforts spanning the last mile to the customer.

◆ *Dell.* Dell was started in 1983 when Michael Dell began selling upgraded personal computers and some add-on components from his dorm room at the University of Texas at Austin. Dell was incorporated in 1984, and went public in 1988. The business model of the organization was (and is) rooted in a straightforward concept—Dell could best understand customers' needs and provide the most effective computer products for those needs by selling its PCs directly to the consumers. The direct-selling method also meant that mass customization, low inventory, incorporation of the latest technologies, and fast cycle times have become staples of Dell's operations. This takes great integration both in the inbound portion of the supply chain (with suppliers) and the outbound portion (with customers). Dell's direct model (seen in Figure 7-4) changed the behaviors of the customers, which resulted in reduced business for many retailers as well as the elimination (deconstruction) of some of them.

◆ *Intel.* Intel was founded in 1968, when Robert Noyce and Gordon Moore resigned from the positions at Fairchild Semiconductor to start their own organization. Noyce and Moore first worked together at

Figure 7-4. Retailers eliminated by Dell.

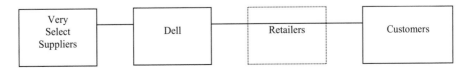

Shockley Laboratories and were later two of the eight founders of Fairchild Semiconductor before starting Intel. At the time of their departure, Fairchild was one of the biggest players in the integrated circuit industry. Intel is typically credited with two of the major postwar innovations in microelectronics that have set the tone for today's e-world: large-scale integrated memory and the microprocessor. More recently, Intel has strategically purchased organizations to increase its share of the motherboard of PCs. For example, Intel bought Chips N Technology to increase its display (graphics) capabilities. This approach has moved Intel's value-added benefits even closer to its customers. (See Figure 7-5.)

Examples of a Constructive Approach

Three examples—involving Apple Computer, CDNOW, and Omahasteaks .com—show how these firms constructed their marketplace structures in their efforts to spanning the last mile to the customer.

◆   *Apple.* Apple was founded in 1976 by Steven Wozniak and Steven Jobs. Wozniak, who dropped out of college to take a job with Hewlett-Packard, and Jobs, who also dropped out of college to take a position with Atari, had been friends since high school. In 1976, Wozniak de-

Figure 7-5. Intel and its strategically purchased suppliers.

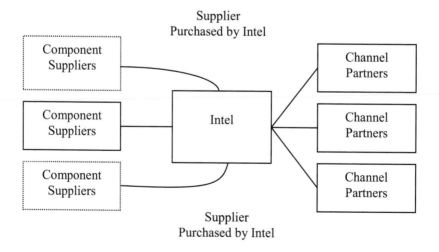

signed what would later be named the Apple I. Although at the time Apple I was merely built in printed circuit-board form, Jobs insisted that he and Wozniak should try to sell Apple I, and thus, on April 1, 1976, Apple Computer was born. From the early beginnings, Apple owes much of its early success to its construction of a very limited and completely different set of partners in the value chain. For example, Apple I (including only its circuit board) was sold to customers through small retailers. A tape interface was available separately, but Apple did not build the case.

- *CDNOW.* CDNOW was created in August of 1994 by Jason and Matthew Olim in the basement of their parents' home. The organization was incorporated in Pennsylvania the same year. Jason Olim started as the president and CEO, while twin brother Matthew became the principal software engineer. CDNOW is an online music destination that offers a comprehensive, personalized connection to the world of music. CDNOW specifically focused on the last mile to the customer by being the first site to offer the sale of music downloads and custom CDs, while at the same time offering both free and saleable music downloads.

- *Omahasteaks.com.* Omahasteaks.com was founded as a separate entity to the Omaha Steaks family business, which started in 1917. The organization markets and distributes a broad variety of premium steaks, meats, and gourmet foods. Their products are custom cut and packaged to deliver on the specific needs of its customers. Omahasteaks.com strives to provide comprehensive service and an incredible shopping experience for customers. Where the butcher shop used to be the place to go in the past, Omahasteaks.com made buying premium meats an overnight-to-your-home experience. Customers soon found out that the quality actually, in many cases, far exceeded that which they could get at the local grocery store or butcher shop, while at the same time providing a much more convenient, "last-mile-to-their-house" shopping experience.

Examples of the Functional Modification Approach

Two examples—involving Virgin Group and Federal Express—provide illustrations of how firms functionally modified their marketplace structure in their efforts to span the last mile to the customer.

◆ *Virgin Group.* Virgin Group operates one of the largest media retail chains in the global marketplace. Led by adventurous founder Sir Richard Branson (of which Virgin Atlantic Airlines is also a business entity), Virgin Group owns twenty Virgin Megastores in the United States. These stores range in size from 35,000 to 70,000 square feet and carry up to 400,000 music CDs, extensive inventories of VHS movies, DVDs, video games, and books. Virgin operates five of the six most heavily trafficked retail outlets around the globe, and it is the second-largest retailer of entertainment media. Overall, the Virgin Megastores exemplify a forward functional integration of activities by providing much more than the typical retail store, instead creating a unique environment that includes music, kiosks, and a more contemporary service-scape.

◆ *Federal Express Corporation.* The Federal Express Corporation was founded in 1973 by Fred Smith as an express-delivery organization. Smith invented the express-distribution industry in March 1973 by capitalizing on the needs of businesses for speed, quality, cost efficiency, and flexibility in deliveries. Its next-day delivery revolutionized the industry, as did its tracking system later on. Over the years, Federal Express has transformed itself into a global logistics and supply chain management company that provides a full-scale, functional integration into other organizations' value chains. Federal Express not only serves as the transportation intermediary in organizations' channels, the organization now also provides value-added, functionally based services to its partner organizations in a seamlessly integrated fashion.

Shaping Customers' Behaviors

Two basic approaches have been identified that would allow an organization to drive the behaviors in the market in which it operates. Based on work by Jaworski, Kohli, and Sahay (2000), these two approaches can be labeled and described as the direct approach and the indirect approach, illustrated in Figure 7-6.[9]

Examples of a Direct Approach

Two examples—involving Ocado and IKEA—show how firms can directly shape marketplace behaviors in efforts to spanning the last mile to the customer.

Figure 7-6. Two approaches to shaping customers' behaviors.

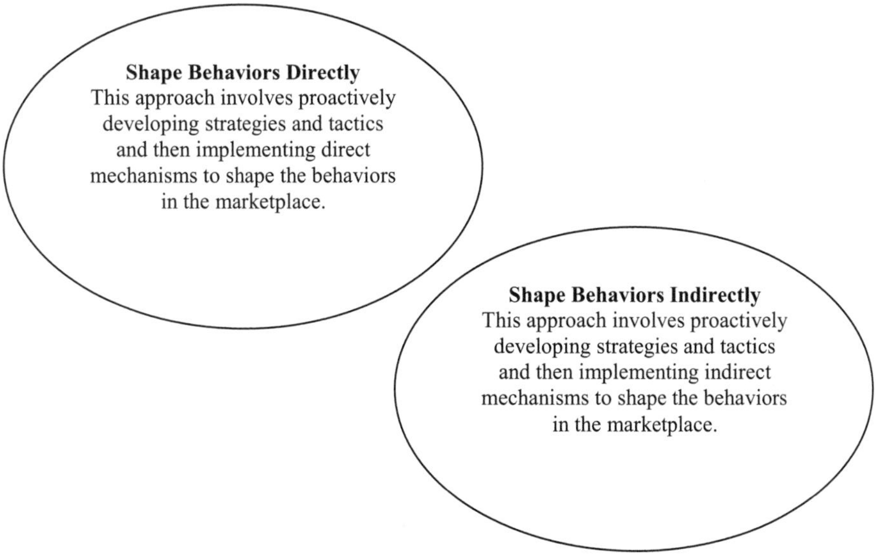

Shape Behaviors Directly
This approach involves proactively
developing strategies and tactics
and then implementing direct
mechanisms to shape the behaviors
in the marketplace.

Shape Behaviors Indirectly
This approach involves proactively
developing strategies and tactics
and then implementing indirect
mechanisms to shape the behaviors
in the marketplace.

◆ *Ocado.* Ocado represents the new breed of online grocery stores. Ocado sells itself as the revolutionary online supermarket in partnership with high-quality, traditional grocer Waitrose. Ocado started operations in January 2002; its service is now available to several million households in the metropolitan area of London in the United Kingdom. Their goal is to change the shopping habits of a lifetime. As such, Ocado forces change to marketplace behaviors by using a distribution system centered on a superwarehouse mentality. It has no traditional stores where its food products can be viewed, and has defined windows of delivery to customers. The organization appears to have a "leg up" on the industry models of previous entrants into the market who no longer exist (Webvan), or who have not consistently increased their businesses since inception (Peapod). Ocado blends a unique supply chain system with effective proactive marketing to aggressively drive the marketplace behaviors it wants to operate within.

◆ *IKEA.* IKEA was founded by Ingvar Kamprad in 1943. When Ingvar was seventeen, his father gave him a present for being successful in his studies. The present was used to establish his own business. The name IKEA was formed from the founder's initials (I.K.) plus the first letters of Elmtaryd and Agunnaryd, the Swedish farm and village where he grew up. IKEA is now the largest furniture manufacturer in the world. Beyond quality furniture for reasonable prices, the organization's trademark is its "forced" shopping experience. IKEA forces customers to "walk around" in a designed path in its oversized stores. The routing system takes the customers on a shopping tour of every aspect of what IKEA manufactures and sells in professionally decorated settings, whether the customer wants it or not, at times. It is very hard to actually enter an IKEA store with the goal of buying a particular furniture piece or kitchen gadget without having to also see outdoor chairs, living room furniture, and other IKEA products. This has resulted in a unique, last-mile-to-the-customer shopping experience, which is rather unusual in today's customer-first mentality.

Examples of an Indirect Approach

Two examples—involving J. Sainsbury PLC and OXO International— illustrate how firms indirectly shape marketplace behaviors.

- ◆ *J. Sainsbury PLC.* The company was established in 1869 by John James and Mary Ann Sainsbury; it is Britain's longest-standing food-retailing chain. Sainbury's strives to be the customer's first choice for grocery shopping by providing high-quality products, value, excellent service, and attention to detail, according to the following scheme, shown in Figure 7-7.[10]

  Sainsbury's diversified its offerings to customers by introducing "Sainsbury's to You" as a way to reach grocery customers in an additional, value-added way. "Sainsbury's to You" helped the organization to indirectly shape customers' behaviors by offering convenient ways to buy Sainsbury's grocery products without having to visit a traditional store. This resulted in traditional, in-store Sainsbury's customers shopping online for groceries, while those customers who became familiar with the online service ended up doing some of their grocery shopping in the traditional stores. In either case, Sainsbury's is the number three grocery chain in the United Kingdom after Tesco and Asda/Wal-Mart.

Figure 7-7. Sainbury's scheme for success.

◆ *OXO International.* OXO began with a few simple questions: Why do ordinary kitchen tools tend to hurt your hands when used as instructed? Why can't there be comfortable kitchen tools that are convenient to use? Sam Farber wondered about these issues and then implemented a solution when he launched OXO Good Grips in 1990. Farber, the founder of Copco, a rather successful cookware organization, had a history of delivering kitchenware products to customers. With OXO, Farber introduced the notion of "universal design" (i.e., design intended specifically for the comfort and ease of use for people of all ages, abilities, and interests) into the kitchenware industry. His innovations continue to be among the most influential elements of the industry more than a decade later. OXO's Good Grips turned the focus of customers from the sturdiness and design of the utensils to the grip—thereby shaping customers' behaviors indirectly by focusing their attention on the handle, as opposed to the typical features of kitchen utensils.

Guidelines for Managers

In this chapter, we argued that a successful, spanning-the-last-mile organization needs to have strategies, structures, and implementation mechanisms in place to take advantage of customers' explicit needs, as well as their latent desires. Going after explicit needs often requires the organization to be responsive in its market-oriented behaviors (and the culture that drives those behaviors). Going after a latent need often requires the organization to be proactive in its market-oriented behaviors (as well as, over time, designing and implementing an organizational culture that can serve as the foundation for those proactive behaviors). This requires the organization to have a total-market orientation, where responsive and proactive actions are taken in coordinated sequences."[11]

Action Steps

◆ Develop a process that allows the organization to effectively implement a "responsive market orientation" to satisfy customers' expressed needs. Ninety percent of the organization's focus should be on responsive market orientation.

◆ Develop a process that allows the organization to effectively implement a "proactive market orientation" to satisfy customers' latent needs. Ten percent of the organization's focus should be on proactive market orientation.

◆ Take advantage of opportunities (or create opportunities) to shape the market structure in which the organization operates.

◆ Take advantage of opportunities (or create opportunities) to shape the market behavior of current and potential customers.

Notes

1. G.T.M. Hult and David J. Ketchen, Jr., "Does Market Orientation Matter?: A Test of the Relationship Between Positional Advantage and Performance," *Strategic Management Journal* (2001) 22 (9), pp. 899–906.
2. John C. Narver, Stanley F. Slater, and Douglas L. MacLachlan, "Total Market Orientation, Business Performance, and Innovation," *Marketing Science Institute Report* (Cambridge, Mass., 2000), Number 00-116.
3. Bryan A. Lukas, G. Tomas, M. Hult, and Mark N. Frolick, "Reducing Cycle Time in the New Product Development Process: A Best Practices Investigation," *Cycle Time Research* (1996), 2 (1), pp. 39–51.

4. Ibid.

5. Ibid.

6. Bernard Jaworski, Ajay K. Kohli, and Arvind Sahay, "Market-Driven Versus Driving Markets," *Journal of the Academy of Marketing Science* (2000), 28 (1), pp. 45–54.

7. John C. Narver, Stanley F. Slater, and Douglas L. MacLachlan, "Total Market Orientation, Business Performance, and Innovation," *Marketing Science Institute Report* (2000), Number 00-116.

8. Bernard Jaworski, Ajay K. Kohli, and Arvind Sahay, "Market-Driven Versus Driving Markets," *Journal of the Academy of Marketing Science* (2000), 28 (1), pp. 45–54.

9. Ibid.

10. From Sainsbury's Web site, see http://www.j-sainsbury.co.uk/about/strategy_update.cfm, October 10, 2003.

11. John C. Narver, Stanley F. Slater, and Douglas L. MacLachlan, "Total Market Orientation, Business Performance, and Innovation," *Marketing Science Institute Report* (2000), Number 00-116.

Supply Chain Design—How to Bridge the Last Mile

Bridging the last mile to deliver direct to customers is a strategy that has been around for a century or more. However, it has largely been eclipsed in the past few decades by the push to build ever-bigger superstores and offer lower and lower prices, albeit at a cost to the consumer in terms of greater effort of acquisition. As we argued in Chapter One, the increased pace of daily life and the extreme busyness of many or most people have created a growing need for such consumer-direct delivery channels.

Simultaneously, new technologies such as the Internet, integrated supply chain software systems, automated sorting hardware, and new management techniques offer the potential to significantly improve the efficiency, speed, and accuracy with which home deliveries can be made. Yet, the supply chain challenges to making this system work are numerous. The goal of this chapter is to provide an overview of some of the major challenges, opportunities, and methods for optimizing systems.

We start with a brief discussion of the three fundamental activities of last-mile supply chains: ordering, fulfillment, and delivery, as shown in Figure 8-1. Because customers are being supplied with a value-added service—order selection and delivery—there is great deal of pressure for these three components of the supply chain to be well integrated and coordinated in a careful manner. The

Figure 8-1. The last mile supply chain.

Ordering
•Internet, phone, fax, mail.
•Needs to be convenient for customers to do with minimal or no assistance from retailer.
•Should become easier with repeat orders.
•Should provide confirmation of item and delivery availability.
•Must provide ways for customers to connect to a "live" human being, but encourage automated ordering when possible.

Fulfillment
•In-store vs. DC.
•Manage product range.
•Different picking methods yield varying productivity and accuracy.
•Must mesh well with delivery schedules and routes.
•Substantially more challenging to pick individual items than large quantities as for DCs supplying stores.
•DCs provide fresher, faster inventory turns and cut costs of shipping and stocking stores.

Delivery
•Direct vs. indirect.
•Density matters.
•Window size and scheduling greatly affect productivity.
•Smart or drop boxes have potential for increased productivity, if consumers can be persuaded to accept them.
•Must balance productivity with building customer relationships.

customer is no longer making her own selections in the store—so any and all mistakes are more likely to be viewed as having been caused by the retailer. When a typical store such as a Wal-Mart, Target, or Kroger is out of stock of a particular item, it is not a particularly huge problem to most customers—they simply select an alternative item, or make do without. However, in last-mile supply chains the entire goal is to raise customer expectations regarding the ease and convenience of shopping—thus leaving less margin for error. Our goal is not necessarily to offer explicit solutions to all the potential challenges in these areas, but in the following sections we will examine each of the three fundamental activities in order to identify key challenges, key advantages, and to suggest approaches that optimize performance.

The Ordering Process

The primary focus of this chapter is on physically managing the supply chain, so we are going to move on to fulfillment and delivery at this point. However, Chapter Nine provides a more detailed look at the three basic principles of ordering: (1) making the transaction simple and easy so that customers can self-source, (2) methods for streamlining customer learning and transactions, and (3) the importance of linking order, fulfillment, and delivery IT systems.

The Fulfillment Process

As shown in Figure 8-1, once an order is received it must be filled—either by manufacturing it to order or by selecting it from the store/distribution center (DC) and assembling a customer's complete order. While there are literally thousands of books, articles, consultants, and Web sites that provide advice on how to set up a distribution center for efficient and accurate picking, last-mile supply chains are substantially different from most DC operations. Since they are picking for direct shipment to the customers, the order sizes tend to be smaller, so rather than picking a pallet of Cheerios, or a box of one hundred Schick razor cartridge packages, the pick quantities tend to be one box of Cheerios and one package of razors for Joe Customer. Second, since orders are shipped directly to the customer, they must be packaged individually rather than loaded on a large truck for delivery to a store. Thus, fulfillment for last-mile supply chains has substantial challenges and opportunities with regard to productivity, accuracy, quality, costs, and substitutions. We will discuss each of these in more detail below.

Store vs. Distribution Center

As examined in Chapter One, the first major choice in fulfillment systems is whether to fill orders from existing stores or from a centralized distribution center. In general, stores are advantageous because they have a lower initial fixed cost. Also, since they already exist, stores provide a tangible point of reference for customers and may benefit from a halo effect where customers do more of their overall shopping in that company's stores and for delivery, and because stores are closer to the customer, thus simplifying delivering. In contrast, stores are also generally less efficient in terms of order-picking efficiency.

They suffer from problems with quality, item availability, and inventory tracking relative to DCs. Distribution centers also offer the ability to custom manu-
facture or assemble products for direct shipment to customers, as described in
Chapter Two—excellent examples being Dell, Lands' End, and FreshDirect.

Companies face two basic choices in designing fulfillment systems. First,
whether to pick in-store or in a DC. This decision hinges on the factors described above, but fundamentally boils down to scalability and volume—at
lower volumes, stores are the only feasible choice, but as volume increases,
DCs offer increasing returns to scale. Second, once the store versus DC decision
has been made, the next decision is how to set up fulfillment operations—how
to route picking of orders, what quantities, how to assign orders, track orders,
etc. Our goal is not to provide a set list of answers to these questions, but to
review the key challenges and offer some useful insights into how to address
these issues.

Productivity

Stores are laid out to appeal to their customers' sense of aesthetics, not for the
efficiency of assembling items. Consider the average grocery store—how many
times have you wondered why the milk (which almost everyone buys) is all the
way in the back? Not to make it convenient for you, but to encourage you to
walk through all (or most) of the store and see more items that you may buy
on impulse. Most retail stores follow similar strategies to get you to make more
impulse buys and expose you to more potential purchases—clothing stores,
music stores, electronic stores, etc.

As expected, picking from stores is relatively inefficient. Grocers use software to develop a coherent and streamlined route through the store. That way,
personal shoppers can move up and down the aisles selecting orders with a
minimum of travel time—in contrast with shoppers (such as myself) who often
do not know the store well and spend a lot of time randomly walking through
aisles looking for an item. Many grocers use handheld computer scanners (essentially a Palm Pilot or BlackBerry-type device) that show the personal shopper the next item to be picked, the location (both which aisle and which
segment of the aisle), and the quantity to be picked. The handheld unit then
reads the bar code on each product and confirms it is/is not the correct product
(often with a loud beeping noise to indicate a mispicked item). Shoppers for
different companies can sometimes pick more than one order at a time. In

short, "professional" shoppers for groceries or other products picked in-store should be more productive than amateur shoppers for two fundamental reasons. First, technology allows them to develop efficient routes and automatically check product accuracy. Second, repetition and learning help shoppers become more familiar with the store—a person who shops the store forty hours a week should become much faster than the once-a-week shopper.[1] Yet, the fundamental problem with in-store picking is that it will always be fairly inefficient relative to DC–based picking. As shown in Figure 8-2, in-store picking rates for groceries range from eighty to 120 items per hour versus 150 to 300 per hour at a DC. These numbers reflect items (i.e., a bottle of milk or a box of crackers), not orders, and since the dollar value per item is fairly small in groceries, the dollars in goods picked per labor hour will also be fairly small.

In contrast, DC–based picking generally has much higher productivity rates. This is primarily because the facility is designed purely for the efficiency of the worker, and products are stored so as to minimize travel distance and effort. This is also due to the ability to use automated equipment. To quote an expert, D. Douglas Graham writes, "Software will choreograph tomorrow's warehouse work. The warehouse of the future will not be technology-dependent but technology-enhanced—a blend of technology, machine, and manpower."[2] Technologies such as automated carousels, sorting systems, pick-to-light, and radio frequency ID (RFID) have had a huge impact on both productivity and accuracy in DCs over the past decade.

As shown in Figure 8-2, DC fulfillment systems tend to be both more accurate and more productive than those that are store-based. While comparing different industries is like comparing apples to oranges, the range of industries shown in Figure 8-2 gives a feel for the relative productivity, accuracy, technologies used, facility size, and number of SKUs stocked. There is also a major difference between what is often called in the industry small-pick/pack versus large-pick/pack operations. Essentially, this boils down to the difference between picking for direct shipment to customers (i.e., consumer-direct) versus picking larger orders that go to individual stores. For example, most retail stores get their goods delivered first to a DC from a series of suppliers/manufacturers. The DC then breaks up these pallet- or truckload-size shipments, stores them, and then assembles individual orders for each store. For example, a pharmacy might receive one order (truck) per day with 500 to 1,000 SKUs on it, but each SKU would consist of multiple items, such as a carton of fifty Schick razors. In short, large-pick (store replenishment) operations tend to pick larger

(text continues on page 178)

Figure 8-2. *Comparison of order picking rates, systems, and accuracy.*

Industry	Home-Delivery Grocers		Seeds	Clothing	Office Products	Novelty and Gifts	Beauty Supplies	Contact Lenses
Pick Method	In-Store	DC	DC	DC	DC	DC	DC	DC
Product Destination	Consumer-Direct	Consumer-Direct	Consumer-Direct	Consumer-Direct	Store Replenishment	Store Replenishment	Store Replenishment	Store Replenishment
Company(s)	Lowes Foods D'Agostinos Albertsons Safeway Tesco	Ocado FreshDirect Grocery Gateway PublixDirect	Park Seed (mail order seeds)	Value Vision Fulfillment Center (for Polo.com)	Sanford and Newell Office Products	Christmas Tree Shops	Avon Canada	Cooper Vision (Contact Lenses)
Pick Rate (Items/ worker hour)	80–120 items	150–300 items	1000 items	67–100 orders	36 cartons	45–60 cartons	94 items	250–600 lines
Accuracy	90%–96%	98%–99.5%	NA	NA	99.5%	NA	99.95%	NA
Systems/Technology	NA	NA	12 Horizontal Carousels	6,500 feet of Powered Conveyor Automated Sorters	Warehouse Management Software (WMS), 2.5 miles of Conveyor with High-Speed Sortation, Pick-to-Light, Radio Frequency Data Communication Terminals	9 Level Storage racks, High-Speed Sortation	Flow & Bin Racks, Carton Forming System, RF and Bar Code Scanning, Warehouse Management System	4 Horizontal Carousels Linked to Order Entry System, Pick to Light, RF transmitter

Facility Size	NA	NA	NA	280,000 sq. ft.	285,000 sq. ft.	250,000 sq. ft.	80,000 sq. ft.
Volume	NA	NA	NA	4,000–6,000 Orders per Day	1,425 Orders per Day	72,000–96,000 Cartons per Day	1.3 Million Orders/Year
SKUs stocked	NA	30,000–40,000	8,000–12,000	NA	6,450	25,000	8,500
Investment in Equipment	NA	$15K—$25K per Store	NA	NA	$6 Million	$3–4 Million	NA

Facility Size	80,000 sq. ft.
Volume	1,500 Order per Day
SKUs stocked	16,000
Investment in Equipment	NA

Data for this table is drawn from several sources. These include the authors' ongoing study of online grocers and the following articles. Tom Feare, "Single DC does it ALL for Sanford," *Modern Materials Handling*, vol. 54, no. 3, March 1999, pp. 42–45; Karen Augustin, "High Tech Handling at Christmas Tree Shops' new DC," *Modern Materials Handling*, vol. 51, no. 15, December 1996, pp. 36–38; "Pick Rates Climb with Carousels," *Modern Materials Handling*, vol. 50, no. 11, September 1995, p. 47; "Carousels Improve Picking Efficiency," *Modern Materials Handling*, vol. 56, no. 12, October 2001, p. 59; Bob Trebilcock, "Makeover Story," *Modern Materials Handling*, vol. 57, no. 13, November 2002, pp. 16–19.

quantities of items for each order, thus making picking more efficient. According to Richard Lancone, professor of logistics at Temple University, "Small package picking is the most inefficient and most labor-intensive method."[3] However, once picked and shipped to the store, these items must again be sorted and placed on shelves—thus adding another source of labor cost that is missing with DC—consumer-direct. If done correctly, the total cost of picking and delivery for consumer-direct versus DC-store-customer can be comparable, and as discussed in Chapters Two and Five, because the supply chain is shorter, products can be fresher and more convenient.

In general, the data for productivity (pick rate) in Figure 8-2 illustrate the higher efficiency of store replenishment over consumer direct. For example, Cooper Vision can pick 250 to 600 lines/items per worker for contact lenses. This is, at least in part, due to the fact that it is picking orders that go to stores—so one store order might consist of three pairs of lens A, four pairs of lens B, one pair of lens C, etc. Thus, much of the efficiency comes from assembling by picking larger quantities and by the similarity of products. In contrast, picking items for Polo.com is primarily a small-pick/pack operation—each customer generally orders, at most, one or two items, and each order has to be individually labeled, packaged, and sorted for shipping. The larger size of the items necessitates greater distance between storage locations. Thus, in general, order picking for consumer-direct applications will be less efficient than for store replenishment at the DC. *However,* the key point is to remember that when shipping to consumers directly, there is no requirement to pay employees to receive, stock, and maintain these items at the store.

Accuracy and Substitutions

Figure 8-2 also provides some data on accuracy. Generally, picking accuracy and in-stock availability run in the 98 percent to 99.5 percent range at a DC. In comparison, on-shelf availability at most retail stores is more typically 95 percent. Clearly, DCs outperform stores on this dimension, which is not surprising given the greater technology investment, the centralized nature of inventory, and the lack of customers to muck up the process (i.e., customers often pick things up and leave them in a different location, or shoplift them). Thus, one would expect fewer substitutions in a consumer-direct order coming from a DC than from a store, and in general, this is true. Consider an order of thirty grocery items to be delivered to a customer's home. The chances of this order being complete (i.e., no missing items or substitutions) when delivered from a store with a 95 percent in-stock rate are only 21.5 percent, while the chances of this order being complete for an order coming from a DC with a 99 percent stock rate are 74 percent.[4] Clearly, DCs outperform store-based picking on this dimension. However, the critical question is how customers perceive this problem.

When customers are shopping in stores for themselves, out-of-stock items are rarely a major problem. Most customers will intuitively switch from one item to another if they are out of stock of something. If there are no 64-ounce boxes of Cheez-Its, a customer might simply take two 32-ounce boxes. For most people, this is not a major problem. Substituting a different size package is generally not a big deal—so consumer-direct grocers generally think of this as an "easy" substitution and will simply give a customer a different package size and adjust the price commensurately. In contrast, substituting for a non-commodity item—like Gouda cheese—is a bit more difficult. An in-store customer might easily decide on a Brie or goat cheese instead. But a customer that has placed an order for home delivery has given up control of this decision.

There are two main weapons that companies have to address this issue. First, they should try to spell out substitution policies as clearly as possible to the customer, and ask the customer in advance for his preferences (i.e., which items a substitution is acceptable for and sometimes which alternative item is acceptable, ahead of time). In a perfect world, the ordering and inventory systems would be linked so the customer would *know* whether the item is in stock, but as we will see in Chapter Nine, this rarely is this case. Whatever the case, companies should clearly communicate to customers what their policies are with regard to substitutions and when substitutions are made. Many grocers bag substitutions in a different colored bag (i.e., a blue bag) to make them highly visible, relative to items that are filled as ordered (a white bag). Second, last-mile retailers that choose to pick orders out of a DC should have a much lower percentage of substitutions overall. This is a major marketing tactic for Ocado, which operates a DC north of London, in its effort to take on the UK and world home delivery grocery leader Tesco. Ocado claims to be operating at a less than 2 percent substitution rate, while companies that pick in-store have substitution rates of 10 percent or more.

It is all well and good to *claim* you are better at substitutions, and it is also theoretically true that delivering from a DC should provide a major advantage, but does this bear out in practice? Data from our study of seven online grocers suggests that it does. Figure 8-3 shows the mean responses to our survey for customers of online grocers clustered in four groups. *New* customers were those who had placed from one to four orders from a particular online grocer, while *loyal* customers were those who had placed seven or more orders. Customers who bought from one of the companies that uses a store-pick model were classified as *store pick* and customers that bought from companies that employed a DC–pick model were classified as *DC pick*.[5] Figure 8-3 shows that for new customers, their perceptions regarding the reasonableness of substitutions (i.e., higher ratings are better) were fairly similar for the DC and store-pick approaches, although DC outperformed store pick by a small margin. In contrast, for loyal customers, the difference was much larger (approximately half a point on a seven-point scale). This indicates that once customers have had sufficient experience with a store, they generally perceive that the DC–based model has fewer substitutions. They also become more accepting of those substitutions that do occur on a less frequent basis. Thus, our data clearly show that DC–based picking minimizes problems with substitutions, if it is done well. This is very important since the score for this question on substitutions correlates quite highly with overall customer satisfaction.

Product Range

Product range is a key challenge in managing any retail business. On the one hand, offering more products offers customers more choices and, particularly in retail stores, creates many more impulse buying opportunities. On the other hand, every additional SKU complicates the inventory-management process by adding complexity to the system and requiring additional shelf or storage space. There is a strong tendency for all companies, particularly retailers, to add products over time without having a good understanding of the effects on sales (are they increasing total sales by creating new sales, or cannibalizing other products) or the effects on inventory-management performance.[6] In a sense, there is always a strong temptation to add a new product(s) because it is almost guaranteed to increase total sales, but it is often very hard to remove products that are underperforming. In other words, how do businesses decide which products are truly profitable and/or necessary, and which should be discontinued in favor of simplification or adding other products?

Last-mile supply chains offer two approaches to this age-old problem. First, many last-mile retailers simply fulfill orders from a DC so that they can carry

Figure 8-3. Comparison of substitutions for store vs. DC pick in grocery home delivery.

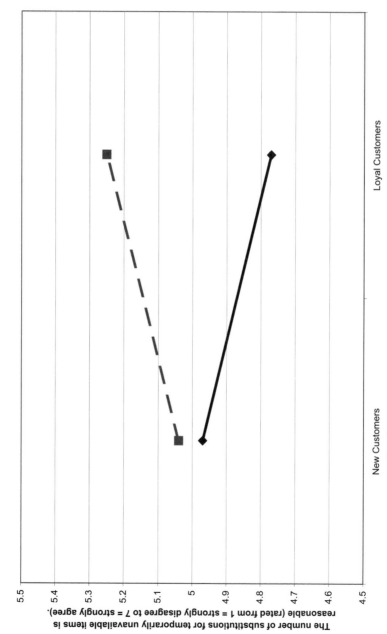

The number of substitutions for temporarily unavailable items is reasonable (rated from 1 = strongly disagree to 7 = strongly agree).

New Customers

Loyal Customers

New Customers = 1 - 4 Orders and Loyal Customers = 7 or more orders.

◆ Store Pick   ■ DC Pick

more inventory and SKUs. Keeping inventory at one or a few central locations is substantially easier than keeping inventory at numerous retail locations. This is true because fluctuations in demand that are highly variable from store to store are buffered by aggregating all the demand in one central location. In addition, safety stock is carried in only one or a few locations, rather than scores or hundreds of sites.[7] This is the fundamental reason why Amazon can offer so much choice—roughly 2 million titles. It stores inventory only at six DCs, rather than at several hundred bookstores around the country, as is the case for Barnes & Noble. Top-selling items are carried at multiple DCs, lesser-selling items are carried at only a single DC, and the lowest-selling items (80 percent to 95 percent of what Amazon offers) is back-ordered from publishers. The end result clearly shows the benefits of centralizing inventory: Amazon turned its inventory 19.5 times in 2002, while Barnes & Noble only turned its inventory 3.8 times.[8] The lower turns at Barnes & Noble are a result of carrying inventory in several hundred stores (although their online division offers a greater range of SKUs and probably has greater inventory turns, but data is not available for this division), and while a Barnes & Noble superstore offers a lot of choice (between 50,000 and 150,000 SKUs), it is not in the same league as Amazon's 2 million–plus SKUs.

Similar examples of increased variety/SKUs for last-mile retailers abound. NetFlix carries over 14,000 DVD titles, while your local Blockbuster or Hollywood Video carries roughly 10 percent of that total. Netflix only has to stock these videos at one of its roughly twenty DCs, while Blockbuster has to stock videos at several hundred stores. Similarly, many of the major catalog operations (LL Bean, Lands' End, Spiegel, etc.) benefit from the ability to offer more SKUs, while keeping a tighter grip on inventory. The ultimate in high variety/SKUs is offered by manufacturers that offer custom products—Dell, FreshDirect, and Lands' End Customer all capitalize on the ability to customize products at their central manufacturing facility. This can be done in fairly high volume as described in Chapter Two.

The second approach that last-mile supply chains offer to manage the increased variety versus more difficult inventory-management trade-off involves *decreasing* the amount of SKUs. Retailers have been trying for years to manage product proliferation with essentially no success whatsoever. The grocery industry spent billions on a major initiative labeled efficient consumer response (ECR) in the 1990s to curb product proliferation, streamline supply chains, and get the right products in stores at the right time. While ECR did lead to improved supply chain capabilities, unfortunately the supply chain increased in complexity faster than grocers could keep up, so the results were often disappointing.[9] Why? The simple answer is that most retail stores look largely alike, sell the same commodity products, and have a hard time differentiating themselves. Thus, they are always trying to influence customers to spend a bit more by offer "new and improved" products. Manufacturers essentially buy space for their new products through slotting fees. In fact, it has been estimated that packaged goods manufacturers (i.e., Coca-Cola, Nabisco, Kraft, etc.) pay grocery stores $25 billion in slotting fees per year.[10] This is a huge number, given that the average net profit in groceries is roughly one percent on about $500 billion of sales per year—or a total net profit of $5 billion. Subtract slotting fees, and grocery stores are losing money, and all the slotting fees accomplish is to push thousands of products per year (20,000 new products introduced every year) that we really don't need, or want, onto shelves.

So how do last-mile supply chains address this problem? Simple: A few innovative companies are essentially telling customers that their service is about convenience and that they will stock a "reasonable" number of SKUs, but not a huge amount. As shown in Figure 8-2, grocers that operate from a DC typically stock 8,000 to 10,000 items versus the 20,000 to 40,000 that traditional grocers stock. Consider FreshDirect, the New York based online grocer. According to Jason Ackerman, president, "The essence of what we're doing is building a manufacturing business on fresh food and doing it as much as possible on a just-in-time and made-to-order basis. We try to do much more fresh products and less packaged foods because we think the piece-pick business of packaged goods is a very difficult and hard business."[11] Thus, FreshDirect concentrates on fresh food, customized to order, where it claims its average gross margin is 40 percent or higher, while carrying a minimal variety of packaged goods, where margins are in the lower 20 percent to 30 percent range. FreshDirect only carries 4,000 packaged goods items and often negotiates exclusive deals with a manufacturer such as Tropicana to exclusively carry their orange juice (sometimes in only one size) to the exclusion of competitors. The message to customers is "Buy your fresh products from us and your packaged goods, but you'll have to be content with a bit less choice on the packaged goods." According to Jason Ackerman, "We envision our target customer as someone who buys their fresh produce, meats, seafood, and dairy from us on a regular, weekly basis and perhaps buys their packaged goods once a month in bulk at a Costco or Wal-Mart."[12]

Product Range/Choice vs. Availability/Substitutions: A Forced Trade-Off?

How do retailers manage the trade-off between range of product choice (number of SKUs stocked or offered) and availability/substitutions? In general, as SKUs increase, availability should go down, and substitutions should go up—but this obviously depends on a number of factors, including the choice of store-based picking versus DC and on the relative skill with which the supply chain is designed and managed. Figure 8-4 offers data from our study of the consumer-direct grocery industry. The graph shows the plot for the mean values for two questions for each of the seven grocers in our study. In a perfect world, customers would agree with the question on the horizontal axis (Grocer X has a sufficient range of products to meet my needs) and also agree with the question on the vertical axis (The number of substitutions for temporary or unavailable items is reasonable). But we do not live in a perfect world, and as we have discussed, offering more choices/SKUs is generally negatively correlated with inventory availability because of increased complexity. The grocers in Figure 8-4 are grouped in three classes:

1. *DC–Based Fulfillment*: Three grocers that fulfill orders from a central DC.
2. *Hybrid:* Two grocers that use a hybrid model (one of which fills some orders from local stores and some from a DC; the other fills all orders from a DC, but is a well-known chain of stores, so customers may perceive orders as coming from stores).
3. *Store-Based Fulfillment:* Two grocers that fill orders from local stores only.

Our expectation would be that DC–based fulfillment would have the best performance (in this case customer ratings) in terms of substitutes, while store-based picking would generally offer more choice of products. Figure 8-4 generally supports these assertions. The grocer with the best performance on substitutions uses a DC–based fulfillment model, but has the worst rating for range. Similarly, the second-best grocer for substitutions also uses a DC–based fulfillment model, but has the third-lowest rating for product range. For product variety, the two grocers with, by far, the highest scores use the store-based fulfillment model. An interesting feature of Figure 8-4 is that the two grocers that seem to do the best job of balancing substitutions/availability and range

Figure 8-4. Product range vs. availability and substitutions—for loyal customers of online groceries.

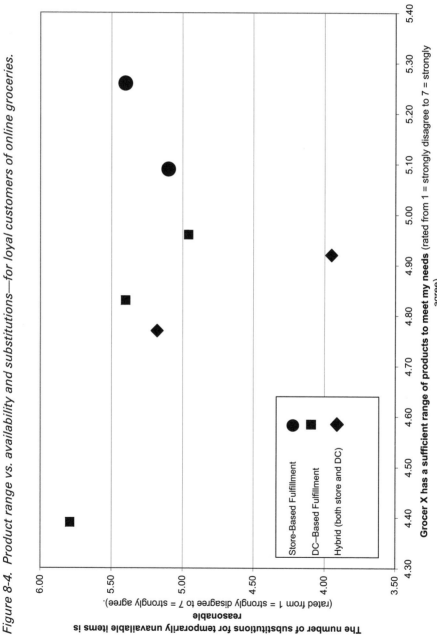

both use the store-based fulfillment model. By far, the worst performers in Figure 8-4 are the two stores that utilize the hybrid model, clearly indicating that they have not mastered the skills necessary for either low substitutions or high product range.

The other thing that Figure 8-4 shows is that there are clearly major differences in the ability to successfully manage both range and substitutions. There are large differences within strategies—for example, the DC–based grocer to the extreme left of the graph is great with substitutions (mean score equaling 5.79), but very bad with range (mean score equaling 4.39). In contrast, another DC–based grocer is almost as good with substitutions (mean score equaling 5.40), but much better with range (mean score equaling 5.26). Clearly, how well a grocer or other retailer manages both availability/substitutions and product range can vary substantially within a strategy. Successfully executing fulfillment and delivery has a great impact on customer perceptions and loyalties. Consider customer loyalty—we asked customers to rate themselves on the following statement: *Loyalty*: "I will use Grocer X's Web site for future orders." (Rated on a scale of one to seven, with one equaling strongly disagree and seven equaling strongly agree.)

We then used the two questions shown in Figure 8-4, plus a third on delivery (the company delivers my order when they promised delivery) to predict a customer's loyalty using linear regression. The result was that the customer response on range, substitutions, and delivery strongly predicted their loyalty to that grocer, explaining over 25 percent of the variation. All three components were significant, with on-time delivery having the largest impact on loyalty, and minimizing substitutions and maximizing product range have roughly equal and strong impacts on loyalty. In short, last-mile retailers must successfully manage fulfillment (availability, substitutions, and range) and delivery to retain customers. Therefore, we now turn to a discussion of delivery to finish our examination of the major components of Figure 8-1.

The Delivery Process

Delivering orders is one of the most challenging aspects of the supply chain because there is a fundamental trade-off between efficiency (delivering the most orders per truck, driver, or shift) and customer convenience (delivering when customers want the order). To illustrate, Figure 8-5 provides a graph illustrating the relative efficiency of eight consumer-direct businesses. These estimates are

Figure 8-5. Delivery efficiency—general comparison for different businesses.

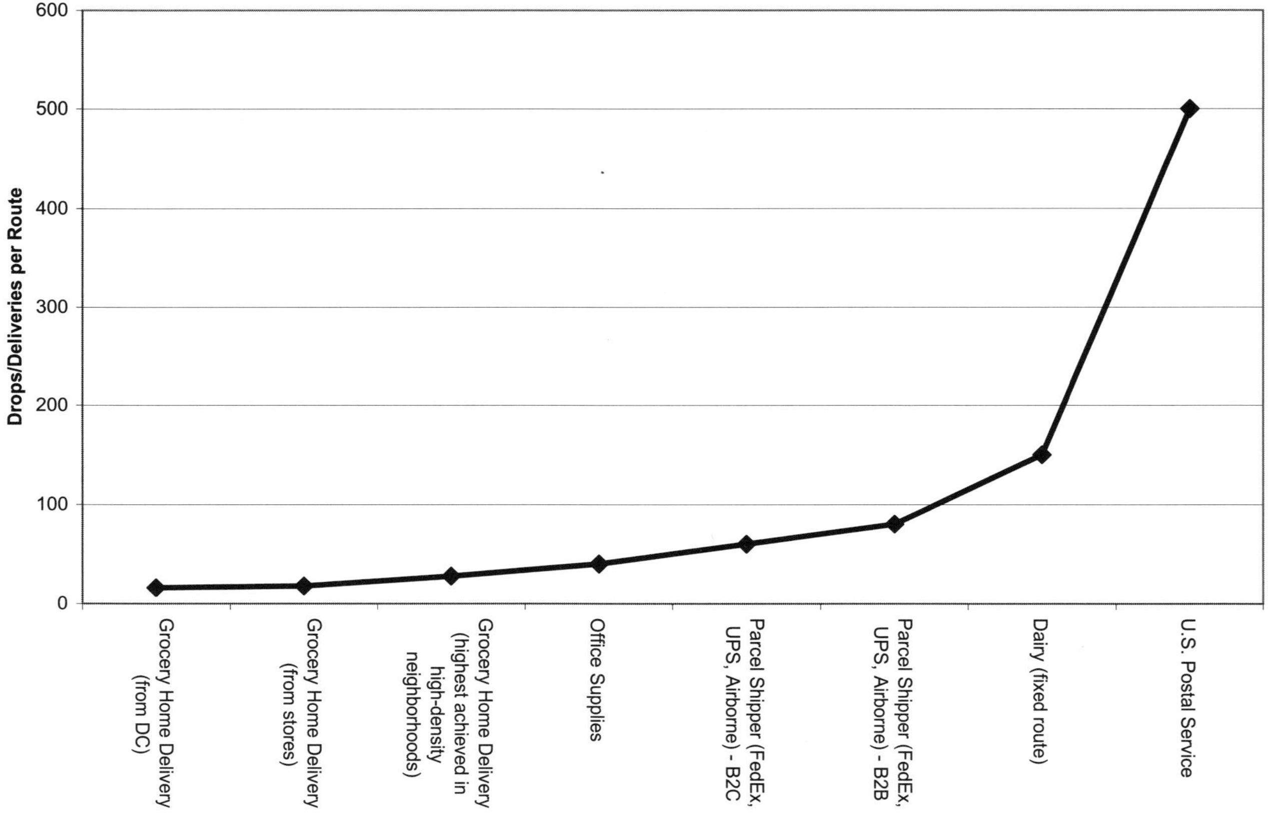

U.S. Postal Service

Dairy (fixed route)

Parcel Shipper (FedEx,
UPS, Airborne) - B2B

Parcel Shipper (FedEx,
UPS, Airborne) - B2C

Office Supplies

Grocery Home Delivery
(highest achieved in
high-density
neighborhoods)

Grocery Home Delivery
(from stores)

Grocery Home Delivery
(from DC)

Drops/Deliveries per Route

600   500   400   300   200   100   0

drawn from our research on the online grocery industry and from discussions with executives in similar industries. They are not meant to be absolute numbers, but they do give a good idea of relative efficiencies. The least efficient routes are those to the left of the graph—those for grocery home delivery. When delivering from a centralized distribution center, most online grocers target between fourteen to eighteen deliveries per route (usually defined as one truck and one driver for eight hours). Grocers that deliver from stores can get slightly higher deliveries (from sixteen to twenty per route) because they deliver from local stores—thus the delivery radius and travel times are much shorter. The best efficiency that we have seen in any grocery home delivery is between twenty-eight and thirty-six deliveries per route. The biggest driver of route efficiency—in a perfect world, a grocer delivering twenty orders on the same street, at the same time block—could increase efficiency greatly, but the limiting factors are drop time (delivering groceries takes quite a while because you are delivering multiple items, not a single package) and the difficulties in getting high density.

Moving farther to the right in Figure 8-5, the next entry is for office supplies retailers (such as Office Depot, OfficeMax, Staples, etc.). Their drops per route is substantially higher, roughly forty per route. This is achieved for two primary reasons: First, most of their deliveries are to businesses, which tend to be located fairly close together and, second, they are not time-constrained. Most businesses have fairly predictable operating hours (i.e., nine to five), so deliveries can be made anytime during that span. This makes it much more efficient to plan routes, as compared to grocers that must arrive during a specific appointment window (i.e., nine to eleven A.M., or one to three P.M.). Moving farther right in Figure 8-5, we see parcel shippers such as Federal Express, UPS, and Airborne. These are separated into two categories: business-to-consumer (B2C) and business-to-business (B2B). Parcel shippers have much better efficiency with B2B shipments because of the more predictable hours and the fact that someone is always there to receive shipments. In contrast, B2C shipments are a problem because a large percentage of customers will not be home to receive the shipment. In this case, the shipper can (A) leave the package (if the customer has approved this option ahead of time) or (B) leave a note saying the customer can either pick up the package at the company's local facility, or have the package redelivered the next day. The second choice results in a substantial percentage of packages that must be redelivered—often two or three times. This hurts both the parcel shipper's efficiency and leaves customers frustrated.

Our estimates are that the difference between B2B parcel shipments and B2C is roughly 33 percent (i.e., seventy to one hundred shipments per route for B2B and fifty to seventy shipments per route for B2C). While these estimates are rough, we will return to this topic when we discuss the efforts (including alternate drop points and smart boxes that allow packages to be dropped in a secure, locked container) that parcel shippers are making to address these gaps.

The final two examples in Figure 8-5 show the value of having fixed routes that do not change on a daily basis. Dairy companies that deliver to homes, such as Oberweis in the Chicago metro area, benefit from fixed routes with high densities. These are possible because deliveries are made in an unattended manner (customers leave a gray-and-white Coleman cooler on the porch) and orders for a given customer are fixed to a given day of the week. Thus, the average route covers 150 stops—a huge improvement over any of the others in Figure 8-5.[13] Not only do they deliver milk, but they also offer other dairy products and the best ice cream, and have been gradually offering some pre-pared meal solutions. The final example in Figure 8-5 is one with which every American is familiar—the U.S. Postal Service. They average approximately 500 drops per route and 2,300 pieces of mail per carrier route.[14] This efficiency is due to the ultimate combination of an absolutely fixed route (i.e., every house, apartment, and condo—thus no skipping and very little travel time between houses) and a fairly easy-to-handle package (i.e., few letters per house that are fairly light). However, even here there is a very good illustration of the difference that delivery design can make in efficiency. In older (pre–World War II) neighborhoods, mail was delivered to customers' doors by carriers who walk. In contrast, most newer constructions (since the 1950s) have mail boxes at the curbside. This allows carriers to deliver from their delivery vehicles (specially built, with the driver on the right side), thus greatly increasing efficiency. While the Post Office does not have figures it releases publicly, the difference in customers served on a walking route versus a driving route ranges from 300 to 600 customers per route—a substantial difference.

Direct vs. Indirect Delivery

Now that we have introduced the idea of delivery efficiency via Figure 8-5, we turn to a discussion of how companies can affect that efficiency. Clearly, one of the biggest factors is whether companies deliver directly or indirectly. The key to efficiency is density; thus the more efficient examples (parcel shippers, dairies, and the U.S. Postal Service) greatly outperform companies or businesses with less density (such as online grocers or even office supplies retailers). The advantage to direct delivery is that is provides an opportunity to build relationships with customers, depending on how it is done. Consider our earlier postal example—many people in older neighborhoods where postal carriers come to their door know their mail carrier by name, but this is much less common in neighborhoods with curbside mail boxes. In other words, there is a trade-off between efficiency and relationship building.

Clearly there are trade-offs between direct and indirect delivery, but once that choice is made, there are several techniques or tactics for improving efficiency. These include order management (choosing the timing and availability of delivery windows), type of delivery (attended or unattended), and routing software that helps develop efficient routes.

Order Management: Window Size and Availability

The most efficient delivery method is to not offer customers any choice when their delivery will occur. Most of us have experienced this with something like furniture delivery, where we are told that the couch we ordered will be delivered sometime on Monday between nine A.M. and five P.M. Efficient for the delivery service, but horrible for the customer because then he has to wait around all day—and Murphy's law says that if you go out for even fifteen minutes, that is when your delivery will come, and you will miss it. So, as customers we appreciate companies that provide us more precise ideas when our order will arrive. Grocery companies that deliver now all offer windows in the one-, one-and-a-half-, or two-hour range, meaning that customers can sign up for a specific slot of that duration. Clearly, this is more convenient, but the question becomes, how does window size affect efficiency and cost? Obviously, the shorter the window, the more challenging it is to meet that constraint, and the more expensive, because the company must have extra resources—more drivers, trucks, etc. A very good example is Domino's Pizza, which, while it built its national reputation on guaranteed pizza delivery in thirty minutes or less, had to cancel the guarantee because of inability to meet it safely and consistently.[15] This is for a business where the pizza store is within two to three miles of all of its customers, so imagine how much harder this becomes when the delivery radius is expanded (as when delivering from a DC), and when the orders become more complicated (i.e., more and bulkier items).

To illustrate the effects of window size, we performed a simple simulation, the results of which are shown in Figures 8-6 and 8-7. We generated forty-five imaginary customers and gave each a location (i.e., an east/west and north/south coordinate), defined appropriate travel times, and a drop time for delivering each order. Each truck/route was given eight hours to complete its route and had to start and end its trip at a central DC. Figure 8-6 shows the routes that were developed when there were no time constraints on orders (customers could receive the order anytime between nine A.M. and five P.M.). This pattern is a classic routing pattern—generally the most efficient routes look like a clover leaf, with each truck following a circular/elliptical path to minimize travel distance. Note that all deliveries can be done with three trucks for an efficiency of fifteen drops per route.

In contrast, Figure 8-7 shows the same problem with time constraints—each customer is assigned to a two-hour window in which their delivery must occur (nine to eleven A.M., eleven A.M. to one P.M., one to three P.M., or three to five P.M.). We assigned an equal number of customers to each window, which makes the problem easier, but may not be realistic, since in actual practice, the demand for certain windows or days of the week varies substantially. As can be seen in Figure 8-7, we now need four trucks/routes and also overtime (in this case, three of the four drivers worked beyond an eight-hour shift for a total of one-and-a-half hours overtime). The routes shown in Figure 8-7 correspond to what experts in home delivery call the "ping-pong effect." In other words, they look like a ping-pong ball bouncing back and forth in an enclosed room. Clearly, the routes are not as efficient distance-wise with all the overlapping and criss-crossing, but this is necessary to meet the delivery windows requested by customers. In terms of costs/efficiency, this solution with two-hour windows is roughly one-third more expensive (four drivers versus three). Obviously, offering more constrained/precise windows or delivery estimates is more expensive/difficult. Plus, when we promise a two-hour window, the chances that we miss it increase. Yet, this is just a simple demonstration of a fairly small delivery situation. We now examine how things like density, window size, and different availabilities of windows effect efficiency.

◆ *Order Density*: The more orders in a given area, the more efficient the delivery, as shown in Figure 8-4. The U.S. Post Office delivers to *every* house and business, so they have the highest efficiency. Consider Figure 8-7 again. What would be the effect of having ten times as many

(text continues on page 194)

Figure 8-6. Route deliveries without specified time windows and no time constraints.

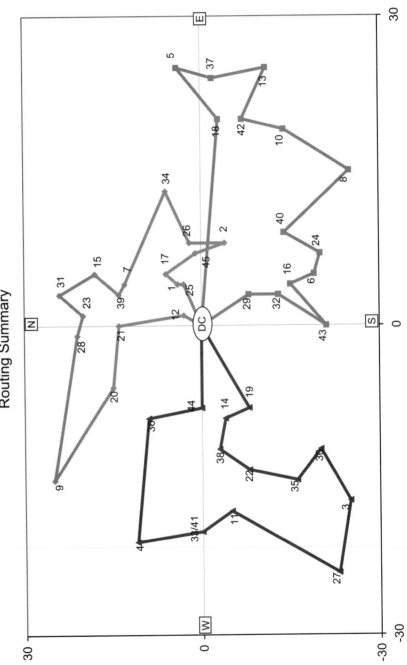

Routing Summary

Figure 8-7. Route deliveries without specified time windows and with time constraints.

Routing Summary

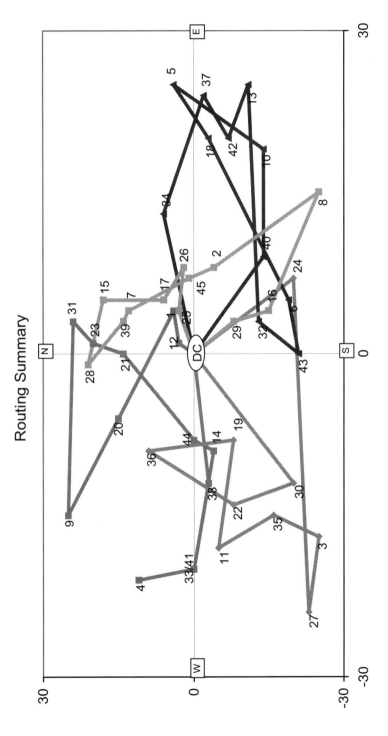

customers in the same delivery area? With the existing forty-five customers and two-hour delivery windows, the efficiency was 11.25
drops/customers (forty-five customers divided by four routes). If there
were 450 customers instead, then there are more options for scheduling
routes. If the 450 customers could be scheduled into thirty routes,
then the efficiency would be fifteen drops/customers per route (450
customers divided by thirty routes). This represents a 33 percent increase in efficiency. In general, as customer density increases, delivery
efficiency increases, but at what rate? A study of home delivery costs
for groceries in Finland estimated that increasing market share in a
given area from 0.05 percent (five customers per 1,000 residents) to
0.48 percent (forty-eight customers per 1,000 residents) would result
in a 24 percent delivery cost reduction when offering one-hour windows. A further increase in market share to 1.44 percent (144 customers out of every 1,000) resulted in only an additional decrease in
delivery costs of 5 percent.[16] Thus, there is great value in increasing the
density in a given delivery area, but at a certain point, the improvements in efficiency become fairly marginal.

The basic lesson is that when offering home delivery it is very
important to target-market particular areas to build a critical density.
That is why many Internet grocers and other direct-delivery retailers
only offer delivery in certain neighborhoods and use a great deal of
targeted marketing (direct mail, door-to-door promotions, local advertising, etc.). Returning to Figure 8-7, the ping-pong effect is lessened
with greater customer density because the delivery scheduler (or software in most cases) has more choices. Thus, the routes are more likely
to look like the clover leaf routes of Figure 8-6.

An interesting illustration of the benefits of density is provided by
the release of the wildly popular Harry Potter book *Harry Potter and the
Order of the Phoenix*. On June 21, 2003, the first date of sale, Federal
Express reported that it delivered 400,000 copies of the book to customers who had ordered from Amazon or Barnes & Noble.[17] While
presenting numerous challenges, this one-time increase in daily business also provided great increases in delivery efficiency. Graye Lewis,
an independent contractor for Federal Express Home Delivery, reports
that his average day's route consists of sixty to seventy packages and

that he drives between 150 and 200 miles. However, on Harry Potter day he delivered 130 packages in one hundred miles.[18]

◆ *Window Size*: Clearly the size of delivery windows has a great effect on efficiency, as illustrated in Figure 8-5. The U.S. Post Office and dairy companies can make a large number of deliveries because they are unconstrained—their window is their entire business day. In contrast, companies that offer prespecified windows are trading efficiency for customer convenience. The key question is, what is the shape of this trade-off curve? In other words, is offering two-hour windows half as efficient as one-hour windows? The answer is—it depends—on several factors. First of all, density, if a region is dense, then shorter windows are not necessarily much more inefficient than longer windows. But if there are few customers in an area, then shorter windows become much more of a problem. Consider Figure 8-7 again—customers nine and twenty-seven are a problem. Not in the sense that they are mean people, but more in the sense that there are no other customers near them. In the solution shown, customer nine requires the driver to drive forty-five minutes, unload the order for ten minutes, then drive forty-five minutes to customer thirty-one. This is clearly inefficient. What's the answer? Either drop customers like customer nine (or regions where there is not much business), offer limited windows for that area, or market heavily to increase density in that area.

Let's examine these options. First, companies can choose not to service certain areas that do not have a sufficient customer base. Both FreshDirect in New York and Ocado in London have taken a phased approach to rolling their services out on a region-by-region basis, as they target neighborhoods with more attractive customer profiles. The advantage is more efficient deliveries; the risk is in upsetting customers who cannot get service, losing potential sales.

Second, companies can offer different window sizes and availabilities in different areas. Peapod has employed this approach. In some areas where it has many customers, it offers two-hour delivery windows and numerous choices. In less attractive areas, it offers longer windows and fewer choices. In some cases, the only choice is unattended delivery (the window is all day), and there is only one day a week. This has allowed Peapod to achieve fairly high delivery efficiencies relative to other home delivery grocers. As an illustration, of eighteen delivery zones in the Chicago area, the top five account for over 60 percent of customer orders, thus these are the zones that get the shortest windows and the most choices.[19] In the extreme case, unattended delivery (no windows, the delivery is simply left whether the customer is home or not) are, by far, the most efficient approach. The Finnish study mentioned earlier found that unattended delivery of groceries resulted in approximately a 33 percent cost reduction.[20] Put another way, unattended delivery is the most efficient for the retailer or carrier, but this has to be balanced against convenience for the customer—a subject we will return to when discussing smart drop boxes below.

The final technique for improving delivery efficiency is to increase density in a neighborhood. The more customers in a given area, the more efficient will be the delivery. Sounds nice, but achieving this goal is relatively hard. As discussed in Chapter Six, this is where marketing and operations need to work together closely to jointly meet their goals. Techniques that have been used successfully include: refer a friend/neighbor, direct/concentrated advertising, and centralized delivery points. One technique that has proven effective is to offer central drop-offs—for example, several grocers now offer services that deliver to work. For a discounted rate, customers of a large company (say an office building with 1,000 employees) can get deliveries at their place of business on a given day (Tuesday from four to six P.M.). The grocer can then bring one truck, park it in the parking lot, and have customers pull their cars up to have orders deposited directly in their trunks. Assuming that one truck can handle sixteen deliveries in two hours, the eight-delivery-per-hour rate greatly beats the average rate of two per hour, achieved by most residential deliveries of groceries. This option works well if it is (A) convenient for the customer and (B) more efficient for the retailer, but only if a way can be found to share the benefits equitably and attract customers. Thus, a delivery fee in this situation might be $3.95 versus $7.95 for home delivery, but since the company is increasing delivery efficiency by a factor of four, it can afford to reduce rates.

◆ *Smart Drop Boxes*: As discussed earlier, unattended delivery is by far the most efficient method; however, it has severe trade-offs in terms of customer convenience. Consider the case of parcel deliveries from UPS or Federal Express; many customers will not allow the shippers to leave packages without a signature. This is because they are afraid to have valuable goods sitting outside, want to visually confirm they received the right item, and/or are afraid the goods will be damaged by exposure to the elements. Unfortunately, for the parcel shippers, this results in a large amount of packages that need a second, third, or even fourth delivery attempt. Customers usually are left a note stating they can sign and leave the note for next-day delivery (for the package to be left), or they can pick it up at the shipper's distribution center— neither of which is a convenient option. To address these difficulties, UPS, Deutsche Post World Net, and Federal Express are all developing new methods for deliveries where customers are not home. United Parcel Service recently bought Mailboxes Etc. and is rebranding its 2,000 stores as the UPS Store. The goal is twofold: (1) to make package returns easier for customers of e-retailers and (2) to simplify delivery for customers who are not home. According to Chris Kelly, a Forrester Research Inc. analyst, "Instead of consumers having to go out to the industrial area outside of town where the UPS warehouse is to pick up the package, there may one day be UPS stores in neighborhoods that serve more of a function of a traditional post office."[21]

Deutsche Post, a major German postal and logistics company, is employing an alternative approach to address missed deliveries. It offers a "Packstation," which is a self-service kiosk equipped with lock boxes that is available around the clock. Customers must register for this service and may choose home delivery or delivery to a nearby Packstation location. When a shipment arrives for them, they are notified via e-mail or a cellular phone text message. Customers then use their ID cards or numbers to access the box, or they can make returns for the carrier to pick up. The benefit for Deutsche Post is greater delivery efficiency, but this must be balanced and matched with customer benefits. As of October 2002, more than 24,000 customers had registered for the service in Mainz and Dortmund, Germany, and further rollouts of trial Packstations were planned in Frankfurt and Amsterdam. The biggest users were e-retailers such as Amazon, Yves Rocher, and Quelle.[22] In the United States, Federal Express is quietly testing a similar concept called "Ship & Get" with many of the same features. Here the Ship & Get locations are similar to the Packstations used by Deutsche Post, but are to be located in grocery stores. Little information is publicly available, but it is safe to assume that Federal Express is testing this concept for further expansion.[23]

In addition to pure delivery efficiencies, such as drops per route, smart drop boxes of this type also offer greater protection of goods from theft or spoilage. E-grocers are particularly interested in the concept because it could help keep refrigerated and frozen items fresher. Similarly, companies that deliver high-value items (such as consumer electronics—think Dell—or prescription drugs) see security as a large potential benefit. Clearly, there are numerous advantages to this approach. Unfortunately, there are also numerous challenges. Among the questions are: (1) Who will pay for the boxes, (2) Where will they be located, (3) How should customers be notified of their shipments, (4) How should customers be encouraged to use this method, and (5) How should shippers/retailers access the boxes (i.e., can they be used by multiple companies or just one)? At this point, there are definitely more questions than answers, but given the possible gains in efficiency and service, there is a good chance that consumers will be seeing more of this option in the future.[24]

◆ *Routing Software*: A final tool for improving delivery efficiency is routing software. As illustrated in our earlier discussion, there are numerous factors that affect routing efficiency, including density, timing, window size, availability, and numerous other things. Developing routes for even a handful of delivery trucks by hand or general software is tremendously challenging—particularly when considering conflicting objectives. For example, what is most important—minimizing drive time, minimizing the number of trucks, maximizing on-time deliveries? Most large last-mile companies employ some third-party software. Two of the largest vendors include Descartes and Paragon Software Systems. Descartes promises this:

> "Efficient service for the last mile. Real-world execution means balancing customer service with operational dynamics—responding to changing orders, shifting priorities, traffic conditions, vehicle breakdowns, the weather—all the things that affect last-mile delivery costs. Too often, companies carefully plan all of the steps leading to order fulfillment but can't

manage final delivery in the way they'd like. Meeting customer expectations is difficult as a result. It's a constant challenge in a competitive market."[25]

Major last-mile customers of Descartes include Best Buy, Schwan's Home
Service, and Ocado. Another leading software solution provider is Paragon
Software Systems whose customers include both Tesco.com and Sainsbury's to
You (the two largest e-grocers in the UK), Dixons, and Domino's Pizza.[26]
Another alternative is to outsource both the routing and the actual delivery—
companies such as Ensenda and Distribution Solutions International provide
third-party logistics solutions to a variety of customers requiring B2C deliv-
eries.[27]

While it is not our goal to evaluate individual software solutions, we can
state that large-scale home deliveries require some type of software, as well as a
good understanding of the algorithms built into it. The people using the software must have good training to understand how it works, and they must have
a clear understanding of the company's marketing and fulfillment strategies. In
other words, as noted in Chapter Six—don't promise more than you can deliver, don't deliver less than you promise, and make sure customers value your
service sufficiently. Finally, as discussed in Chapter Nine, it is also critical that
order-fulfillment software be carefully integrated with order-delivery software,
since a truck that gets the wrong orders (or the right orders, but late) can never
deliver the right orders on time.[28]

A Note on Technology

There has been a plethora of new technologies developed and introduced over
the past decade or so that have had a huge impact on the ability to coordinate
and manage various supply chain activities. We could easily name a lengthy list
of acronyms and technologies: Enterprise Resource Planning (ERP), Flexible
Manufacturing Systems (FMS), bar coding, Automated Storage and Retrieval
Systems (AS/RS), pick-to-light, etc. Most, if not all, of these technologies rely
heavily on computerization and information systems. Consider the humble bar
code, which is really just a series of short and long lines, but when read by a
scanner into a computer is incredibly useful in providing information for a
variety of purposes. The use of bar codes has had a huge influence on the
ways both retailers and manufacturers conduct business. Many retailers and

manufacturers are eagerly tracking the development of RFID, which would allow the same benefits as bar-code scanning, without employees actively needing to scan individual bar codes, and which could store vastly increased amounts of information.[29]

Technology is often a driver for supply chain change, particularly within last-mile supply chains. However, we want to offer two points of caution. First, there is no such thing as a magic technology that solves all of a company's problems. It is only as good as the people using it and their abilities to creatively harness its powers. Thus, companies must carefully manage both technology and the people who use it to optimize the results. Training and empowerment are critical—without these it is similar to giving a thirteen-year-old child a Ferrari—a great car, but likely to be crashed into something quickly. Second, we have not spent much time discussing specific technologies. This is because they change quickly, and we are examining strategies for last-mile supply chains, not specific technologies. If you are looking for a good source on specific technologies, we suggest consulting journals such as *Modern Materials Handling, Frontline Solutions,* or *Logistics Management,* all of which offer looks at specific fulfillment and delivery technologies that vendors are currently offering.

Action Steps

This chapter has examined the three critical components of the last-mile supply chain: ordering, fulfillment, and delivery. We have not tried to provide a complete review of all aspects of any one of these components, since that clearly could be an entire book in and of itself. Rather, our goal in this chapter has been to examine how consumer-direct businesses must manage these activities in a different manner than traditional companies that require the customer to physically come to them. We have shown where there are opportunities, and where there are challenges.

Ordering must be a simple, easy-to-complete process that offers the customer a time savings. Fulfillment of orders must combine elements of efficiency, accuracy (availability of items), and range or choice. Finally, once the order is taken and fulfilled, it must be delivered. This is often the most expensive and challenging of the three steps. Last-mile supply chains are not just ordering, fulfillment, or delivery—they are the sum of all three. Mistakes or inefficiencies in any area spill over into customer perceptions and actions. Thus, we close this chapter with a list of action steps:

◆ Decide how you want to take orders (phone, fax, Internet) based on a careful analysis of the benefits and challenges from both the customer's and company's perspective. Then work to design and offer a system that is simple and enjoyable for the customer to use, while streamlining order entry and processing for the company.

◆ Link order, fulfillment, and delivery IT systems, and minimize human data entry points and handoffs.

◆ Choose whether to fulfill orders from a store or a DC, then be clear about the benefits *and* disadvantages of that choice.

◆ Limit product proliferation and the number of SKUs offered. When offering customization, make sure it is *meaningful*, not about *minutia*.

◆ Carefully balance the choice of customer convenience against loss of operating flexibility when deciding on delivery options.

◆ Choose delivery availability (e.g., window length) based on value to customer, and do *not* overpromise.

◆ Remember density, density, density when offering home delivery, and force marketing to emphasize this over simply increasing sales.

Notes

1. More detail on specific applications is available in K. Boyer and M. Frohlich, "Ocado: An Alternative Way to Bridge the Last Mile in Grocery Home Delivery," teaching case published by *European Case Clearing House* (September, 2002), Case # 602-057-1.

2. D. Douglas Graham, "Warehouse of the Future," *Frontline Solutions* (April 2003), Vol. 4, No. 4, pp. 20–24.

3. Ibid.

4. The chances of a complete order with a 95 percent fill rate are calculated as $0.95^{30} = 0.2146$, and the chances for a complete order with a 99 percent fill rate are $0.99^{30} = 0.7397$.

5. There were 179 new, store-pick customers; 795 new, DC customers; 699 loyal, store-pick customers; and 472 loyal, store-pick customers in our sample.

6. Marshall Fisher, "What Is the Right Supply Chain for Your Product?" *Harvard Business Review* (March–April 1997), pp. 105–116.

7. Kenneth K. Boyer, "E-Operations: A Guide to How the Internet Streamlines Operations," *Business Horizons* (January–February 2001), Vol. 44, No. 1, pp. 47–54.

8. Inventory turns are based on calculations for total sales and inventory data presented in the respective annual reports of Amazon and Barnes & Noble.

9. Ken Partch, "A Vision of a 'Frictionless' Marketplace," *Supermarket Business* (September 15, 1999), Vol. 54, No. 9, p. 185.

10. Glen A. Terbeek, *Agentry Agenda: Selling Food in a Frictionless Marketplace* (Breakaway Strategies, Inc., 1999).

11. Dana Dubbs, "Catch of the Day," *Operations & Fulfillment* (July 1, 2003), see http://opsandfulfillment.com.

12. Author's personal conversation with Mr. Ackerman.

13. David Philips, "Oberweis Dairy: Special Delivery," *Dairy Foods* (September 2001), Vol. 102, No. 9, pp. 60–63.

14. The U.S. Postal Service has numerous fascinating facts and details on their Web site at www.usps.com. It is worth a few minutes of your time to gain a new appreciation of this service, which most Americans take for granted. For example, the U.S. Postal Service delivers more than 200 billion pieces of mail per year and over 40 percent of the world's card and letter volume.

15. Michael Janofsky, "Huge Jury Award Ends Speedy Pizza," *The New York Times* (December 26, 1993), p. E2.

16. Hannu Yrjola, "Physical Distribution Considerations for Electronic Grocery Shopping," *International Journal of Physical Distribution & Logistics Management* (2001), Vol. 31, No. 9/10, pp. 746–761.

17. "400,000 Harry Fans received books from Amazon, BarnesandNoble.com Saturday," *Internet Retailer* (June 23, 2003), see www.internetretailer.com.

18. Kristin S. Krause, "FedEx's Welcome Home," *Traffic World* (August 28, 2003), Vol. 263, No. 9, pp. 11–12.

19. Data drawn from Kenneth K. Boyer, G.T.M. Hult, and M. Frohlich, "An Exploratory Analysis of Extended Grocery Supply Chain Operations and Home Delivery," *Integrated Manufacturing Systems*, Vol. 14, No. 8 (2003), pp. 652–663.

20. Hannu Yrjola, "Physical Distribution Considerations for Electronic Grocery Shopping," *International Journal of Physical Distribution & Logistics Management* (2001), Vol. 31, No. 9/10, pp. 746–761.

21. "Evolution, Not Revolution, Likely to Broaden Delivery Options for Consumers," *Internet Retailer* (Mary 29, 2003), see www.InternetRetailer.com.

22. Toby Gooley and James Aaron Cooke, "Deutsche Post Introduces Unique Parcel Service," *Logistics Management* (October 2002), Vol. 41, No. 10, p. 17.

23. Basic data drawn from http://www.fedex.com/us/shipandget/.

24. Good sources of information on smart drop boxes include Tim Laseter, David Torres, and Anne Chung, "Oasis in the Dot-Com Delivery Desert," *Strategy & Business* (2001), Issue 24, Third Quarter; Tom Laseter and Roy Shapiro, "eShip-4U," *Harvard Business School Press* Teaching Case, N1-603-076 (October 22, 2002); and the Web site http://www.smartbox.com.

25. See www.descartes.com/solutions/routing/.

26. See www.paragonrouting.com/client.htm.

27. Information available at www.ensenda.com/ or www.dsii.com.

28. Andrea McKenna Findlay, "When It Absolutely, Positively Has to Be There, E-retailers Turn to Outsourcing," *Internet Retailer* (January 2001), see www .internetretailer.com.

29. "They're Small, Techie, and Revolutionizing Pick-and-Pack Warehouse Operations," *Internet Retailer* (April 2003), see www.internetretailer.com.

CHAPTER 9

Information Technology—Facilitating Learning and Streamlining Transactions

The objective for this chapter is to examine the role of information technology in extended supply chains. Taking orders over the Internet or an automated phone system has the potential to streamline and lower transaction costs for the company selling goods or services, while simultaneously making the purchase experience more pleasant, informative, and efficient for the customer. Unfortunately, such disintermediated approaches that do not involve direct interaction with the customer also have great potential to create errors, misunderstandings, lose customers, and foment ill will. Therefore, this chapter focuses on three key concepts. First, we examine key approaches for designing Web sites that are simultaneously simple for customers to use and provide valuable information and opportunities for cross-selling, if appropriate. Ideally, the goal is to get customers to self-source—place orders on their own with little or no intervention from representatives of the company. To make this occur, there has to be something to attract the customer—quicker ordering, more features, or a more informative/fun experience. Second, we examine the need to streamline transactions so that customers gain comfort and efficiency as they make repeat purchases. The learning curve that customers follow is critical—the faster customers become comfortable with the Web site, and the quicker they can order, the happier and more loyal they become. Finally, we examine the critical importance of integrating the order taking system (either Web- or phone-based) with the operational systems that support the fulfillment of customer orders.

Principles for Building Effective Web Sites

There are hundreds of books, magazines, and journal articles that provide advice on how to design Web sites for commercial purposes. There are sources that give general layout advice, technical coding advice, and advice regarding hardware. Our purpose in this chapter is not to give a detailed how-to guide, but rather to provide some general principles and discuss some Web sites and techniques that have been proven to be particularly effective.

A good starting point is provided by the Webby Awards, which are presented annually by the International Academy of Digital Arts and Sciences. Since their inception in 1996, the Webby Awards have become one of the leading and sought-after awards for Web sites—"Better than the Oscars," according to *Vanity Fair* magazine. In its own words, "The Webby Awards works year round to identify the best of the Web. Examining the many sites visited daily for information, entertainment, and the best business practices online, we help daily users and business professionals make the most of their time and investment online."[1] Awards are given in twenty-nine diverse categories, including activism, games, humor, government and law, and TV. For our purposes, we are most interested in the awards given in the commerce category, and the criteria used for judging competitors. In fact, while the Webby has been awarded for seven years, the fall of 2003 marked the initial offering of a second program—the Webby Business Awards, designed to "honor the best business practices online, identifying the leading trends in online business, highlighting the companies and professionals using the Web as an innovative and effective business tool."

The Webby-judging process uses six criteria for evaluating Web sites: Definitions of these criteria are posted on their Web site—www.webbyawards .com. We use these criteria as a rough framework for designing an effective Web site for commercial purposes. Note that we are interpreting these criteria primarily for the commerce category because there are clear differences in what a Web site for activism or humor is trying to achieve. Note also that we are simply trying to provide a broad overview of principles—for an IT professional working full-time on a Web site, there are numerous resources that are far more detailed. Our goal is to provide a manager with a general overview. So, we will briefly review each of the criteria as they apply to Web sites for last-mile retailing, and will provide one or two examples of companies that employ them effectively.

◆ *Content.* Web sites need to engage customers and get their attention. However, the key trade-off for business Web sites is between offering too much content/information and offering a simple purchasing process. Content should aim to educate customers regarding a company's products—particularly when customization is a key feature—as is the case with companies such as Dell, Art.com, FreshDirect, and Lands' End. However, content should be balanced against the need for speed—users don't want to wait excessively long for pages to load. Alternatively, content should seek to increase customer purchases. Amazon is a master at offering additional books based on a customer's past purchases and at offering lists of similar books purchased by other customers. This technique can greatly increase customer sales.

◆ *Structure and Navigation.* Web sites should be easy to comprehend and to navigate. Customers should be able to figure out where they want to go quickly and efficiently. There should be a careful balancing of breadth with depth. Consider online grocery shopping—should sites be organized like a store with aisles for meat, produce, canned goods, etc., or should they be organized in a different manner? Web site designers have to carefully balance the amount of information and graphics offered with the speed of loading and searching. Too much information can be burdensome, and too little can inhibit purchases.

A key to navigating Web sites that sell many items and where orders tend to be for multiple items (groceries, office supplies) is to offer saved lists of past orders. When customers tend to buy the same items repeatedly, retailers want to take advantage of the ability to standardize that transaction. A second key is to make searching easy and offer alternatives—for example, a search by product name, SKU, or category.

◆ *Visual Design.* Visual design should be appropriate for the audience. Many designers get carried away with fancy graphics, videos, and other flash media. Customers in different businesses want different things. For example, Art.com puts a premium on showing customers what their final, customized product will look like. Art.com lets customers choose one of several hundred thousand photos or prints of well-known artwork, then choose the type of frame, the type of matting, etc. The end result is a completely customized piece of art—imagine Monet's water lilies customized with your choice of framing style, matting, and glass. The ability to see a visual representation of the final product is very important, since customers can not physically handle the product. The real value of Art.com is not so much in the art itself (all of which consists of reproductions), but in the ability of customers to frame it the way they want. This is important, since this is a primary selling feature. Companies selling more standardized products will want a more text-based shopping cart, but will want to think carefully about what information is shown to customers. A common practice is to show basic information on the first screen, and then allow customers to click down to get further information. For example, Amazon shows the cover of a book, the title, publisher, author, and major reviewer information. Customers can then click to get customer reviews of that book, or to download sample pages.

◆ *Functionality.* For a commerce site, functionality may be the most important criteria. For entertainment purposes, people are there to browse, but fundamentally, commercial Web sites want to get people to complete a transaction. Functionality involves quick-loading pages, live links, access to communicate with the company in multiple manners, and, above all, transaction efficiency. Customers should always be one click away from their shopping cart.

◆ *Interactivity.* This is one of the primary features that separates online ordering from phone or in-store ordering. Interactivity ought to be used to make the customer feel in control of the process, and it is extremely important for companies using decoupled supply chains. This is what allows product customization, and it is one of the few direct linkages with the customer. A good illustration can be found at numerous Web sites including Amazon, Office Depot, or Lands' End. One form of interactivity is feeding back to customers their order information and flagging in a visible, intuitive manner when something has been entered incorrectly. For example, if a customer enters a city, name, or credit card number that is invalid, it is much better to get the customer to correct the error right away.

Just a few years ago, most Web sites were not set up to check customer information for either accuracy or conformity to standards. Yet considerable progress has been made over the past three to five years to simplify and improve these processes. Similarly, when offering customized products, letting the customer feel in control of the process and showing a picture or rendition of the final product is critical. As noted earlier, Art.com is excellent at this. The final screen shows what the final product looks like. Compare that to one of our experiences only three years ago—when ordering an award plaque online, the ordering mechanism was a big text box that asked the user to type in the desired copy that would be used. There was no feedback or picture of what the final plaque would look like (how the text would be formatted, laid out, which fonts would be used, etc.). In essence, ordering the plaque was a one-way process where the customer was taking blind faith it would turn out well. Unsurprisingly, it did not—thus no repeat orders from this author.

- ◆ *Overall Experience.* This is the sum of all the other criteria listed above. Different users will place different weights on the criteria, but fundamentally, overall experience is about whether the customer was comfortable with the online experience, enjoyed the Web site, and was able to place an order easily. Metrics used to track this include whether customers set a bookmark, signed up for newsletters or e-mail updates, passed information on to friends, and, most important, came back often to make repeat purchases.

There were five finalists for the 2003 Webby Award in the commerce category. These were chosen from several hundred Web sites that were submitted for consideration. While the award committee does not release detailed scoring information, Seth Gordon, the category chair of nominating judges for the commerce division of awards, was kind enough to provide a short commentary on each of the five finalists:

"Tire Rack makes it easy for customers to select tires appropriate for their vehicle. The site has good information and selection tools. The company provides great choice on hard-to-find and specialty tires. Red Envelope provides distinctive and high-end gifts. The site has food guidance tools to select by person, event, or price. FreshDirect: Of all the food sites, they are the most appetizing and give the best product information. They offer great ability to customize on meat products and offer the best seasonal fruits and vegetables. Art.com offers an immense amount of choice; the ability to customize frames, mats, and materials, etc., is excellent. The Web site provides a simple, intuitive, and easy-to-use process to get to the end product. Amazon: They have been the clear leader in the market since their start. They are one of the innovation leaders. Very good with customer retention and upselling, they spend a lot of time looking at the psychology of user purchases. They are constantly tinkering and looking to improve—much of which may not be obvious to the customer, but will be beneficial in the long run."[2]

Examining Customer Perceptions of Web Sites

Figures 9-1 to 9-6 show data from three different studies conducted by the authors. Figure 9-1 shows four questions on the perceived ease of Web site use. Most of the ratings are fairly high (all averages are above five and are closer to seven, with seven equaling strongly agree and one equaling strongly disagree). Customers generally felt that it was easy to remember how to use the Web site (D1) and that the sites overall were easy to use (D4). However, the ratings for the question about whether it is easy to get the Web site to do what the customer wants it to do (D2) were substantially lower. This suggests that using a Web site and getting it to do exactly what you want it to can be two quite different things. In general, the ratings for all four questions were fairly good; however, one can also see a clear progression from the office supplies retailer to the major city symphony orchestra to grocers, with ratings improving in that order. There are two possible explanations: (1) Grocers have better Web sites than the symphony and office supplies retailer, respectively, or (2) the timing of data collection affects perceptions. Notice that the office supplies study was conducted in 2000, while the other two were conducted in 2001 and 2002/ 2003, respectively. We believe that the large differences between the office supplies retailer and the other two are due to rapid improvements in both Web technology and customer comfort with this ordering medium. In short, the

Figure 9-1. Perceived ease of Web site use in three industries.

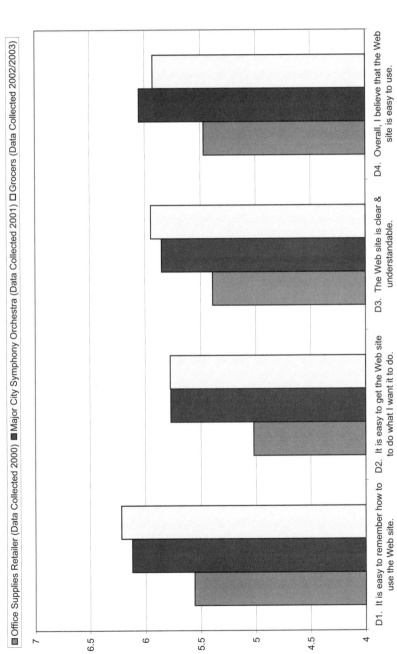

■ Office Supplies Retailer (Data Collected 2000) ■ Major City Symphony Orchestra (Data Collected 2001) □ Grocers (Data Collected 2002/2003)

D1. It is easy to remember how to use the Web site.

D2. It is easy to get the Web site to do what I want it to do.

D3. The Web site is clear & understandable.

D4. Overall, I believe that the Web site is easy to use.

Questions rated from 1 = Strongly Disagree to 7 = Strongly Agree.

sites of all retailers have gotten better as a general rule, and customers have become much better versed in ordering various items online.

Figure 9-2 looks at five questions relating to Web site ease of use. Customers are generally happy with the ability to get on the site when they want to (E1); however they are less satisfied with other aspects, such as loading speed (E2), navigation ease (E3), and the steps for placing an order (E4). The lowest ratings tend to be for searching for products and information (E5). This is disappointing, but not surprising; given the large number of SKUs many Web sites carry, it would be next to impossible to design a "perfect" search system. However, this underscores the importance of getting repeat customers to use saved lists and to streamline their ordering process—something we will talk about in the next section. Finally, Figure 9-2 shows a trend similar to Figure 9-1—as time has passed, retailers have generally improved both the technology behind their sites and the design, so there appears to be improvement from 2000 to 2003. There is a particularly strong pattern of improvement for ease of navigation (E3) and steps for placing an order (E4). This is probably because software and hardware vendors have been able to improve and offer more standardized products—for example, many Web sites use the same underlying technology to manage their shopping baskets. Another important factor has been the rise of broadband or cable access rather than dial-up—faster connection speeds make site loading in particular (E2) much quicker and generally simplify and speed up numerous aspects of the ordering experience. As an illustration, a general rule of thumb in 1999 was the "eight-second rule"—customers were much more likely to abandon if a Web page did not load in eight seconds. At that time, a survey by Nielsen/Netratings found that home users had to wait an average of twenty-eight seconds for a page to load on the 109 most visited e-commerce sites. In contrast, business customers waited an average of only eight seconds—likely due to faster access through T1 lines.[3] Obviously, standards have become tougher over the past four years as people have more ordering experience and often faster access.

In many ways, the most important measure of Web site ease of use is the ability to finalize a transaction. Five to seven years ago, the most heard metric was simply how many hits a site was getting. Now, companies do deeper-level analysis to track how customers progress through a Web site, but surprisingly only 16 percent of companies measure activity all the way through to order conversion.[4] The key to success is often called "stickiness," or the percentage of visitors who actually make purchases. Companies want to do all they can to

Figure 9-2. Web site ease of use.

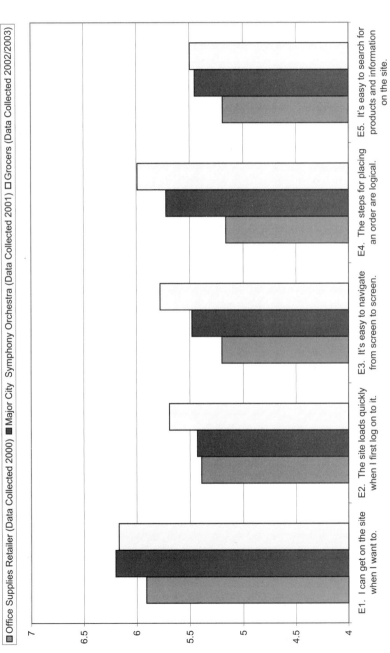

■ Office Supplies Retailer (Data Collected 2000) ■ Major City Symphony Orchestra (Data Collected 2001) ☐ Grocers (Data Collected 2002/2003)

E1. I can get on the site when I want to.

E2. The site loads quickly when I first log on to it.

E3. It's easy to navigate from screen to screen.

E4. The steps for placing an order are logical.

E5. It's easy to search for products and information on the site.

Questions rated from 1 = Strongly Disagree to 7 = Strongly Agree.

ensure that customers are not just browsing, but actually buying. They also need to make sure that transactions, when made, run smoothly.

Figure 9-3 shows results from the E-Commerce Transaction Performance Index. These results are for the top sites by market share and involve repeated access attempts in which software measures the average time to load a page and the proportion of transactions that were completed.[5] The data shown in Figure 9-3 indicate that page load times commonly violate the eight-second rule. More important, the number of transactions that went through successfully is often substantially lower than 100 percent. Note that the study uses automated software and defines criteria for how long a transaction can take—so a human customer might be more or less likely to abandon a transaction in the same circumstance. Either way, the lower-performing Web sites (Best Buy and Office Max) do not look good, with over 10 percent of transactions being lost. Imagine if 10 percent of the people in a line in a traditional store bailed out.

In contrast to Figure 9-3, Figure 9-4 shows the results from our studies of customer perceptions for the ease of transaction placement. For the symphony and grocers, this chart presents a much more pleasant picture—the means for all three questions are around two, or lower. Thus, customers are disagreeing with the statements that they sometimes have difficulties placing an order (E6), have payment problems (E7), or navigation problems (E8). In general, customers appear to be fairly happy with the transaction methods. In contrast, the office supplies retailer had substantially higher mean response for its customers. Now there can be two reasons for this: (1) that its Web site and systems are poorly designed and hard to use, or (2) that the difference in time is a major

Figure 9-3. Results from the keynote E-Commerce Transaction Performance Index, week of August 11, 2003.

	Response Time			Success Rate	
Rank	**Site**	**Time (seconds)**	**Rank**		**Success Rate**
	INDEX	**13.31**		**INDEX**	**96.23%**
1	Eddie Bauer	6.70	1	JC Penney	99.64%
2	Amazon	10.43	2	Eddie Bauer	99.55%
3	Target	11.48	3	Office Depot	99.37%
4	Office Depot	11.58	4	Sears	98.99%
5	JC Penney	13.39	5	Target	98.56%
6	Wal-Mart	15.59	6	Wal-Mart	98.55%
7	Sears	16.9	7	Amazon	98.35%
8	Best Buy	22.12	8	Best Buy	86.94%
9	Office Max	22.61	9	Office Max	84.76%

Figure 9-4. Ease of transaction placement.

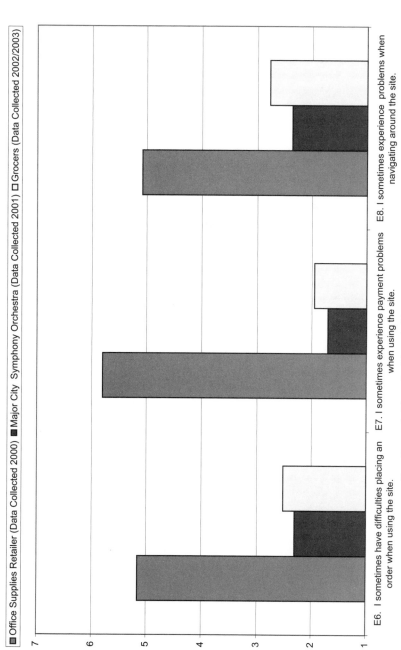

■ Office Supplies Retailer (Data Collected 2000) ■ Major City Symphony Orchestra (Data Collected 2001) □ Grocers (Data Collected 2002/2003)

E6. I sometimes have difficulties placing an order when using the site.

E7. I sometimes experience payment problems when using the site.

E8. I sometimes experience problems when navigating around the site.

Questions rated from 1 = Strongly Disagree to 7 = Strongly Agree.

factor (data collected in 2000 is on less-experienced online shoppers than for 2003). We strongly believe in the second explanation for two reasons: First, the office supplies retailer has continued to grow its online business at roughly 40 percent to 60 percent per year, which suggests customers do not have major transaction problems. Secondly, the data in Figures 9-1 and 9-2 exhibited a similar pattern. Thus, we believe that the data in Figure 9-4 illustrate that Web sites, hardware systems, and customers have all developed to a point where transactions are fairly routine.

Rather than looking across different types of businesses, Figures 9-5 and 9-6 show a comparison of Web site ease of use and ease of transaction for different online grocers. Both figures show large variations between grocers. In Figure 9-5, grocers B and E have the lowest scores on all five questions, while grocer A is generally the best. In Figure 9-6, grocer B is by far the worst, but grocers D, E, and F have substantial problems with site navigation (E8). It is important to note that higher scores for the questions in Figure 9-6 are worse because they indicate customers have had more problems, not less. In summary, Figures 9-5 and 9-6 show that there is substantial variation between companies in the same industry regarding aspects of their sites. More important, this variation correlates strongly with customer retention. Our study finds that about 25 percent of the customer loyalty can be explained by differences in customer perceptions of questions E1 through E8. This is a fairly substantial number given that it does not include any of the fulfillment (picking and delivery) aspects of online ordering. In short, simply making it easier and more efficient for customers to order has a substantial impact on loyalty. If only it were a simple process to design a Web site that appealed to a wide range of customers!

Streamlining Transactions for Repeat Purchases

One of the most important things for e-commerce is to streamline transactions for repeat purchases. This is why Amazon tried so hard to patent its one-click order process. First-time users of a Web site are almost always at a disadvantage because of two things: the need to learn about the site and the need to enter personal information to complete an order. When buying something in a store, all we need is cash, but when we buy online we need to provide name, address, credit card number, complete information for the product(s) we are buying, and often other information. This can be perceived as intrusive, but necessary.

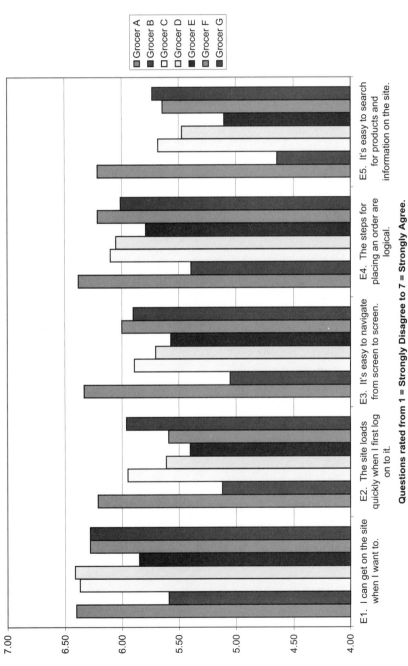

Figure 9-5. Web site ease of use within Internet grocer industry.

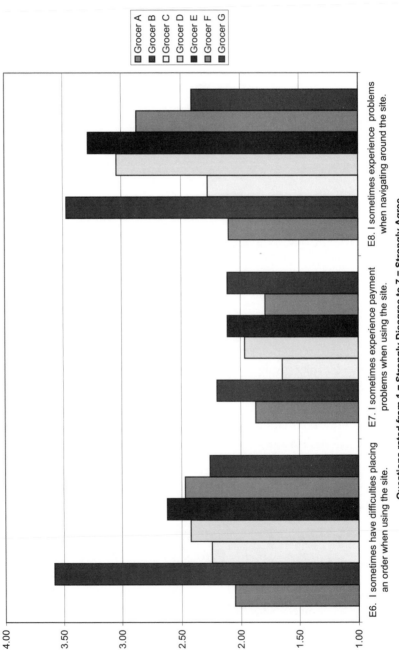

Figure 9-6. Ease of transaction placement for Internet grocers.

More important, it is time-consuming and offers numerous opportunities for errors. Fortunately, this is also an area where repeat transactions become much easier if the retailer designs its Web site appropriately and offers saved lists and information on past orders.

Amazon has been widely cited as a leading e-commerce retailer, and their one-click ordering is also a widely copied innovation. However, the most important question is: How do repeat users change in terms of purchase time/ efficiency, and how does learning affect the purchase process? In a study of several Internet booksellers, the efficiency (basically the speed with which an order can be placed) of several thousand customers was measured, and customers were rated on their efficiency (essentially time spent placing an order relative to time spent browsing a site). The study found that customers became much more efficient as they made repeat purchases, with a strong correlation between efficiency and the repeat purchase ratio. Just as important, the study also found that the percentage of repeat customers for two Web sites increased from roughly 10 percent to 40 percent. This is important since retaining an existing customer is generally less expensive than marketing and recruiting a new customer. In addition, while specific numbers for customer efficiency were not revealed, the strong correlation between efficiency and repeat purchases indicates that improving customer efficiency—both through improved site design and through customer education efforts—is extremely beneficial for increased sales and customer loyalty.[6]

Lands' End has been discussed earlier in this book as a company following a decoupled supply chain strategy. They have been fairly successful with their offering of custom clothing, such as men's and women's chinos. This is due both to effective manufacturing and delivery systems, but also to a Web site that makes first-time orders fairly easy and intuitive. More important, follow-up orders are very easy and intuitive. Let's compare a first-time order with a follow-up order:

- ◆ *First-Time Order.* To place a first order, there are at least seven Web pages that one must navigate through. Most of these are pretty standard to online ordering, but the two most important are the pages that ask customers to choose a fabric, color, fit, rise, front style, and hem/cuff (six choices). These are neatly laid out with pictures that explain each choice. Next, the customer must enter measurements for waist, inseam, height, weight, sport coat size, shirt neck size, sleeve length, shoe size, seat shape, and body proportion—a total of eleven choices! Some of these choices may seem superfluous and unnecessary—what does sport coat size have to do with pant size? Lands' End uses specialized software that checks for incongruous measurements or possible data entry errors. The final two steps include a review of the order information (sizes and styles), entry of billing information (name, address, phone, credit card, etc.) and order confirmation. The total process takes between ten and twenty minutes—depending on the user. The process is laid out to be fairly simply and easy to interpret.

◆ *Follow-Up Orders.* For follow-up orders, the process is simplified since, after logging in, customers can view a list of all their recent past orders. The choice is given to start from scratch, or from a previous order. When starting from a previous order, you are shown the information from the previous order on preselected buttons, which you can leave as is or change—at least for color style choices. In contrast, the size choices force you to explicitly enter some information. However, this is greatly simplified since the size information requested is now for inseam, waist, rise, seat, thigh, and bottom leg opening. Customers *must* actively select a size for each, but the drop-down boxes give choices for waist dimensions (tighten three inches, tighten two-and-a-half inches, no adjustments, loosen two-and-a-half inches, loosen three inches), thigh dimensions, and inseam dimensions. The idea is to allow customers to pick all of the same dimensions, or change one that did not fit right. In my case, my first pair fit almost perfectly, but overindulgence had led to a larger waist, so I chose to "loosen by a half inch." This system is quick, and it forces customers to think (at least briefly) about what should be changed to make their pants fit better.

Of course, nothing is ever perfect. When asking customers for their waste size on repeat orders, the drop-down menu starts at "tighten three inches," and then offers choices in half-inch increments down through "no adjustments," and finishing with "loosen three inches." It would seem better to start customers with no adjustments, and have them move up/down to tighten or loosen. The current system offers too many opportunities for a customer to pick the first option, without realizing that he is making a major change.

Generally speaking, the more a Web site can simplify and streamline both the initial and the repeat ordering process, the more likely customers are to return. Many Web designers/retailers have made much progress in using things like one-click ordering, retention of past orders, and standardized shopping carts to make the ordering process simpler. However, most readers of this book can easily remember a bad experience they have had with a particular site—navigational problems, poor directions, nonworking links, inaccurate information, etc. These are to be avoided at all costs, or else customers will avoid these Web sites.

Streamlining of orders becomes even more critical in situations where customers are buying numerous items and where they make frequent purchases. Figures 9-7 and 9-8 show data from our study of online grocers that clearly illustrate this point. As has been discussed, a primary attraction of ordering groceries online is saving time, yet Figure 9-7 shows that the average time to place a first order is between sixty and eighty-five minutes. This does not represent much of a time saving for customers, if any, over going to the store themselves. Yet, this finding is not surprising when one considers how fundamentally different ordering groceries on the Internet is from physically selecting them in the store. Thus, grocers must do all they can do to help customers familiarize themselves with the ordering process.

The grocers in our study offer a variety of supporting features. One grocer offers three helpful approaches: (1) They will key in your first order from a receipt from your last store visit (even from a competitor), (2) they will guide you through the process with a customer agent on the phone, while you place your order, or (3) they will even send a representative to sit with you in person and help place that first order. All of these measures, and many others taken by other retailers in other industries, are designed to increase customer retention—i.e., the number of customers who place future orders. The bottom line in Figure 9-7 shows the average order time for the most recent order placed by customers who have placed multiple orders with that grocer. This clearly shows that customers quickly become more comfortable with the ordering process. In all seven cases, the time for the most recent order is 30 percent to 50 percent of the time for the first order! This is critically important since there is a high correlation between both the first order time and the most recent order time (and their ratio) and customer satisfaction/retention.

Figure 9-8 shows how quickly customers learn and become comfortable with ordering groceries on the Internet. This graph groups customers by the number of orders they have placed on that grocer's Web site (one, two, three, four, or five, etc.) and by whether they make use of the saved-list option. The

(text continues on page 224)

Figure 9-7. A comparison of first and last order times.

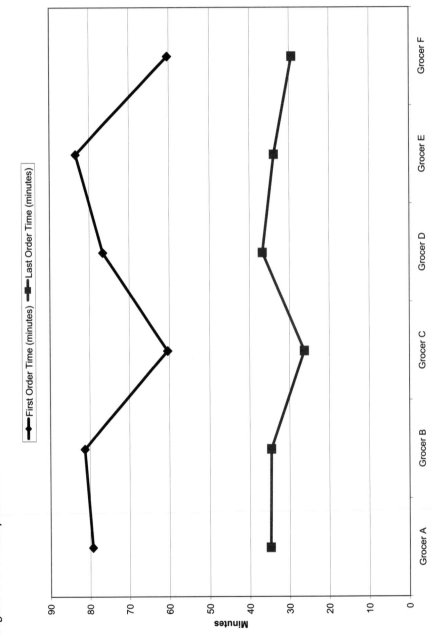

Figure 9-8. The effects of saved lists on order time.

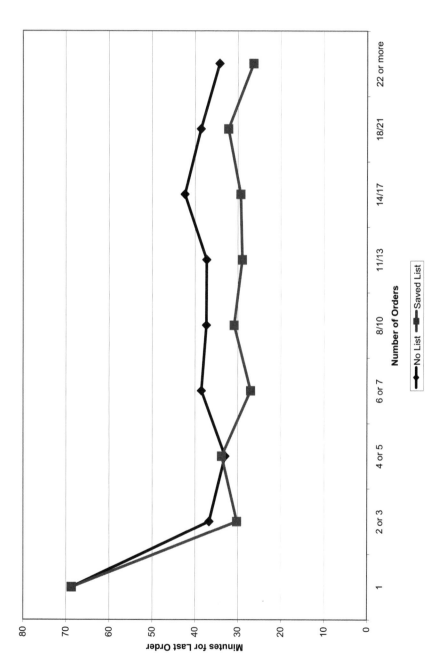

saved-list option varies by grocer, but all of them offer some method of using a previous order as a base for making another order. One grocer even sends out reminder e-mails that have the customer's most commonly purchased items in it. Figure 9-8 shows two things very clearly. First, by the fourth or fifth order, customers become much faster, with the average order time dropping from seventy minutes to thirty-three minutes—a substantial savings of time. Second, customers using the saved-list features uniformly place orders quicker, and are more satisfied with the service. In fact, Figure 9-8 shows that the average order time for customers employing saved lists drops below thirty minutes for very established customers. Note, this is just the average—for the approximately 600 customers in our survey (across all seven grocers) who had placed more than seven orders and who used the saved-list feature, over 50 percent reported that their most recent order took twenty minutes or less. That's twenty minutes for an entire week's shopping—the average shopper in our study placed an order for 37.2 items at a cost of $117.77.

Web designers and retailers must think through the entire ordering process carefully—clearly the time it takes to order is a big factor for customers. First-time orders generally take longer—both because the customer must learn the system and because they must enter personal data (name, address, billing information) that they do not need to enter when making an in-store purchase.[7] However, once this first order or hurdle has been surmounted, the next order should be much simpler—as illustrated by our examples from the book retailing industry, Lands' End, and online grocers. Unfortunately, this is not always the case since many retailers consciously (or unconsciously) do not make efforts to reap the advantages of the learning curve. In short, it is imperative that customer order time be reduced for repeat orders.

Integrating Ordering and Fulfillment

This behind-the-scenes aspect of last-mile supply chains is one that is fairly invisible to the customer, yet critical for success. Too many Web sites can be described as what is commonly known as "brochure ware"—pretty-looking sites that do not link to any actual inventory or fulfillment systems. For example, many hotels have Web sites that allow you to "book" a room online, but what they are really doing is taking an e-mail, having a reservation agent enter it into their reservation system, check availability, and then sending a confirmation/denial message to the customer. This process takes fifteen to twenty minutes at best, sometimes twenty-four hours or more. Obviously, the customer would prefer a site that gives instantaneous confirmation that a room is available or not. It comes as a surprise to many people that less than 10 percent of retailing Web sites have real-time links to inventory.[8]

Many sites are not linked to inventory and delivering systems because often there are proprietary systems or old, difficult-to-change systems that have been cobbled together over a long period of time. It is all well and good to say that everything should be linked, but often the software development to link things together is exceedingly complex and expensive. Consider the airlines, which have been one of the leading examples of Web ordering and fulfillment. For example, as far back as 2000, Delta and Northwest both saw more than 5 percent of their sales come in through their Web sites, with online transactions saving as much as 80 percent in processing and commission costs.[9]

In October 2003, Northwest reported that 26 percent of its tickets were sold online and that it checked in 63 percent of its passengers via the Web or self-service kiosks.[10] Clearly airlines are benefiting and taking advantage of opportunities to have customers' self-source ordering and check-in. This is easier for airlines to do because their reservation systems have long been auto-mated and accessible by travel agents and reservations agents of the company. Thus, when developing Internet-ordering systems, they could concentrate on building a customer interface that linked well with an existing reservation sys-tem. Airlines also benefit from selling an intangible product—they do not have to deliver anything (they used to have to mail paper tickets, but increasingly with e-tickets, there is no delivery function whatsoever). Airlines have been able to reduce the size of their call centers considerably because many of the ticket orders and questions that were handled by customers phoning the airline have been transferred to the Internet. Northwest Airlines recently announced that is was closing a reservation center with 570 employees in Livonia, Michi-gan, because of decreased call volumes associated with increased usage of the Internet for booking flights.[11]

Retailers of tangible products have a different set of challenges. Not only do they have to check inventory for availability, but they have to check delivery schedules and/or exchange information with third-party logistics providers (for example, Federal Express or UPS). This adds at least another layer of interfaces. Many companies have been very proactive about adding links for tracking or-ders—for example, Amazon, Caremark, Lands' End, Omaha Steaks— particu-larly when linking with a third-party carrier. Yet few companies have actual, real-time links with inventory systems. This is because inventory is fast-moving and often dispersed in several locations. This is an especially challenging problem for companies following a semi-extended or fully extended supply chain strategy (fulfilling orders from stores). Here, inventory must be tracked at numerous stores rather than a single or few distribution centers.

Again, consider Amazon. They do not have real-time inventory linkages. Book orders are typically shipped in "twenty-four hours," "two to three days," or "two to three weeks." This corresponds to a simple ABC inventory system. The fastest-moving items (the top 1,000 to 2,000 sellers) are likely stocked at each of their distribution centers (they have six).[12] The next tier of items (say the items ranked 2,001 to 10,000 in sales) may be held at only a single distribution center—thus requiring longer shipment times on average. Finally, the lowest tier of items (those ranked 20,001 to 2 million) are not stocked at Amazon at all, but are stocked or printed on demand by the publisher—thus requiring the longer lead time. While it would be preferable for a customer to get real-time feedback on whether a book was available immediately, in reality, this is not feasible. Instead, Amazon (and numerous similar companies) make up for this gap by communicating the order status with the customer at several stages. A clear confirmation of order receipt is provided at checkout, an e-mail is sent when items are shipped or back-ordered, and often a confirmation e-mail is sent upon receipt by the customer.

A similar example is provided by Caremark, a mail/Internet/phone order provider of prescription drugs for millions of people in thousands of health plans. Obviously, prescription drugs are a product for which customers have a high degree of concern regarding timeliness and safety of fulfillment. Refill orders can be placed online (remember from Chapter Three that new orders cannot because of the need to send a written prescription), but the customer is not given instant visibility into when they will receive their order. Instead, the customer gets an e-mail noting when the drugs have been shipped, a tracking number, and the ability to check status online or over the telephone. This system works well because of the relatively long gap between ordering and receipt. In contrast, consider a local pharmacy taking an order online or over the phone that does not have real-time linkage to the inventory fulfillment system (as many do not). A customer may place an order and either assume or be told by the automated phone system that it will be ready in two hours. On arrival at the store to pick it up, the order is *not* ready—either because the pharmacy was swamped with other orders or because the item was out of stock, or because the item could not be renewed because of insurance issues. The result is a very unhappy customer who was expecting her prescription on arrival. What was the cause? Obviously, it is extremely difficult to link not only the order system and the inventory/fulfillment system, but, in this case, there needs to be a link to the insurance company's system too—usually involving several different systems.

Action Steps

This chapter has provided an overview of three key principles for the use of information technology in supply chains.

The first key principle is to encourage customers to self-source, i.e., place their own orders with no or minimal involvement with employees of the retailer. When ordering systems (whether Internet, telephone, kiosk, or other) are well designed and executed, customers will enjoy this method of ordering because it is convenient, quick, and easy. The key is to get customers to accomplish most of the input with a minimal involvement on the retailer's side, while doing this in a manner that is attractive to customers.

The second key principle is to encourage repeat business and do everything possible to turn first-time customers into repeat customers. In most automated transactions (either online or telephone, or kiosk), there is a substantial learning curve. First-time customers will take longer, feel less comfortable, and make more order-entry mistakes. However, in most cases, customers get much more efficient (fast), accurate, and comfortable sometime between their third and fifth orders. Thus, companies that can get customers through the first few orders without undue troubles have much better retention rates for their customers.

The final key principle is to connect IT systems as much as possible so that customers get an accurate read on whether their order is in stock or not. Too many Web sites are just pretty-looking sites that do not link to any actual inventory or fulfillment systems. Truly effective last-mile supply chains *must* have interconnections between the ordering, fulfillment, and delivery systems. Ideally, customers have near-perfect insight into exactly when and how they will receive their orders. Alternatively, many retailers do not have real-time links—customers can't see whether an actual item is currently in stock, but the retailer provides clear and informative information that reports when orders are ready for shipment and when they ship, and allows customers to track these orders readily. In short, the IT aspects of last-mile supply chains must be interconnected to facilitate a seamless flow of information, just as the supply chain components discussed in Chapter Eight should facilitate a seamless flow of orders and goods.

We close with the following action steps:

- Balance Web site design with both attractive features that excite the customer and features that simplify ordering. Cool graphics may get their attention, but completing the order should be straightforward and simple.

- Streamline transactions. Customers will not return if placing an order is cumbersome.

- Look for ways where added information can benefit customers and/or lead to incremental sales.

- Link ordering and confirmation of orders to supply chain software. When promising orders, customers want to know *actual availability* and *actual delivery times*—not guesses.

- Think of the Web site as serving both first-time and return customers. More experienced customers may be ready for enhanced features, while providing new customers with enhanced support or guidance is critical to turning them into repeat customers.

- Consider ways to build an online community—shared experience or recipes, enhanced user information, interactive components—but do not go overboard. Customers must be able to complete transactions quickly.

Notes

1. From the Webby site, see www.webbyawards.com.
2. Author's personal conversation with Seth Gordon on September 22, 2003. Mr. Gordon served as the 2003 category chair for the group of nominating judges for the e-commerce category. He is a consultant in user research and can be reached at seth@gordy.com.
3. B. Tedeschi, "For Internet Shoppers, Speed Counts," *The New York Times* (June 14, 1999), p. C4.
4. "Customer Retention Metrics Still Often Overlooked, Survey Finds," *Internet Retailer* (August 26, 2003), see www.internetretailer.com.

5. From *The E-Commerce Times*, reprints available from www.ectnews.com/about/reprints.shtml.

6. Data on Internet booksellers drawn from Mei Xue and Patrick T. Harker, "Customer Efficiency: Concept and Its Impact on E-Business Management," *Journal of Services Research* (May 2002), Vol. 4, No. 4, pp. 253–267.

7. Kenneth K. Boyer, "E-Operations: A Guide to How the Internet Streamlines Operations," *Business Horizons* (January-February 2001), Vol. 44, No. 1, pp. 47–54.

8. Kurt Peters, "Telling Online Customers It's on the Shelf," *Internet Retailer* (April 2002), see www.internetretailer.com.

9. Chris Murphy and Christopher T. Heun, The Results are In," *Information Week* (January 29, 2001), No. 8222, pp. 22–24.

10. Martin J. Moylan, "NWA Ad Campaign Touts Ease of Travel," *Detroit Free Press* (October 2, 2003) p. 5C.

11. "NWA's Livonia Calling Center to Close," *Detroit Free Press* (September 26, 2003), p. C1.

12. Note: These numbers are for illustrative purposes only. We have no direct information on Amazon's stocking policy but have talked to people in the industry who agree that this is the fundamental approach used.

CHAPTER 10

The Future of the Extended Supply Chain

At the beginning of this book, we started off with a nostalgic look at the 1950s and the numerous businesses that delivered products and services straight to customers' homes. This service was high-touch, highly appreciated, and highly inefficient compared to most of the major retailers in existence today. Today's retail landscape is dominated by big-box retailers like Wal-Mart, Home Depot, Best Buy, Target, Tesco, etc., all of whom have tremendous supply chains that offer very low prices for commodity products. The shortcoming of this landscape is that customers are not treated as individuals, but as consumers who must navigate large parking lots, huge stores, long lines, and an experience that is almost completely impersonal.

We laid out the challenge for companies seeking to differentiate themselves in some manner—by offering better quality, more convenience, or more personalized service. The extended or last-mile supply chain seeks to combine high technology and high touch to offer the personalized and convenient service offered by so many "local" companies in the 1950s. Amazon is a "virtual" company—meaning that most of its customers have never talked to, much less met, a company employee, yet there are millions of extremely loyal customers who love Amazon. Similar examples can be offered, ranging from high-technology manufacturers such as Dell to companies such as Netflix, which delivers rental DVDs via mail. These companies follow the decoupled supply chain approach that provides advantages in ability to manage inventory, customization, and fulfillment, but is distanced from the actual customer via the use of a third-party logistics provider (such as UPS, the U.S. Postal Service, or Federal Express).

In other cases, the retailer "reaches out to customers by making deliveries directly to them. Companies such as Office Depot, FreshDirect, Tesco, and Schwan's Dairy all deliver directly to consumer homes via either a distribution center or a local store. Here the goal is to offer both convenience to the customer and a chance to connect and build a relationship. Since interaction with the customer occurs at a single time and place, it can be managed carefully to nurture a relationship that does not exist in the big-box stores. We have presented data from our studies of online grocers and from OfficeDepot.com that illustrate both the challenges of last-mile supply chains and the potential benefits.

Advantages of Last-Mile Supply Chains

Think about your own favorite retail Web site and then think about why you like it—what does it offer that its real-world competitors do not? In Chapter One we argued that last-mile supply chains potentially offer four major advantages: convenience, customization, quality, and experience. Convenience means different things to different people. Last-mile retailers need to be aware of the trade-off between instant gratification (i.e., if I order it online, I can*not* get it right now) versus the ease of ordering from a computer, anytime, anyplace, and have it delivered to my house. Customization is another powerful advantage for last-mile supply chains, but it has to be meaningful customization, not minutiae. A diverse array of companies including Dell, FreshDirect, Lands' End, and Art.com use the separation between customer ordering and delivery to use central manufacturing or fulfillment centers to customize on demand. This is only feasible on a fairly large-volume, low-cost basis because of the ability to aggregate volume/manufacturing operations in a single location and the smooth, convenient, low-cost linkage of orders from a wide market of customers provided by the Internet.

Quality for last-mile supply chains is exhibited in three ways. First, by carefully managing the point of customer contact, customers often feel like they are getting better service (not more, just better). Second, by cutting a link from the supply chain, retailers and manufacturers can move products to customers faster—a characteristic that Dell has exploited to cut down on obsolete inventory of computers, and FreshDirect has exploited to offer fresher produce and meats. Third, Web sites can provide more detailed information and develop a sense of community for products that have many subjective characteristics. (Amazon and its customer review system is just one example.)

Finally, experience is essentially a combination of the other three advantages. Where purchases are routine and monotonous, the last-mile supply chain can be used to take the drudgery out of the experience—i.e., online grocery shopping is faster, and it can provide one pleasant interaction when groceries are delivered versus two hours of schlepping to, through, and from the store. Where purchases are more personal, or have more possibilities, experience can be refined through last-mile supply chains to be fundamentally different than in traditional stores. The user communities that have grown up around Amazon or eBay are good examples, as is the loyalty that many customers feel to a manufacturer, such as Lands' End or Dell, that allows the consumer to customize her product.

Strategies

As described in Chapter One, there are four strategies for bridging the last mile, based on fulfillment (either via DC or store) and delivery (direct or indirect). In-store picking tends to be closer to customers, requires less fixed investment (assuming stores already exist), and has a halo effect that can improve the organization's overall standing with customers. In contrast, DC–based picking tends to be more efficient and more accurate. It allows more product range to be stocked or manufactured and has a shorter supply chain that allows it to ship fresher products faster.

Similarly, the differences between direct versus indirect delivery can be generalized, but they need to be carefully applied to specific situations and industries. Indirect delivery is more efficient, and it can encourage customers to enter stores and buy additional products. In contrast, direct delivery is much more convenient for customers, but far less efficient and more costly for the retailer.

The combination of fulfillment and delivery choice creates four last mile strategies: semi-extended, fully extended, decoupled, and centralized. Companies need to carefully evaluate which option best fits their overall goals. Many companies have failed because they used existing facilities without adequately mapping out their goals. For example, many companies outsource delivery, and then they wonder why customers do not form a strong bond with them. The problem is the lack of experience at the point of delivery, or in interaction with the customer. Many companies utilize hybrid strategies in different markets—for example a DC approach in high-density urban areas, combined with a store-based picking approach in more suburban or rural areas. This can be an effective strategy, but it can also lead to conflicts within an organization. Chapters Two through Five provided detailed examinations of the ins and outs of each of the pure strategies, as well as profiles of two or three companies that have employed them successfully.

Making the Last Mile Supply Chain Work

While all supply chains are under more pressure these days to be integrated, seamless, and efficient these days, last mile supply chains are more exposed to that pressure—both in negative and positive ways. Any deficiencies in the last mile supply chain are highly visible at its end—the customer. This has immediate consequences because customers who have had a bad experience are quick to revert to their "traditional" shopping habits. On the other hand, when the last mile supply chain works, providing increased convenience, customization, quality, and/or a more enriching experience, it offers a way to connect and win over customers that is fundamentally different from the every–store-looks–the-same, big-box approach that is prevalent in modern society.

We identified and examined in some detail four key areas for perfecting last mile supply chains in Chapters Six through Nine. They are:

- ◆ *Strategy.* The need to seamlessly mesh strategy so that marketing and operations work together in partnership.
- ◆ *Marketing.* The need to market to customers' latent desires, or to tap into needs that customers may not explicitly know they have.
- ◆ *Design.* The need to carefully design the last mile supply chain to meet the strategic objectives and to minimize potential problem areas.
- ◆ *Information Technology.* The need to use information technology (the Internet or automated phone systems) to allow customers to self-source in a manner that they benefit from and that creates a richer experience for them.

All four of these areas must be well done, or last mile supply chains will break at the weakest link. We have highlighted the key concerns in each area, and provided a broad map for how to begin to address the challenges in each one.

Bridge to the Future

The last mile supply chain offers tantalizing prospects, as well as daunting challenges. Much like the builders of famous bridges such as the Brooklyn Bridge, the Golden Gate Bridge in San Francisco, or the Akashi-Kaikyo in Japan (the world's longest bridge), businesses offering consumer-direct solutions must master both a grand plan and thousands of smaller, yet critical details. Otherwise, the bridge or supply chain collapses.

Figure 10-1 illustrates the keys to mastering this task. In the center of the "Last Mile Wheel" are the four primary advantages of last mile supply chains: convenience, customization, quality, and experience. On the interlocking outer edge of the wheel are the four supply chain keys: (1) meshing operational and

Figure 10-1. Rolling across the last mile.

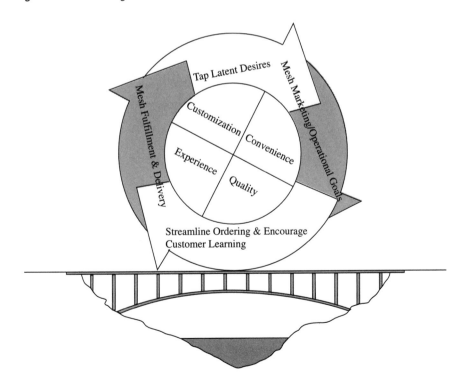

marketing goals, (2) tapping the latent desires of customers, (3) facilitating learning and streamlining transactions, and (4) meshing fulfillment and delivery (i.e., picking and effectively implementing the correct last mile strategy).

Numerous last mile retailers have already prospered using many of these principles. Notable leaders include Dell, Office Depot, Amazon, NetFlix, Omaha Steaks, and FreshDirect. Each of these companies has exploited one of the four major advantages of last mile supply chains. Office Depot provides a time-saving convenience for busy workers in businesses around the world. Dell offers convenience and customization. Amazon offers convenience and a customer experience that differs substantially from traditional bookstores, but manages to achieve a strong feeling of community. NetFlix offers convenience and increased choice of DVDs. Omaha Steaks and FreshDirect utilize last mile supply chains to offer both customization and increased quality/freshness of perishable foods.

Change in life, and business, is constant. Much as we acknowledge that fact, it also scares us. We tend to resist it. However, last mile supply chains present an opportunity to take advantage of change. Companies are experimenting with numerous techniques for managing the last mile, but there are three things that are truly essential for driving this change. First, companies, and consumers, need Internet access and other forms of electronic communication, which continue to proliferate and become more common. Sales via direct ordering over the Internet will continue to grow rapidly as a new generation of consumers becomes proficient with these technologies. Second, home delivery needs to become more efficient and standardized—much like the home mail delivery from the post office that most of us take for granted. Finally, customers need to be retrained to be more demanding—to ask for and expect personalized service versus the homogenized, faceless service so common with today's big-box retail experience.

As discussed in Chapter Nine, facilitating transaction speed is a critical driver of last mile transactions. If a customer is seeking convenience, there is little point in trading the time to travel to a store, shop, and return home simply for an extended, difficult ordering experience. Thus, companies must offer ordering methods (whether via the Internet, fax, or phone) that give customers the features they are looking for and are quick and easy to use. However, the factor that is outside of the company's direct control is the speed of information flow. As more customers convert to broadband, wireless, and mobile phone access, the market for online ordering should open up accordingly. As an illustration, the Pew Internet and American Life Project found that nearly a third of U.S. citizens with a home Internet connection have converted to broadband. This represents approximately 16 percent of the total population, and a 50 percent increase in the past year.[1] Figure 10-2 shows how this type of faster access can affect sales. This figure outlines the type of Internet access that was used and the percentage of all grocery shopping that was done at one home-delivery grocer in our study. The slowest type of Internet access in Figure 10–2 was for customers with dial-up access (in which the average order time was thirty-seven minutes). This corresponds to the lowest percentage of grocery shopping (24 percent for the question, "What percentage of all of your grocery shopping do you do with Grocer X?). Clearly, the type of Internet access that is used is related to the propensity of customers to order online. Though companies are limited in their ability to affect this relationship, increased broadband, wireless, and cell phone access should spur increased sales for all. In addition, individual companies can look into cross-marketing opportunities with Internet or cell phone service providers.

The second major change that must be facilitated to make last mile supply chains truly soar is greater efficiency and standardization of home delivery. As discussed in Chapter Eight, the delivery of orders to consumer homes suffers from numerous challenges and generally is much more costly than delivery to businesses. The primary challenge is delivering to a customer who is not home. If a customer is forced to be home, then the convenience of getting home delivery is greatly hampered. Currently, home delivery companies, such as UPS, Federal Express, and Airborne, and retailers who make their own deliveries, such as Office Depot, all utilize a mishmash of techniques to work around the challenge of missing customers. These techniques include leaving goods on the customer's doorstep, repeat delivery attempts, and scheduled delivery windows. No one technique, however, truly solves the problem of allowing for efficient deliveries for the provider, while simultaneously making the delivery convenient for the customer.

Most, if not all, of the major third-party delivery companies are testing methods for unattended deliveries involving some type of controlled access smartbox. By way of analogy, let's consider early postal deliveries. In the early twentieth century, the Unites States Post Office delivered door-to-door and left mail with an actual customer in a person-to-person handoff. At some point, this became unworkable as more and more housewives went to work, and more people worked outside the home. Thus, the post office mandated that

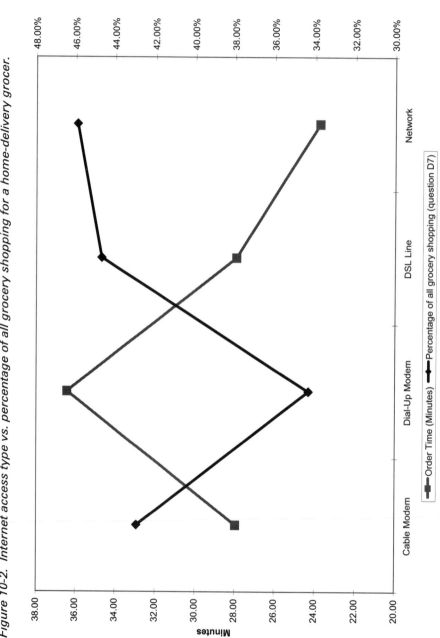

Figure 10-2. Internet access type vs. percentage of all grocery shopping for a home-delivery grocer.

each house would have an attached mailbox for receiving letters. While most of us never think about it, this simple innovation led to greatly increased delivery efficiency, yet it had to overcome some barriers. When the change was first introduced, there must have been numerous people who wondered if their mail was safe in an unattended mailbox. Sure, the U.S. government (and most governments) has laws stating that tampering with federal mail is illegal—but this is difficult to enforce on a wide scale. The safety of our mail is attributable more to social convention—we operate in a society that takes this for granted and in which people generally do not tamper with other people's mail. A similar change must occur for last mile deliveries to grow widespread. The U.S. Post Office prohibits any other carrier from using mailboxes. Even if other companies could use mailboxes, they are generally not of sufficient size, and they are not secured for valuable shipments of computers, clothing, groceries, etc. It is our belief that some type of larger, access-controlled box that is available to a wide variety of home delivery companies is an important hurdle for growing last mile deliveries. This type of box must be sponsored either by one of the large third-party carriers or by a joint partnership of several home-delivery grocers.

The third fundamental change for building last mile supply chains involves reorienting customer attitudes. The last half of the twentieth century can be characterized as a period where manufacturers and retailers relentlessly lowered costs and prices by cutting the amount of service offered. While exceptions certainly exist, major success stories such as Wal-Mart, Home Depot, Kroger, Tesco, etc., have grown by getting customers to do more of the work involved with shopping in exchange for lower costs. Customers have to navigate stores the size of warehouses, stand in long lines (or use self-checkout), and navigate parking lots that look like a demolition derby. Clearly, home delivery offers a very different experience. However, customers must be convinced of the value of greater convenience, and they must be educated about the difficulties of "traditional" shopping. There is a reason why large proportions of customers say they hate grocery shopping, drugstore shopping, and shopping in general, yet most tolerate the difficulties because they do not know any other way to shop. Last mile supply chains require time to change these lifelong habits. Changing shopping habits requires two fundamental things: (1) good alternatives (i.e., competitors who offer home delivery in a easy-to-use and reasonably cost-effective manner) and (2) changing customer attitudes. Once a sufficient base of companies offering home delivery is built and proves that it can offer the service expected, the customers will follow. In the short term, however, it is important for last mile retailers to work to educate customers and communicate the benefits of their service to them . During part of the Christmas 2003 season, 62 percent of online retailers had experienced at least a 25 percent growth in sales from the same period in 2002, and about a quarter of them had experienced at least an 80 percent growth in sales, according to a Shop.org survey.[2]

There are numerous companies experimenting with last mile solutions. Given the time pressures on most people in developed nations, timesaving choices that offer increased convenience have excellent potential for growth. As introduced in Chapter One, the two fundamental ways to compete in business are based on offering low prices and differentiating the company's products and services in customers' minds. The pendulum in modern society has swung too far to the side of price. Most consumers have a surplus of goods and a shortage of time. For many people, spending an extra hour to shop in a megastore may save them five dollars or ten dollars on a $200 purchase, but if that hour of time could be saved instead, it would be more beneficial for them personally.

Many of the early efforts to bridge the last mile resulted in spectacular failures. So did the Tacoma Narrows bridge—the infamous suspension bridge that collapsed due to wind-induced vibrations on November 7, 1940.[3] But the builders of that bridge did not give up; they went on to learn from their mistakes (as have bridge designers around the world) and built a second, and later a third, bridge to replace the first failure. Last mile supply chains are quite similar—some have failed, some have succeeded, but we can all learn lessons from studying both the failures and the successes. Whether you are a customer or a retailer, we encourage you to keep pushing the envelope to master the last mile supply chain. We'll see you on the other side.

Notes

1. "Americans Lap up Broadband Access," BBC News, see news.bbc.co.uk, May 20, 2003.
2. "Online Retailers Expect Another Strong Holiday Season, Shop.org Reports," www.InternetRetailer.com, November 24, 2003.
3. For a description of the bridge collapse and some pictures and video footage, the following Web site is very informative: http://www.enm.bris.ac.uk/research/nonlinear/tacoma/tacoma.html.